Transformations in Irish Culture

Luke Gibbons

UNIVERSITY OF NOTRE DAME PRESS
in association with
FIELD DAY

For my father
and in memory of my mother

Published in the United States in 1996 by
UNIVERSITY OF NOTRE DAME PRESS
Notre Dame, Indiana 46556
All Rights Reserved.

and in Ireland by
CORK UNIVERSITY PRESS
University College Cork, Ireland

The paper used in this publication meets the minimum requirements of the
American National Standard for Information Sciences–Permanence of
paper for Printed Library Materials, ANSI Z39.48–1984

Library of Congress Cataloging-in-Publication Data

Gibbons, Luke.
    Transformations in Irish culture / Luke Gibbons.
        p. cm. — (Critical conditions)
    Includes index.
    ISBN 0-268-01893-6 (alk, paper)
    1. Ireland—Civilization—20th century.   2. Nationalism—Ireland—History—
20th century.   3. Ireland—Politics and government—20th century.
4. National characteristics, Irish.   I. Title. II. Series.
DA959.1.G53 1996
941.50824—dc20   96-11708
                                                                        CIP

CONTENTS

List of Illustrations   ix

Preface   xi

1 Introduction: 3
Culture, History and Irish Identity

2 Synge, Country and Western: 23
The Myth of the West in Irish and American Culture

3 Back Projections: 37
John Hinde and the New Nostalgia

4 From Kitchen Sink to Soap: 44
Drama and the Serial Form on Irish Television

5 From Megalith to Megastore: 70
Broadcasting and Irish Culture

6 Coming Out of Hibernation?   82
The Myth of Modernization in Irish Culture

7 Labour and Local History: 95
The Case of Jim Gralton, 1886–1945

8 The Politics of Silence: 107
Anne Devlin, Women and Irish Cinema

9 'Lies that Tell the Truth': 117
Maeve, History and Irish Cinema

10 Narratives of No Return: 129
James Coleman's guaiRE

11 Identity Without a Centre: 134
Allegory, History and Irish Nationalism

12 Race Against Time: 149
Racial Discourse and Irish History

13 Montage, Modernism and the City 165

14 Unapproved Roads: 171
Ireland and Post-Colonial Identity

Notes and References 181
Index 209

LIST OF ILLUSTRATIONS

Fr Browne, 'The Shadow of Progress', courtesy Irish Picture Library   x

1.1	Robert Janz, 'The Day After' (1983)	2
2.1	Seán Keating, 'Men of the West' (1916), courtesy Hugh Lane Municipal Gallery of Modern Art	25
2.2	Cartoon, *Dublin Opinion*	35
3.1	From *The Quiet Man* (1952) and 'Collecting Turf from the Bog, Connemara', John Hinde, courtesy John Hinde Ltd	36
3.2–3.7	Postcards, courtesy John Hinde Ltd	38–43
5.1	Cartoon, *Dublin Opinion*	71
6.1–6.8	IDA advertisements	87–91
7.1	James Gralton (1886–1945), courtesy Pat Feeley	94
7.2	Jim Gralton on arrival in New York, August 1933, courtesy Pat Feeley	98
7.3	Selection of newspaper cuttings relating to Jim Gralton, courtesy Pat Feeley	101
8.1–8.3	From *Anne Devlin* (1984)	109–15
9.1–9.4	From *Maeve* (1981)	119–26
10.1	Olwen Fouere on stage in James Coleman's 'guaiRE' (1985), courtesy Marian Goodman Gallery, New York	128
12.1	Seán Hillen, 'The Executioners' (1996)	148
13.1	Seán Hillen, 'The Oracle at O'Connell St. Bridge' (1996)	164
14.1	Cartoon, *Dublin Opinion*	170
14.2	Philip Napier, 'Ballad no. 2' (1992–94)	173
14.3	From *Illustrated London News* (29 October 1881)	173
14.4	Alice Maher, 'Familiar 1' (1994)	175
14.5	Willie Doherty, 'Evergreen Memories' (1989)	177
14.6	John Kindness, 'Belfast Fresco Series' (1994)	178

Fr Browne, 'The Shadow of Progress'

PREFACE

There is an important sense in which a culture has not found its own voice until it has expressed itself in a body of critical as well as creative work. 'It is one thing for a race to produce artistic material,' wrote the great African-American writer W. E. B. Du Bois, 'it is quite another thing for it to produce the ability to interpret and criticize this material.' Irish culture in the twentieth century has displayed no shortage of creative energies, but as if bearing out the stereotype of the anti-intellectualism of the Celt, it has been less successful in generating its own criticism, or its intellectual terms of reference.

One of the most encouraging signs in recent years has been a willingness to break with this demeaning self-image, and this book is very much the product of the rejuvenation of critical debates in Ireland. In bringing together a range of essays written originally for a variety of purposes, and different readerships, there is a danger of imposing order where none was intended, as if there was a book in the making from the very outset. I did not have to work too hard to dispel this illusion, since it takes some stretch of the imagination to link up *The Riordans* with the Whiteboys in the eighteenth century, and John Hinde postcards with montage and modernism (I leave the latter to the versatility of artists such as Seán Hillen and John Kindness). Nonetheless, I have sought where possible in the introduction to indicate various points of intersection in the essays, and different interpretations of a number of recurrent themes. This admittedly makes for a certain amount of repetition, but if it helps to demonstrate the degree to which some discussions take up where others leave off, and other seemingly unrelated topics overlap, it serves its purpose. Such corrections and minor amendments as have been made are also designed to add to the coherence required by the publication of the essays in book form.

Since the essays were written for diverse publications dating from the early 1980s, some of the discussions undoubtedly bear the traces of their time of publication. This is particularly true in assessments of film and broadcasting, where shifts in policy and practice can often change the contours of debate within a few years. The temptation in cases like this is to bring the arguments into line with recent developments, updating the references and examples to give them a contemporary gloss. The difficulty here is that this may not be a matter of simply adding new material, but may call for a whole new set of perspectives on the subject in question. Thus, for example, in the essay on the television drama serial in Ireland, the discussion might be extended by indicating the changes of

direction taken by *Glenroe* (1983–) and *Fair City* (1989–) and, indeed, by the
drama serial elsewhere. This, however, would have to be set against a more
general set of questions, investigating whether the capacity to illuminate the
darker corners of Irish society passed from television to film and radio in the
1980s and 1990s – a trend which I hope to examine in a forthcoming study of
Irish cinema. As it stands, the discussions of film and broadcasting in the book
are central to the overall argument that media representations, and cultural forces
in general, act as transformative forces in society, rather than as 'reflections' or
mimetic forms at one remove from reality.

The fact that some of the essays are marked by the circumstances in which
they were originally written is also clear from the scepticism expressed at various
points about the belated modernization of Irish society. This is partly a response
to the conservative backlash of the 1980s or, more particularly, to the possibility
that the downturn was not an aberration but may have been a logical development of the truncated version of modernity which has been credited with the
'liberalization' of Irish society since the 1960s. To what degree recent developments in Ireland – the election of Mary Robinson as President in 1990; the
undoing, in however limited a fashion, of the abortion (1983) and divorce (1986)
referenda, in 1992 and 1996 respectively; the Catholic Church's fall from grace
due to successive sexual and institutional scandals; the new political climate in
Northern Ireland – give greater cause for optimism is an open question. These
developments leave unresolved, however, many of the theoretical issues which
inform the original discussions, particularly the crisis in modernity, and in per-
ceptions of progress and enlightenment, as we approach the end of the twentieth
century. The extent to which the various discussions throughout the book have
a shelf-life beyond the original circumstances of their writing depends on their
capacity to raise such theoretical issues, and to engage with wider questions
which admit of no easy solutions.

I have incurred many debts in the process of bringing this book to completion.
My first debt is to my parents, to whom the book is dedicated, and my loss is that
my mother did not live to see its publication. Thanks are also due to the other
members of my family, at home and abroad, from whom I learned at an early
stage the valuable lesson that disagreement is not the end of dialogue.

That there is a book at all is due to the persistence of Seamus Deane, and to
his enabling example as both friend and editor. When I first saw Seán Hillen's
extraordinary images, I felt he had almost second-guessed the contents of some of
the essays, and I am grateful to him not only for the book cover, but for the use of
other works originally conceived with something entirely different in mind. The
Marian Goodman Gallery (New York), The Municipal Gallery (Dublin), The
Green on Red Gallery (Dublin), James Coleman, Willie Doherty, Pat Feeley, Bob
Janz, Pat Murphy, Philip Napier, Martin Walsh at John Hinde, McConnell's
Advertising Service, and Wolfhound Press generously gave me permission to
reproduce other images and illustrations in the book.

The interdisciplinary nature of many of the essays is a testimony to the open spirit of enquiry fostered by the School of Communications at Dublin City University. I have benefited considerably from exchanges with many students and colleagues in the Faculty of Humanities, both formally and informally, and Farrel Corcoran, Michael Cronin, John Horgan, Stephanie McBride and Brian Trench have been adept at ensuring that good fences are not necessary for good neighbours in an academic community. This is also the place to say a long-overdue thanks to Pam Galvin, Louise McDermott, the late Maeve MacCarthy, David O'Callaghan, and to Seán MacPhilibin in Library Services.

One of the rewards of working in different fields of research is meeting up with many scholars, practitioners and friends who have given me the benefit of their expertise (and, on many occasions, the benefit of their doubt): Jeff Chown, Liz Cullingford, Mary Doran, Tom Duddy, Terry Eagleton, Maud Ellmann, Michael Foley, Richard Kearney, Joep Leerssen, Sharon O'Brien, Peggy O'Brien, Mary O'Connell, Kevin O'Neill, Ann Rigney, Eamon Slater, John Waters, Kevin Whelan, Jennifer Wicke, Paul Willemen and Trisha Ziff. Angela Bourke, Luke Dodd, Anne Kearney and Tanya Kiang have been a constant source of encouragement and stimulation, and more recently, the warm support and critical acuity of Siobhán Kilfeather, Marjorie Howes, David Lloyd and Clair Wills have helped me not only to see reason, but beyond it. My longest standing debt is to Tadhg Foley, whose intellectual integrity and generosity have sustained me over a long period and have taught me how to take ideas, but not myself, too seriously. If I single out Niamh O'Sullivan for special thanks, it is because she will recognize throughout the book echoes of many unfinished conversations. Her friendship and enthusiasm have been crucial in bringing about that minor miracle in Irish culture – the transition from speech to print.

My last and most profound debt is to those who had to live through this difficult transition at first-hand, to Laura and Barry who cheerfully reminded me that all work and no play makes theory a killjoy, and above all to Dolores, whose serenity and sharing of her own time over many years has made event the most trying of tasks a labour of love.

It remains to express my gratitude to the editors and publishers who were initially responsible for the publication of these essays. The order of publication is as follows:

'Lies that Tell the Truth: *Maeve*, History and Irish Cinema', *The Crane Bag*, vol. 7, no. 2, 1983.

'Synge, Country and Western: The Myth of the West in Irish and American Culture', in Chris Curtin, Mary Kelly, Liam O'Dowd, eds. *Culture and Ideology in Ireland* (Galway: Galway University Press, 1984).

'From Kitchen Sink to Soap: Drama and the Serial Form on Irish Television', in John McMahon and Martin McLoone, eds, *Television and Irish Society* (Dublin: RTE/Irish Film Institute, 1985).

'The Politics of Silence: *Anne Devlin*, Women and Irish Cinema', *Framework*, no. 30/31, 1986.

'From Megalith to Megastore: Broadcasting and Irish Culture', in Tom Bartlett, Chris Curtin, Riana O'Dwyer, and Gearóid Ó Tuathaigh, eds., *Irish Studies: A General Introduction* (Dublin: Gill and Macmillan, 1988).

'Labour and Local History: The Case of Jim Gralton, 1886–1945', *Saothar: Journal of the Irish Labour History Society*, no. 14, 1989.

'Coming out of Hibernation? The Myth of Modernity in Irish Culture,' in Richard Kearney, ed., *Across the Frontiers: Ireland in the 1990s* (Dublin: Wolfhound Press, 1988).

'Race Against Time: Racial Discourse and Irish History', *The Oxford Literary Review*, no. 13, 1981.

'Montage, Modernism and the City', *The Irish Review*, no. 10, Spring 1991.

'Identity Without a Centre: Allegory, History and Irish Nationalism', *Cultural Studies*, vol. 6, no. 3, October 1992.

'Narratives of No Return: James Coleman's guaiRE', *Artforum*, vol. xxxiii, no. 4, December, 1993.

'Back Projections: John Hinde and the New Nostalgia', *Circa*, no. 65, Autumn 1994.

'Unapproved Roads: Ireland and Post-Colonial Identity', in Trisha Ziff, ed., *Distant Relations: Chicano/Irish/Mexican Art and Critical Writing* (New York: Smart Art Press, 1995).

Now, once I feel myself observed by the lens, everything changes: I constitute myself in the process of 'posing,' I instantaneously make another body for myself, I transform myself in advance into an image. This transformation is an active one: I feel that the photograph creates my body or mortifies it, according to its caprice.

ROLAND BARTHES, *Camera Lucida*

They said, 'You have a blue guitar,
You do not play things as they are.'

The man replied, 'Things as they are
Are changed upon the blue guitar.'

WALLACE STEVENS, 'The Blue Guitar'

1.1   Bob Janz 'The Day After' (1983)

1. INTRODUCTION:
Culture, History and Irish Identity

It is impossible to change the factual, thing-like side of the past, but the meaningful, expressive, speaking side can be changed, for it is unfinalized and does not coincide with itself (it is free). The role of memory in this eternal transformation of the past . . .

Mikhail Bakhtin

Ireland is a First World country, but with a Third World memory. It is with this paradox that many of the essays in the present book deal: the dislocations between periphery and centre, the country and the city, tradition and modernity.[1] Though it is usual to present these as opposites, both the strengths and weaknesses of Irish culture derive from its confounding of such neat polarities. The 1916 Rising, with its invocation 'of God, and of the dead generations', may now itself be relegated to the memory of the dead (that is, when it is remembered at all), but it is often forgotten that it was staged in a modern post-office, amidst all the trappings of early communications technologies.[2] There is an emblematic moment in *The Promise of Barty O'Brien* (1951), a didactic film on the need for rural electrification scripted by Seán O'Faoláin, in which a son with some obvious oedipal problems surreptitiously installs electricity in the family cottage, and turns on the radio to impress his father, a veteran of the 1916 Rising. To his horror, the voice of England comes on the airwaves, electrifying his traditionalist father in more ways than one. The son rushes to the dial and retrieves the situation by tuning into Radio Éireann, on which, as it happens, a commemorative programme on the Rising is being broadcast. His father is assuaged, and is reluctantly brought into the modern world. From this it is clear that the media can act as a means of anglicization (or Los Angelesization), spreading foreign influences, but they can also consolidate national culture, bringing technology to bear on tradition. O'Faoláin's point is that modernization is not solely an external force, but also requires the active transformation of a culture from within, a capacity to engage critically with its own past.

This theme of 'transformation from within' is taken up in many of the essays. Contrary to a prevalent view which sees Ireland as a 'periphery dominated centre', with the periphery signifying the dead weight of tradition, and the centre the dynamism of change, I argue that it is often the integration of Ireland into the new international order which activates some of the most conservative forces in Irish society. The co-ordinated campaigns in defence of the constitutional prohibitions on abortion and divorce, with their sophisticated use of television and public

3

relations, owe as much to the televangelism of the American 'New Right' as to what Marx once referred to as 'the idiocy of rural life'. By the same token, fundamentalism is not simply a throwback to the past, a relic of an obsolete social order, but may well exemplify the release of righteousness from the fluidity of custom or the contingencies of history. As Martin Woolacott observed acutely in the wake of the Oklahoma bombing, one of the more ominous shifts taking place in modern societies is a conjunction between technology and the politics of reaction:

> [This involves] the escape of religion, and to some extent nationalism, from traditional controls and from traditional thinking. Fundamentalism today, many argue, is post-literate. In spite of its claims to be based on the Book or the Word of God, it is based much more on image and oratory transmitted by modern electronic means. This is not the fundamentalism of the Monkey Trial or of the nineteenth-century mullahs, but the fundamentalism of the sound-bite. It is less rational than its predecessors, more selective of its 'Truth', less open to argument even on its own terms.[3]

This is important to bear in mind, in view of uncritical adulations of the role of the media as modernization agencies in Irish society. It may well be that in combating 'tradition', the mass media and related versions of modernity are often tilting at windmills of their own making. What such linear models of social change overlook is that tradition itself may often have a transformative impact, particularly if it activates muted voices from the historical past, or from marginalized sections of the community. It is in this context that I argue, in relation to the influence of television on Irish society, that it was home-produced programmes, not imported products, that posed the greatest challenge to taboo areas in Irish society. These programmes often borrowed heavily from formats and genres evolved elsewhere, such as the American-style 'talk show' or the British and American drama serial, and this exposure to 'external' forms was vital to their success. However, the innovative thrust of these programmes did not entail a blanket repudiation of 'traditional' or national values, but rather allowed them to re-work the specificity of Irish culture. It was the rural-based television serial, *The Riordans* (1965–79), as against the earlier, urban *Tolka Row* (1963–8), which set the agenda for much of Irish television drama, while *The Late Late Show* (1963–) drew much of its digressive, unpredictable power from Irish oral culture, albeit on terms which addressed a mass audience as against the more familiar codes of local knowledge. At a different level, in my discussion of Pat Murphy's films *Maeve* (1981) and *Anne Devlin* (1984), I argue that their ability to question traditional stereotypes of landscape and history, women and nationalism, derives not from an outright rejection of their falsity, but rather involves a process of recasting them from within. In *Maeve*, landscape is freed from the mythic patriarchal narratives secreted within it by Victorian versions of Irish nationalism and by loyalist ideology; in *Anne Devlin*, the figure of the silent, suffering woman is endowed with a moving, visual eloquence, and redefined as a figure of strength rather than as a forgotten, submissive victim.

The point here is that transformations induced by contact with the new may activate a transgressive potential already latent in the old, in the cast-offs and rejects of history. In my essay on 'Labour and Local History', I argue that it was the unlikely appearance of the spectre of communism in the Leitrim countryside in the early 1930s which galvanized the state into the unprecedented action of deporting an Irishman, the remarkable James Gralton, from his native country. Gralton's radicalism was imbued with international socialism from his experience of the United States, but was also deeply interwoven with clandestine traditions of agrarian protest in the Irish countryside. Such was the alarm caused by Gralton's escapades – the mixture of carnival and communism at his Pearse-Connolly Hall in Gowel – that he brought about an unholy alliance between church, state, and the IRA, all of whom sought to put a stop to his activities. The controversy surrounding his deportation had far-reaching consequences, for it may well be that it helped to precipitate the split in the republican movement that led to the formation of the left-wing Republican Congress in 1934.

At the basis of all these discussions is a rethinking of tradition, at least as it manifests itself in a country with a fractured, colonial past. It is because tradition is associated with order, stability and the inherited wisdom of the ages, the sluggish evolution of a society over a long duration, that it becomes the antithesis of the modern, against which both 'progress' and 'enlightenment' must define themselves. This may indeed be true of Burkean notions of tradition formulated in a British context, a nation unscathed by invasions which prides itself on the continuity of its political institutions, and in which even such revolutions as took place managed to lead to social stability. Faced with a cultural conformity based on notions of a homogeneous, uninterrupted past, it is not surprising that the left in the heartlands of the major European powers has often distanced itself from nationalism, and even from any expression of cultural specificity.[4] Yet while tradition may appear orderly and reassuring from the privileged vantage point of the imperial centre, that is not how it presents itself to countries on the other side of the imperial divide. Writing at the turn of the century, the unionist historian C. Litton Falkiner lamented that the shattered remains of Irish history leave a lot to be desired by comparison with their pristine English counterparts:

> Irish topography is in general deficient in that wealth of historical or literary association which lends so much charm to a summer's ramble in rural England, and invests with so much romantic interest so many of the ancient cities and boroughs of Great Britain. . . . Historical continuity has been lost in the endless civil distractions of the island, and tradition itself speaks in confused and scarce intelligible accents.[5]

As the nationalist Alice Stopford Green retorted, Falkiner is somewhat coy as to the reason why Irish ruins are not in the same charming state as British antiquities: 'How was it that these Englishmen left none of their "romantic charm" there [in Ireland]? What strange history lies hidden behind this saying?'[6]

Stopford Green is alluding here to what Brendan Bradshaw has described as the 'catastrophic' dimension in Irish history – 'seared as the record is by successive waves of conquest and colonization, by bloody wars and uprisings, by traumatic dislocations, by lethal racial antagonisms, and, indeed, by its own nineteenth-century version of a holocaust'.[7] As I argue in 'Montage, Modernism and the City' and 'Race Against Time: Racial Discourse and Irish History', the attrition of Irish history has the effect of removing any semblance of order and harmony from the passage of time. 'The truth is', as one nineteenth-century commentator lamented, 'the whole condition of Ireland is disjointed':

> Ireland has long been a country of agitation. The elements of discord were sown early in her history; and throughout her course, they have been nourished, and not eradicated. . . . We observe in the structure of Irish society, not merely that the elements of it are fragmentary, but antagonistic.[8]

One of the consequences of this is that Irish society did not have to await the twentieth century to undergo the shock of modernity: disintegration and fragmentation were already part of its history so that, in a crucial but not always welcome sense, Irish culture experienced modernity before its time. This is not unique to Ireland, but is the common inheritance of cultures subjected to the depredations of colonialism. As Paul Gilroy suggests in relation to the traumatic legacy of the 'Black Atlantic', 'the concentrated intensity of the slave experience is something that marked out blacks as the first truly modern people, handling in the nineteenth century dilemmas and difficulties which would only become the substance of everyday life in Europe a century later'.[9] Due to a similar uprooting of Irish experience after the atrocities of the 1798 rebellion and the devastation of the Great Famine, Irish literature in the nineteenth century (especially in its romantic or gothic register) often evinced a 'proto-modernist' outlook, whether in the dishevelled, multiple narratives of Charles Maturin or William Carleton, the colloquy of voices in Bram Stoker's *Dracula*, or the heightened, montage effects of Boucicault's melodramas. This calls for a reversal of the standard view which presents the modernist movement – particularly as represented by Joyce and Beckett – as turning its back on the torpor of tradition in Ireland in order to embrace the exhilaration of the metropolitan avant-garde: if anything, these writers' vital contacts with mainland European culture proved productive precisely because they were carrying with them the nightmare of Irish history, the 'ruin of all space, shattered glass and toppling masonry' of the Irish political landscape.[10]

It follows from this that nationalism, as it emerges in an anti-colonial frame, is radically different from the imperious, aggrandizing forms it assumes in the great colonial or world powers. Xenophobic expressions of identity, with their ideas of racial purity and domination, come easily to countries with habits of authority and a secure, organic basis in tradition, but make little sense in cultures whose national narratives are already porous and open-ended, and in which even natives were considered strangers in their own land. It is, of course, true that to win recognition and gain respectability, emergent nationalisms in subaltern cultures have tended to mimic their masters' voices, and reproduce in their own idioms the closed, univocal expressions of identity articulated in the imperial centre. If there are 'invented traditions', as E. J. Hobsbawm and other critics of nationalism delight in discovering, they usually take this form of an integrated, self-validating past.[11] But as I argue in relation to Ireland in 'Identity without a Centre: Allegory, History and Irish Nationalism', threaded through these totalizing images is a much more complex set of narratives, often figuring the self-images of a culture in *allegorical* terms, with all the contestation of identity and openness towards the other which that entails. As Barbara Johnson describes it, drawing on the etymology of the word allegory: *allos*, 'other'; *agorein*, 'to speak in the open or public square':

> Allegory is speech that is other than open, public, direct. It is hidden, deviant, indirect – but also, I want to emphasize, public. It folds the public onto itself. It *names the conflictuality of the public sphere* and the necessity of negotiating these conflicts rhetorically.[12]

Allegorical versions of identity evolved in seventeenth- and eighteenth-century cultural practices and modes of protest which explicitly contested the public sphere, and it was the carrying over of these unresolved energies into nineteenth- and early twentieth-century literature which was largely responsible for the 'proto-modernist' strategies of Irish romanticism.

Of course, the fact that political consciousness in Ireland did not match up to the high standards set by its more 'advanced' European neighbours is sufficient for some commentators to point to the inferior, primitive modes of organization on the periphery. According to Hans Kohn, the purpose of nationalism in the modern west 'was to create a liberal and rational civil society representing the middle class and the philosophy of John Locke'. When, he continues

> nationalism, after the Napoleonic wars, penetrated to other lands – Central and Eastern Europe or to Spain or Ireland – it came to lands which were in political ideas or social structure less advanced than the modern West. . . . While English and American nationalism was, in its origin, connected with the concepts of individual liberty and represented nations firmly constituted in their political life, the new nationalism, not rooted in a similar political and social reality, lacked self-assurance. Its inferiority complex was often compensated by over-emphasis.[13]

The fact that for English and American nationalism, individual rights only extended to cultures recreated in their own image, and that otherwise – as John Locke explicitly ordained – they were simply in a 'state of nature' and ripe for colonization, does not trouble Kohn. Equality extended to individuals, but there was less magnanimity in extending it to cultures. Beyond the pale lay *terra incognita*: in effect, no culture at all.

The politics of representation

For a recent restatement of this view, we need go no further than the response of James Molyneaux, former leader of the Official Unionist Party, to his party's defeat in the North Down by-election in June 1995, perhaps the first significant test of unionist public opinion since the ceasefire was announced in Northern Ireland in 1994. Molyneaux attributed his party's poor showing to the complacency of the largely Protestant electorate in the constituency: if they lived in what he referred to as 'the frontier counties', they might have been less cavalier in exercising their political preferences.[14] In this unguarded remark, it is possible to detect the kind of psychopathology of power which has underpinned some of the most intractable political conflicts in Ireland. Beyond a *border* lies another culture or nation: beyond a *frontier* lies simply waste land, a wilderness awaiting the progress of civilization and 'God's frontiersmen'.[15]

Faced with an invidious frontier myth from the onset of colonization, it is not surprising that culture in Ireland became ineluctably bound up with politics, a pattern that has persisted in many contentious and divergent forms down to the present day. All culture is, of course, political, but in Ireland historically it acquired a particularly abrasive power, preventing the deflection of creative energies into a rarefied aesthetic or 'imaginary' realm entirely removed from the exigencies of everyday life. To engage in cultural activity in circumstances where one's culture was being effaced or obliterated, or even to assert the existence of a civilization prior to conquest, was to make a political statement, if only by depriving the frontier myth of its power to act as an alibi for colonization. For this reason, the successive affirmations of Irish culture since the early modern period – from Geoffrey Keating's opening salvo in the 1630s, to the first cultural revival in the eighteenth century, the romantic nationalism of the nineteenth century, and the Literary Revival and its aftermath in the twentieth century – have assumed a political cast, with greater or lesser degrees of intensity.[16] Contrary to W. H. Auden, poetry did indeed make things happen, to the extent that even W. B. Yeats, the subject of Auden's famous elegy, was tormented late in life by the possibility that his creative works may have made a lethal contribution to the events that culminated in the Easter Rising of 1916, and the subsequent birth of the Irish state.

It is in this sense, in the essays that follow, that I insist on the transformative capacity of culture in society, its power to give rise to what was not there before. Cultural representations do not simply come after the event, 'reflecting' experience or embellishing it with aesthetic form, but significantly alter and shape the ways we make sense of our lives. This would be unproblematic were it not for the fact that to make culture a material force in this way is often construed as an attack on the autonomy of art. For culture to be effective as 'equipment for living', in Kenneth Burke's phrase, it has to be grounded in the material conditions of society, but this runs counter to those familiar currents within literary and cultural criticism which, under various invocations of 'the aesthetic', see the creative imagination as entirely transcending its social and political circumstances, gathering itself up, as Yeats expressed it, into 'the artifice of eternity'. Though this approach sees itself as eschewing politics, in the past it has provided the rationale for a very distinctive colonial agenda. In the Celticism of Matthew Arnold, for instance, Irish identity was reduced to a cultural imaginary, in a restricted aesthetic sense, all the more to remove it from more quotidian matters of power and self-determination.[17] Culture was fine, so long as it concerned itself with denizens of the Celtic twilight rather than with citizens of the real world – or rather, imperial subjects attempting to become citizens. The radical politicization of culture during the Literary Revival may be seen as a repudiation of this idea, an attempt to bring cultural identity down to earth from its more ethereal flights through the Celtic cosmos.

As against this essentially idealist aesthetic, there is an opposing approach, adopted by the dominant methodologies in historical research and the social sciences, which relegates questions of culture entirely to the margins of the social process. Culture is, at best, a mere reflex of more manageable, 'objective' realities (as in the approach which views paintings or novels as mere windows on the world, 'documenting' ethnographic details), or, at worst, a smokescreen, concealing economic and political truths through myth and other rhetorical excesses. Either way, cultural representations are at one remove from society, and hence are in no position to act as agents of historical change, or to help us understand social processes.[18] In an Irish context, such reductionist approaches have set themselves the task of explaining away cultural practices, or symbolic aspects of behaviour, in terms of the 'hard facts' of politics and economics, as if questions of ideology and meaning conveniently evaporate as soon as class and power come on the agenda.

Far from contesting idealism, this is simply its mirror-image, for ideology and cultural identity are still conceived primarily in 'spiritual' or mentalistic terms. On this logic, nothing of significance intervenes – be it narrative structures, generic conventions, linguistic practices, symbolic forms, media institutions, collective memory – between representations and reality, or if it does, it only helps to cloud the issues, rendering society through a glass darkly. It is with this in mind that Raymond Williams stressed the need to 'de-etherialize' culture, asserting its importance as a material force in its own right in negotiating the structures of experience. As he puts it in relation to the traditional Marxist approach to culture, the difficulty is not that it is materialist, but that it is not materialist enough. Hence his advocacy of 'cultural materialism', an approach emphasizing the institutional and material forms taken by culture which would contest two seemingly opposed, but actually mutually supportive, traditions:

> one which has totally spiritualized cultural production, the other which has relegated it to a secondary status. My aim was to emphasize that cultural practices are forms of material production, and that until this is understood it is impossible to think of them in their real social relations – there can only be a second order of correlation.[19]

This has important consequences in reconsidering the relations between culture and history in Ireland, particularly as they impinge on the deeply contested issues of cultural and national identity. It is clear from this approach that identity does not just involve consciousness, or even self-consciousness, but also the realm of *representation*, i.e. the capacity to be realized in material form. Identity is not simply a given which springs into position, fully formed, like Minerva from the head of Jupiter, and still less is it transmitted through telepathy, by a mystical communion between members of a culture. Rather, as Mikhail Bakhtin observes, 'cultural and literary traditions are preserved and continue to live, not in the subjective memory of the individual nor in some collective "psyche", but in the objective forms of culture itself'.[20] Cultural identity, therefore, does not pre-exist its representations or material expressions, but is in fact generated and transformed by them – whether they take the form of the mass media, literary genres such as the novel and drama, visual representations, or other cultural or symbolic practices. Though much valuable work has been done on Irish society from the point of view of economic development, political mobilization, and administrative structures, very little has focused on culture as a set of material practices informing and constituting the social environment. Culture, for the most part, is limited to 'artistic' works, and refined out of existence, while historians and social scientists get on with the business of studying the facts, and determining how society really operates. This narrow division of labour is of little use in understanding the wider ramifications of movements such as nationalism in which symbolic structures themselves are constitutive elements, exerting a profound influence on the logic of social action. As Anthony D. Smith reminds us:

> we cannot understand nations and nationalism simply as an ideology or form of politics but must treat them as cultural phenomena as well. That is to say, nationalism, the ideology and movement, must be closely related to national identity, a multidimensional concept, and extended to include a specific language, sentiments and symbolism.[21]

As an example of such a 'specific language, sentiments and symbolism', we might cite the impact of the mass media on nationalism. Historians are adept at using media sources as evidence or as primary data, but rarely examine the ways in which newspapers and the broadcasting media orchestrate and construct their messages – other than to discern 'externally' induced biases, or direct political interference. The manner in which newspaper stories, for example, are structured in distinctive ways by journalistic codes and conventions that make them different from, say, religious sermons, folklore, legal discourse or indeed pamphlets and other literary forms, is seldom given adequate attention.[22] By the same token, the fact that the different mass media are not just neutral observers but are major participants in politics in their own right, locked into competition with other powerful ideological agencies such as the churches, educational institutions and the family, is also rarely attended to. The fact that, as the social historian Samuel Clark demonstrates, newspaper editors and correspondents were the most over-represented professional category among those arrested at the height of the Land War in 1881 would indicate that the press was far from being an 'impartial spectator' in this formative phase of nationalism. The power of the press at this critical juncture also helps to explain its relative autonomy from clerical influences, and from forms of state control, a course the media were to chart through different though equally troubled waters in the twentieth century.[23]

To say that the media, and culture in general, generate and constitute the objects of their concern is not to concur with Oscar Wilde's dictum that life imitates art. Culture *transforms* what it works on: it does not produce it *ex nihilo*. Representations draw their 'raw materials' from extra-cultural spheres of activity (such as politics, economics, kinship systems), but then subject them to symbolic transformations of their own making. It is from this perspective that I analyse the role of Synge's writings in charting the imaginative geography of the west of Ireland at the turn of the century, and, closer to our own time, the strange, self-conscious evocations of nostalgia in the postcards of John Hinde in the 1950s and 1960s. These images do not just illustrate but rather *exemplify* the areas of experience they address through their representational and rhetorical innovations. In the two main essays dealing with the development of the media in Ireland, I argue that it was the formats, generic conventions and production contexts of key programmes such as the television serial *The Riordans* and the talk show *The Late Late Show* which allowed them to ventilate certain controversial topics, thus helping substantially to mould public opinion on these issues. Had the programmes' styles and modes of representation been different, it may have proved much more difficult to challenge prevailing attitudes, and lift the taboo off sensitive issues regarding the family, sexuality, property, and the traditional pieties of faith and fatherland.

The Riordans, for example, dealt sympathetically with almost every transgression of the Irish family as enshrined in the 1937 Constitution – mixed marriages, marital breakdown, 'living in sin', extra-marital affairs, illegitimacy, contraception – but its approach to these issues was greatly enhanced by the generic convention that the family (rather than, for example, the individual) is the centre of dramatic action in the television serial. Moreover, the open-ended, diffuse narrative structure, which is a hallmark of the serial, prevented any neat or authoritative solutions to the issues raised, thus acting as a solvent of traditional Catholic authority, with its rigid, almost Euclidean, approach to moral problems. The related convention of naturalistic time, according to which Christmas scenes are screened at Christmas and so on, gave an additional journalistic immediacy to its treatment of social problems, removing the 'aesthetic distance' which in other circumstances might have safely relegated these problems to other times and other places.[24]

But it was the innovations introduced for its target audience, the inflections given to the genre by its precise Irish context, which opened up the most valuable spaces for airing social issues. The serial originated as a didactic vehicle for agricultural instruction, designed to break the grip of habit and conformity on farming methods, so that when it subsequently shifted its focus to social issues, it already had a captive audience disposed towards questioning conventional wisdom. The fact that the family farm operated not just as a site of economic production but also as a locus for deep, affective ties enabled the serial to re-figure the boundaries of public and private space, projecting into the social arena issues that might have been safely sealed off as personal or domestic concerns in other soaps.[25]

From this it can be seen that it is the distinctive features of a cultural work, the forms and representational patterns by virtue of which it is constituted as 'art', that allow for the most complex, critical engagements with social reality. This is important to emphasize, in view of the common assumption that works of art are only of social or historical relevance insofar as they efface their formal qualities, giving clear, unmediated access to their 'content'; or, conversely, are only of interest to the connoisseur or the critical purist when their aesthetic aspects and stylistic techniques are foregrounded.[26] It was precisely the sifting and processing of recalcitrant areas of social experience through their stylistic codes and narrative conventions which enabled *The Late Late Show* and *The Riordans* to revise the moral history of Ireland, in however limited a fashion, in the first two decades of Irish television.[27]

National narratives and historical experience

Though the transformations effected by culture are given their exemplary form in specific works, their sphere of influence is not confined to artistic texts but may percolate through social experience, informing responses to everyday situations at many different levels. As Richard Slotkin describes it:

> Historical experience is preserved in the form of narrative; and through periodic retellings those narratives become traditionalized. These formal qualities and structures are increasingly conventionalized and abstracted . . . [but] at the same time that their form is being simplified and abstracted, the range of reference of these stories is being expanded. Each new context in which a story is told adds meaning to it, because the telling implies a metaphoric connection between the storied past and the present.[28]

Slotkin is writing about the Western genre here, about the manner in which its ideological resonances are not restricted to the cinema screen and popular literature but enter into the deepest recesses of American experience. According to Slotkin, the colonial mission into the wilderness was transferred from its original agrarian setting and reformulated to meet the needs of a rapidly industrializing society in the nineteenth century. Frontier ideology was conscripted into class conflict and race relations, with strikers, blacks and immigrants being portrayed as savages and social misfits, anachronistic barriers on the road to progress.[29] In the twentieth century, when these national narratives seemed to have come to the end of the trail, they received a new lease of life from foreign policy, supplying the rhetoric that was required to justify expansionism abroad in the name of freedom and the American way of life. Redskins were replaced by reds under the bed, or, more latterly, by mad mullahs or despots inhabiting oil-rich deserts that looked suspiciously like the landscapes of classic Westerns. Under President Kennedy, the initial territorial co-ordinates of the errand into the wilderness were re-asserted, but this time transposed onto outer space, the last frontier, where manifest destiny was finally given the room to manoeuvre denied it on earth. As Slotkin points out, these myths and narrative formulae exist in a complex relationship both with actual historical developments, and with fictive representations on the big (or the small) screen. Defeat in Vietnam, Watergate, and the oil crisis in the 1970s, for instance, virtually eliminated the Western as an active genre in popular culture, but with the installation of Ronald Reagan in the White House, it came into its own once more, albeit in a grim, parodic form.

It is against this backdrop of powerful national narratives, infusing and animating the self-images of a people, that I contrast the myths of the west in Irish and American culture. For all their similarities as foundational myths – sharing agrarian ideals, an aversion to law and order and to the centralization of the state – it is the differences between them that are most striking. The wild west is an outpost of individualism, extolling the virtues of the self-made man that lie at the heart of the American dream. By contrast, the recourse to the west in Ireland is impelled by a search for community, a desire to escape the isolation of the self and to immerse oneself in the company of others. It is the loner who reaches for his gun in the western, standing up against mob rule, but it is collective violence, in the guise of 'Captain Moonlight' and his cohorts, which stalked the Irish countryside, with the individual only making his appearance in the guise of an informer, or an unwelcome stranger.[30] Above all, however, the western genre is a hymn to the wilderness, an exercise pre-eminently of the *spatial* imagination which finds its images of freedom in the open expanses of the supposedly uninhabited great plains. Its Irish equivalent, however, looks for its authenticating images in *time*, extending its horizons through the accretions of history which acknowledge, rather than deny, the pre-colonial presence on the landscape.

At this point it becomes clear that the most important correspondences between the respective myths of the west lie in the affinities between the native Irish and the native Americans – and, on the other side of the colonial divide, between the proponents of the frontier myth in the new world and their forbears, the Cromwellian planters and the Scots-Irish in seventeenth-century Ireland. These are not just analogies but, as I argue in 'Race against Time' and 'Unapproved Roads', are part of a shared historical experience of colonization. As the leading Irish-American paper, the *Irish World*, expressed it in 1875, defending Sitting Bull against the calumnies heaped on him by the American press following the Battle of Little Big Horn:

> If SITTING BULL is a savage[,] JOHN BULL is a hundred times a greater savage
> . . . 'Exterminate them' [say the journalists about the Indians] . . . are these
> journalists civilized? . . . the descendants by blood or in spirit, of the brutal
> Tories of a century ago who warred against justice and sought to perpetuate a
> reign of fraud and wrong over men of all sizes . . . SITTING BULL is said to be
> a savage; and the simple fact is that he stood between his people and
> extermination.[31]

On the other side of the divide – or the stockade – we find loyalist ideology in Ireland even in modern times identifying with the frontier ethic, and, indeed, attributing its success in America to the efforts of the Ulster Scots, or Scots-Irish, in transplanting their 'civilizing' skills from Ireland to the new world:

> Ideally suited for their new life by reason of their experience as pioneers in Ulster,
> their qualities of character and their Ulster Scottish background, they made a unique
> contribution to the land of their adoption. They became the frontiersmen of colonial
> America, clearing the forests to make their farms . . . [As] President Theodore
> Roosevelt described them . . . 'they suffered terrible injuries at the hands of the
> redmen, and on their foes they waged a terrible warfare in return . . . they were of
> all men the best fitted to conquer the wilderness and hold it against all comers'.[32]

Given this 'romance' of colonization, it is not surprising to find a resistance to the cult of the wilderness, and the idealization of solitude and nature, in Irish culture, a dissident current in romanticism which I examine in 'Synge, Country and Western', 'Lies that Tell the Truth' and 'Race Against Time'.[33] Where the colonizer saw nature, the colonized saw culture. Accordingly, land-scape in Irish romanticism answered not so much to the call of the wild as to the return of the native, its ruins, antiquities and associations with myths and legends testifying to the existence of disparate national narratives which exerted a tenacious hold on popular memory.

According to Roy Foster:

> Again and again in Irish history, one is struck by the importance of the narrative
> mode: the idea that Irish history is a 'story', and the implications that this carries
> about it of a beginning, a middle, and the sense of an ending.

'The compelling logic of a Story of Ireland,' he continues, 'with its plot, narrative logic and desired outcome, reached its apogee in the nineteenth century' in books such as A. M. Sullivan's *The Story of Ireland* (1867), which rapidly sold 50,000 copies and went into several editions. Foster is correct to insist on the importance of the narrative mode in Irish history, but seems to confine its operations to what came after the events, to *books* and the *writing* of history as against the lived experience of popular memory. Sullivan's book, with its upbeat promise of national redemption, 'constructed (often by careful exclusion) the accepted national memory. . . . In so doing, it supplied the canon for Irish history as taught for generations by orders like the Christian Brothers.' 'All conformed,' Foster continues, 'determinism was explicit. The formula brilliantly popularized by Sullivan from 1867 created the terms learned by the succeeding generation.'[34] It is not entirely accurate to say that 'all conformed', for what Foster fails to point out here is the precise nature of Sullivan's conservative political project, and in particular, his sustained opposition to Fenianism and popular insurgency. As I argue in the case of Sullivan's and Standish O'Grady's Victorian reconstructions of the past in 'Lies that Tell the Truth', their orderly stories can be seen as an attempt to co-opt and control the more unruly and refractory narratives of vernacular history, in which the past was embossed in material form on the landscape and worked into the very texture of social experience. As William O'Brien, one of Sullivan's most implacable opponents, expressed it, with characteristic heightened language:

> When the framers of the penal laws denied us books, and drew their thick black veil over Irish history, they forgot that the ruins they had themselves made were the most eloquent schoolmasters, the most stupendous memorials of a history and a race that were destined not to die. They might give our flesh to the sword, and our fields to the spoiler, but before they could blot out the traces of their crimes, or deface the title deeds of our heritage, they would have had to uproot to their last scrap of sculptured filigree the majestic shrines in which the old race worshipped; they would have had to demolish to their last stone the castles which lay like wounded giants through the land to mark where the fight had raged most fiercest; they would have had to level the pillar towers, and to seal up the sources of the holy wells.[35]

As against the contention of several leading critics in recent historiographical debates that narrative does not belong to experience and action, but only to its subsequent re-ordering in writing or representations, O'Brien is here insisting that life itself is infused with narrative forms, albeit of a fragmented, wayward kind.[36] The most telling expressions of these inchoate structures lie not in the tightly controlled 'Stories of Ireland' discussed by Foster, but rather in the proto-modernist tales of terror which haunted the gothic fiction of Charles Maturin, Lady Morgan, William Carleton and others, and the abrupt transitions and reversals of popular melodrama alluded to above.[37] In order to cast Sullivan's and O'Grady's histories as the templates of nationalist memory, Foster feels obliged to diminish the importance of popular celebrations, such as the street demonstrations and expressions of collective memory that accompanied the centenary of the 1798 rebellion. As recent research has shown, however, these offered powerful alternative perspectives on the past to the official versions, and may be seen as the modern equivalents of the endangered 'history from below' eulogized by William O'Brien.[38] The fact that this history is staged and contrived, rather than being an organic legacy from time immemorial, is precisely the point; these are often the kind of symbolic practices through which culture effects its most radical transformations of society.

By pursuing, then, the oblique and often recondite ways in which social forces and historical events are inflected by cultural forms, their characteristic figures and narrative patterns, it may be possible to give a belated hearing to voices or patterns of experience that have escaped the nets of official knowledge, or have been muted by the dominant ideologies of the day. As an example of this, we may cite the pertinent questions raised by F. S. L. Lyons some years ago in his lecture 'The Burden of our History'. Stressing the need to broaden the definition of culture to include the whole mode of life of a community, Lyons asked:

> Though our days are filled with the actualities of communal strife, how much do we really know, in historical terms, about how a community evolves and how it interacts with, or reacts against, another community? Oh, we know about community politics all right, we know about parties and elections . . . and the rest of the pseudo-democratic paraphernalia. But about the essence of a community we know, I repeat, all too little outside our immediate, personal and highly fallible experience.[39]

This observation is central to genuine historical understanding, but Lyons does not follow his own argument to its logical conclusion. For no sooner has he emphasized the desirability of 'cross[ing] the barriers imaginatively between one community and another' than he proceeds to write off a community's own understanding of itself, the narratives through which it attempts to make sense of its past. These, from his perspective as a professional historian, are best construed as simply fiction, 'the false history', as he puts it, 'that has for too long masqueraded as the real thing'. Complaining that 'we can no longer distinguish the realities of what has happened on this island from the myths we have chosen to weave around certain symbolic events', Lyons makes it clear that in this contest between darkness and light, truth lies firmly in the hands of the academic historians rather than the benighted cultures they purport to represent.[40] This denigration of popular history, the immensely complex ways in which communities organize their own lives, received perhaps its most authoritative expression in T. W. Moody's canonical article, 'Irish History and Mythology':

> Nations derive their consciousness of the past not only – and not mainly – from historians. They also derive it from popular traditions, transmitted orally, in writing, and through institutions. I am using the word myth to signify received views of this kind as contrasted with the knowledge the historian seeks to extract by the application of scientific methods to his evidence.[41]

Yet, as the American scholar Joel C. Weinsheimer comments in a related context, there is something troubling about formulations of this kind, particularly if they are meant to be of any benefit to the communities they are supposed to enlighten:

> First, the overcoming of prejudice occurs on only one side of the equation, that of the historian. While the object of historical understanding is conceived as other people's prejudices, not their knowledge or insights or truths, the historian manages to escape his own [historical positioning] . . . If the historian's overcoming of his prejudices means overcoming his particularities, then it is history itself that he is escaping . . . history is not just the object of understanding but the very thing that impedes it.[42]

The historian's fear, in other words, is not simply of myth, but of history itself, particularly when it is not easily incorporated into the controlling, seamless narratives that allow communities to smooth over, or even to deny, their own pasts.

If we are to acknowledge history as a living force rather than a dead letter, we have to free ourselves, as Brendan Bradshaw advises, from 'the sheer dullness of the clinical style to which value-free discourse lends itself'.[43] Understanding a community or a culture does not consist solely in establishing 'neutral' facts and 'objective' details: it means taking seriously *their* ways of structuring experience, their popular narratives, the distinctive manner in which they frame the social and political realities which affect their lives. Even the 'facts' themselves, where a communal *mentalité* or world view is concerned, risk serious misunderstanding if their meaning is taken as self-evident, as beyond interpretation. As Robert Darnton writes of the attempts to reconstruct the world view of the French peasantry under the Old Regime:

> Precision may be inappropriate as well as impossible in the history of mentalities, a genre that requires different methods from those used in conventional genres, like political history. World views cannot be chronicled in the same manner as political events, but they are no less 'real'. Politics could not take place without the preliminary mental ordering that goes into the common sense notion of the world. Common sense itself is a social construction of reality, which varies from culture to culture. Far from being the arbitrary figment of some collective imagination, it expresses the common basis of experience in a given social order.[44]

Darnton is not denying the importance of precision: he is saying that a literal, one-dimensional approach may be suitable for some restricted fields of enquiry, but may often miss out on what is most characteristic and profoundly important about a society.

Thus when Lyons protests that 'myth' has obscured 'reality' in our understanding of certain 'symbolic events', he does not seem to realize that the very existence of a *symbolic* dimension in human action requires a historical method that goes beyond literalist assumptions, and scientific norms of causality and certainty. For this reason, it is important not only to re-think but to *re-figure* Irish identity, to attend to those recalcitrant areas of experience which simply do not lend themselves to certainty, and which impel societies themselves towards indirect and figurative discourse – narratives, generic conventions, rhetorical tropes, allegory, and other 'literary' modes of composition.[45] It may well be that these constitute a society's way of evading the truth: if so, one would like to hear more from historians why the truth is so painful.[46]

Allegories of identity

It follows from this that historical accounts or social explanations that gloss over the multiple ways in which cultural practices intervene in the unfolding of events do less than justice to the diversity and complexity of human behaviour. It is not just that such investigations are incomplete; rather, they are distorted without due provision being made for cultural factors. Hence, for example, in the discussion of agrarian insurgency in 'Identity Without a Centre', I argue that accounts of secret societies such as the Whiteboys and their later successors – couched exclusively in economic terms – fail to grasp the full measure of the political threat they presented to colonial hegemony. This was derived from their cultural filiations, which were threaded through their more immediate economic objectives having to do with enclosures, tithes, rent, and so on. Agrarian protest based its legitimacy on its intricate associations with peasant rituals, with groups such as the Molly Maguires mobilizing at wakes and weddings,[47] and was interwoven with important seasonal festivals in the cultural calender such as Mayday, Halloween (Samhain), and the aftermath of Christmas (Wrenboy's Day, New Year's Eve). Describing the almost imperceptible shifts between masquerading in the festive costume of mummers and Wrenboys, and dressing up in the menacing garb of Ribbonmen, Sir William Wilde wrote:

> It was really a sort of melo-dramatic exhibition. Those who wore cut paper round their hats, as wren-boys, when they grew up to be young men decorated themselves with ribbons and white shirts to act the May-boys – and, as mummers, painted their faces, and went through the Christmas pantomime with old rusty swords. These were the mechanists, stage-managers, wardrobe keepers, dressers, scene-shifters, and 'property' manufacturers of the Roscommon ribbonmen . . . meeting, thus attired, with an old gun, or a yeoman's rusty halbert, of a November night, and marching, by moonlight, to the sound of the fiddle or bagpipes, though what end was to be attained thereby, the great majority of them neither knew nor cared.[48]

It is clear that to appreciate this far from humorous display of moonlighting, it is necessary to make use not only of the causal explanations of the positive sciences, but also the interpretative protocols deployed in understanding melodrama and folk theatre. If we shift locale and turn our attention to the reincarnation of the Molly Maguires in the United States in the 1870s, it is clear that the actual events which took place in the Philadelphia coalfields, as they are mediated through legal investigations and subsequent trials, are so charged with symbolic import as to make the very notion of an accurate account depending on these 'reliable' historical sources deeply problematic. Pre-ordained formulae depicting the Molly Maguires 'as a band of Irish cut-throats, engaging in violence for its own sake, for money, or for revenge', and indeed linking them in time-honoured fashion to the 'savagery' of 'the Red men',[49] featured so prominently in the trial speeches, newspaper reports, and local histories, that one of the vital tasks facing the historian is to uncover the buried narratives in which the 'facts' are mired. The understanding of genres, key tropes and figures afforded in literary contexts is central here to the pro-cess of social explanation.[50] In this respect, as Michael Denning argues, the innumerable popular fictions in 'story papers' and dime novels which dis-played their narrative structures openly, and explored the events from different angles, broke with this one-dimensional approach and, precisely by virtue of their artistic licence, introduced a far greater degree of complexity into the shadowy proceedings of the Philadelphia coalfields. Questions having to do with who bore ultimate responsibility for the violence, with motivation, mean-ing, and patterns of organization, were addressed in ways that did not surface in the more highly regarded factual registers of legal and journalistic dis-course, patrolled as they were, by dominant power interests:

> In many ways, the story papers allow a more complex response to cases like the Molly Maguires than did the newspapers. Whereas the newspapers, both com-mercial and labour, were caught within the conventions of crime reporting and the narrow, if vital, issues of guilt and innocence, the story papers could weave elements of the court testimony into a wider narrative of . . . miners in gener-al, to the Irish, to the miners' organizations, and to the social and production relations of the mining community.[51]

In their original Irish setting, these popular modes of resistance derived their legitimacy from the kind of vernacular history adverted to by William O'Brien above, drawing on an extended repertoire of folk motifs, popular justice and collective memory. The fact that their political awareness did not raise itself to the level of an idea, or to clearly stated objectives, did not make it any less sophisticated, for instead of invoking political concepts such as 'the nation' or, indeed, 'Ireland', insurgent movements and the cultural politics they inspired owed their allegiances to a series of enigmatic, allegorical figures, be they 'Queen Sieve', 'Dark Rosaleen', or 'Cathleen Ní Houlihan'. This is not just 'pre-national' consciousness but in an important sense constitutes the sub-stratum of all national sentiment, or any nationalism 'from below'. As Miroslav Hroch writes, taking issue with the widespread notion that nationalism is a set of ideas imposed from the top down by the urban intelligentsia:

> Intellectuals can only 'invent' national communities if certain objective preconditions for the formation of a state already exist. Karl Deutsch long ago remarked that for national consciousness to arise, there must be something for it to be conscious of . . . [These] may be verbalized, but below the level of 'high politics' they are often unverbalized.[52]

Allegory in an Irish context belongs to the politics of 'the unverbalized'. It is not just a poetic device, but a figural practice that infiltrates everyday experience, giving rise to an aesthetics of the actual. When five Whiteboys were hanged in Waterford, they declared that by the mysterious Queen Sieve, they did not mean a poetic abstraction but a 'distressed harmless old woman, blind of one eye, who still lives at the foot of a mountain in the neighbour-hood'. Allegory of this kind is not a veil that can be lifted at will, but involves a refusal, or rather an inability, to name a reality too painful for clear and distinct ideas: 'The very extravagance of the allegory employed on these occasions', wrote Edward Hayes, 'is an unmistakable index to the intensity of the persecution which produced it in the first place.'[53] This is a corrective to the common misapprehension that the 'figural' is implacably at odds with the 'real', as if something only possesses allegorical – or symbolic – resonances to the extent that it is emptied of its own materiality, be it a sign, an object, or the body of a person. I deal with these questions in 'The Politics of Silence' and in 'Narratives of no Return: James Coleman's guaiRE', showing how in some of the finest achievements in contemporary Irish cinema and the visual arts, allegory and signification derive their power from their dense connections with the physicality of the flesh, and in particular, the maternal body.

There is an important issue here for feminist politics, given the often voiced criticism that female figures are endowed with allegorical status at the expense of the interests of living women in the real world. Clearly, to cite an obvious example, the personification of 'Justice' as a female holding a weighing scales has done little, historically, to advance the cause of women in society. In this case, there is simply a mechanical correlation between the image and the concept, and the figure is not at all necessary to an understanding of the idea, which exists independently of its allegorical expressions. This is indeed what happened when the identification of Ireland as a woman ossified into 'Mother Ireland' and related images under the official ideology of faith and fatherland. But this is not how all figurations work. For allegory to retain its critical valency, it is vital that there is an instability of reference and contestation of meaning to the point where it may not be at all clear where the figural ends, and the literal begins. As Edward Hayes again describes the recourse to allegory under colonization, in his nineteenth-century anthology of Irish ballads:

> It was this persecution of the bards by Elizabeth and Cromwell, which led to the dreamy allegory in which national hopes were shrouded. Ireland was the poet's

> love . . . and so consistent were his political rhapsodies, on some occasions, with the wailings of the tender passion, that it is almost impossible to discriminate whether they were intended for his country or his mistress. Of this class is [James Clarence] Mangan's 'Dark Rosaleen', which some consider political, but which we have placed among the Ballads of the Affections.[54]

According to Miroslav Hroch, the intensity of this relationship to the nation arises 'in conditions of acute stress' so that the experience of the body politic 'comes to be lived as part of the individual memory of each citizen, and its defeats resented as failures that touch them. One result of such personalization is that people will regard their nation – that is, themselves – as a single body in a more than metaphorical sense'.[55] This blurring of the boundaries between the personal and the political, inscribing the physicality of the body in public space, may not be at all to the detriment of feminist politics, or at least that project which calls for an entire transformation of the public sphere to allow women to participate in it as 'real women'.[56]

Moreover, unlike the statue of Justice (or Liberty), which is placed on a pedestal in order to remove it from structures of power, allegory in a colonized culture is part of the symbolic ordering of life itself and hence, for all its visionary tropes, is in a position to unmask power relations. The figuration of Ireland as a woman intensified under a system of cultural apartheid in which the entire native population, both male and female, shared the condition of women in the metropolitan centre. In these circumstances, the recourse to female imagery in poetry and popular protest turns the colonial stereotype against itself, positing an alternative 'feminized' public sphere (imagined as the nation) against the official patriarchal order of the state. This conjunctural reading is important to understanding how cultural representations are inflected by history. As the examples of allegory cited by Hayes indicate, the instability of reference is such that it may not always be possible, on *textual grounds* alone, to decide whether a work is functioning allegorically or not, and hence we have to go 'outside' the text, to its *historical conditions of meaning*, in order to give full scope to its semantic potential. The multiple references are not, in the strict sense, inherent in the text, nor are they simply added by ingenious critics in retrospect: rather they derive from the historical contiguity of the text to other narratives and symbolic forms that are working their way through the culture.[57] As James Clifford describes it:

> There is no way definitely, surgically, to separate the factual from the allegorical in cultural accounts . . . reading is indeterminate only to the extent that history in itself is open-ended. If there is a common resistance to the recognition of allegory, a fear that it leads to a nihilism of reading, this is not a realistic fear. It confuses contests for meaning with disorder.[58]

It is, then, only by bringing history to bear on a work that its semantic richness, its capacity for proliferating meanings is realized. So far from being a reductionist exercise, the placing of texts in their wider generic and historical settings releases their manifold interpretations, reminding us, in the process, that there is no one way of mapping out an experience, even if some ways are more appropriate in specific contexts than others. For historians whose relation to the past extends beyond the provision of a minimalist chronicle, the irreducible cultural dimension in experience insists that the 'logic' of social explanation is essentially contested terrain, in which certainty is often achieved at the expense of complexity. At the other end of the spectrum, the attempt to make culture impervious to history and politics, insulating it from the contingencies of context and social change, makes the imagination itself a closed book, converting the autonomy of art into a pretext for aesthetic fundamentalism. Art is at its most autonomous when it negates the official boundaries between private and public experience, text and context, bridging the gap between what can be said and what often goes without saying.

2. SYNGE, COUNTRY AND WESTERN: The Myth of the West in Irish and American Culture

We have no prairies
To slice a big sun at evening . . .

Seamus Heaney, 'Bogland'

In a lecture on Irish visual culture delivered in 1980, the artist Robert Ballagh has singled out the idealization of the west of Ireland as being perhaps the greatest inhibiting influence on the development of twentieth-century Irish art. The equation of rural life with all that is truly Irish has dominated the work of many modern Irish painters, but is particularly evident in the work of Jack Yeats, Paul Henry and Seán Keating. In one of Keating's pictures, a romantic portrayal of a group of armed republicans entitled 'Men of the West' [Fig 2.1], the artist's imagination runs away with him to such an extent that the gunmen, in Ballagh's words, 'are more reminiscent of being west of the Rio Grande than west of the Shannon'.[1] In Keating's eyes, apparently, there is little difference between the two: the playboy could just as well become the cowboy of the western world.

The cowboy and the playboy: the west of both worlds

The invocation of the west as the source of heroism, mystery and romance goes back at least to antiquity, and is found in many different cultures under such varied names as Atlantis, Elysium, El Dorado or the English Land of Cockaigne. In modern times, however, Ireland and the United States would seem to be the outstanding examples of countries in which the myth of the west has been elevated to the level of a national ideal.[2] It is easy to see, moreover, how confusion could arise between the two different versions of the western world. Both concern themselves centrally with sites of cultural survival, the sole remaining enclaves of traditional values in a world corrupted by progress and industrialization. For this reason, the country is extolled at the expense of the city and the past venerated rather than the present. In the old west, there is a general distrust of everything connected with modernization – the preacher, the 'schoolmarm', the pony express, the stagecoach, the steamboat and, more ambiguously, the railroad or the iron horse. In the Irish equivalent, things are no different. On the Aran Islands, Synge assumed the role of a latter-day Canute, attempting to hold back 'the filthy modern tide' (in

23

Yeats' graphic phrase). He expressed his profound dismay at 'the thought that this island will gradually yield to the ruthlessness of "progress"'. 'How much of Ireland', he goes on to ask, 'was formerly like this and how much of Ireland is today Anglicized and civilized and brutalized'.[3]

The most striking resemblance, however, between the Irish and the American myths of the west lies not in their aversion to progress as such, but in their pronounced hostility to law and order, and the forces of centralization. In both, there is a preoccupation with violence or any other means of taking the law into one's own hands. In the typical western scenario, the lawyers and judges hightail it out of town at the first sign of trouble, an underlining of the irrelevance of the 'due process' seen to greatest effect in the bumbling character of the tinhorn lawyer in John Ford's *The Man Who Shot Liberty Valance* (1962). Nor is Synge any more sanguine about the consolidation of law and order in the west of Ireland. Witnessing an eviction on one of the Aran Islands, he writes that 'these mechanical police, with commonplace agents and sheriffs, and the rabble they had hired, represented aptly enough the civilization for which the homes of the island were to be desecrated'. He goes on to remark:

> It seems absurd to apply the same laws to these people and to the criminal classes of a city. The most intelligent man on Inishmaan has often spoken to me of his contempt of the law, and of the increase of crime which the police have brought to Aranmor.[4]

These then are some of the assumptions common to both the Irish and the American versions of the agrarian ideal. However, it would be unwise to conclude on the strength of this that one can simply lift the conventions of one genre and transpose them unaltered onto another. For, as we shall see, despite all their similarities, the differences between the Irish and American interpretations of the west are even more profound and far-reaching.

In its American form, the western is a hymn to individualism, a celebration of self-interest and personal liberty evoked in visual terms by the limitless expanse of the great plains and the vast open prairies. In marked contrast, the image of the west of Ireland elaborated in the Anglo-Irish contribution to the Literary Revival represents the precise opposite: an escape from individualism and the fragmentation of community which Synge believed to be endemic in the modernizing process. In the American myth, we find the classic formulation of the puritan ethic – self-interest and liberty are only given free rein insofar as the passions, and sensual pleasure in general, are controlled and subordinated. It is this spartan code of conduct which insulates the cowboy against what is perhaps the greatest threat to his personal freedom – women. By way of contrast, the appeal of the west of Ireland for writers like Synge and Yeats lay precisely in the fact that it offered a refuge from such a puritan ethos, from the suffocating moral atmosphere of an Ireland dominated by the emergent bourgeoisie, both Catholic and Protestant. This gives a radically different inflection to the animosity towards

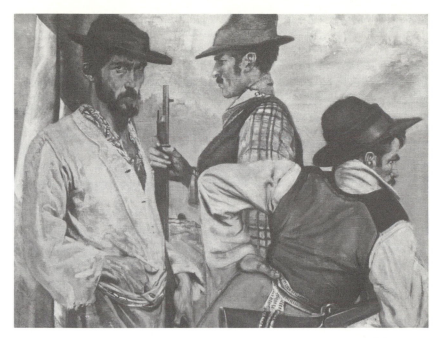

2.1   Sean Keating, 'Men of the West'

law and order which we find in both idealizations of the west. For Synge, the glorification of violence and lawlessness so evident in *The Playboy* was animated by Yeats' 'dream of the noble and beggar-man', by a desire to return to the pre-lapsarian world of Ascendancy Ireland, when the rule of law and the centralizing structures of a developing capitalist economy had still not brought about the landed gentry's fall from grace. The distrust of the law in the old west is also motivated by a fear of big government, but for very different reasons: here the operating principle is a mixture of republican self-reliance and *laissez-faire*, the ideology of the smallholder and the sovereign self which found expression in the image of the hard-riding cowboy, but which was so inimical to the values of Yeats' rakish 'hard-riding country gentlemen'.

Reaganism revisited: the ideology of the old west

In his interesting study of the myth of masculinity, *White Hero Black Beast*, Paul Hoch has identified two dominant archetypes of the male which recur with almost cyclical regularity throughout history. There is, he claims

> on the one side a sort of hard-working, hard-fighting, 'puritan' hero who adheres to a production ethic of duty before pleasure; and, on the other, a more aristocratic 'playboy' who lives according to an ethic of leisure and sensual indulgence.[5]

The former corresponds to what Hoch calls an 'ethic of production', the latter to an 'ethic of consumption', and the oscillation between the two archetypes may be attributed, in his view, to the shifting power relations between the two social classes governing these outlooks on life – the bourgeoisie during the entrepreneurial phase of capitalism, and the leisured aristocracy of a slowly disintegrating feudalism.

The western is quintessentially the expression of the restless individualism which lies at the heart of the great American dream. The myths of the Lone Ranger, the trailblazer, the pathfinder and the frontiersman, all crystallize in their various evocative images the pioneering spirit of agrarian capitalism, the austerity and moral endeavour of the colonial errand into the wilderness, and the ruthless social Darwinism of the eastern businessman. The cowboy is the product of all these influences, taking the form, in one Hollywood western after another, of an 'upright, clean-living, sharp-shooting . . . White Anglo-Saxon Protestant who respects the law, the flag, women and children' – usually in that order.[6]

Hence the western hero, the moral entrepreneur, the man of vision who single-handedly cleans up a town overnight. The cowboy is his own man, settling his own scores, the very epitome of self-help and individual initiative. He is a crusader against all those vices which threaten his independence and self-control – drink, gambling, lust, greed and communal violence. Characteristically he allows himself to be subjected to temptation, but in these situations evil is only advertised, as Barthes would say, all the more to exorcise it. The cowboy buys himself a bottle of whiskey, but unlike the bandit or Doc Holliday, leaves it virtually full on the counter behind him. He may guard payrolls or ride with Wells Fargo, but he never thinks of lining his own pockets. It is at cards, however, that his greatest single attribute comes into play – his poker face. There is not a flicker of emotion or enthusiasm; to publish one's feelings is to perish in this autistic environment. It is not for nothing that Clint Eastwood is said to have learned his trade at the Mount Rushmore school of acting: like God, the cowboy knows that to be inscrutable is to be invincible.

This codification of the flesh, this emotional paralysis, is seen at its starkest in the cowboy's attitude towards women. The old west is a male preserve – Marlboro country.

> With woman [writes Peter Homans of the cowboy] there is no desire or attraction. He appears somewhat bored with the whole business, as if it were a line of duty. He never blushes or betrays any enthusiasm; he never rages or raves over a woman. His monosyllabic stammer and brevity of speech clearly indicate an intended indifference.[7]

As a rule, the cowboy leaves home at an early age (Davy Crockett taking to the woods at the age of three, apparently) and learns to fend for himself from the outset, in what Jim Kitses refers to as 'a dream of primitivistic individualism'.[8] If anything threatens to sabotage this dream, and destroy this pursuit of loneliness, it is the proximity of a woman. For this reason, it is essential in the western that the main female character be desexualized, taking the form of a blond, virginal figure from the east, the female counterpart of the puritan hero. Her role is to act as a brake on violence, attempting to convince the hero to hang up his guns, but as soon as the shooting starts, it is clear that her protests are to no avail. The one female character whom the cowboy does feel at ease with is the saloon girl, who always comes from a non-WASP background. Her very remoteness from serious relationships ensures that there are no fears of complications. She alone understands the hero's compulsions and inner torments. For her trouble, she usually ends up, like Marlene Dietrich in *Rancho Notorious* (1952) and *Destry Rides Again* (1939), stopping a bullet that was intended for him. When it comes to the final showdown, the cowboy has only one stable companion – his horse. In a characteristic scene from a 'Hopalong Cassidy' novel, a young female admirer pleads with Hoppy to abandon the trail of the lonesome pine for a normal, humdrum existence:

> 'But you can't always move on, Hoppy!' Lenny protested. 'Some day you must settle down! Don't you ever think of marriage?'
> 'Uh-huh, and whenever I think of it I saddle Topper and ride. I'm not a marrying man, Lenny.'[9]

The puritan ethos of the western represents the frontier myth of colonial ideology reworked for a project of agrarian capitalism, the homespun philosophy of the smallholder or self-made man which presided over the great push west in the aftermath of the Civil War. It is in this light that we should consider the ambivalent attitude towards progress in the western, for obviously the pioneers and settlers themselves represent the thrust of civilization against the 'primitivism' of the Indians, the previous inhabitants of the great plains. It is not, therefore, progress itself which the western opposes, but the particular form it assumed in the development of American capitalism. In this sense, it soon become apparent that the power and ruthlessness of big business and monopoly capital posed a greater threat to the livelihood of the smallholder than the dark, brooding presence of the Indians. Hence the stock situation in films such as *Shane* (1953) in which the 'small man', the homesteader or sheep-farmer, is pitted in struggle against the rancher, the cattleman or the great railway-baron from the east. The moral of the western, however, is that in the face of big business or corporate interests, the peace-loving smallholders stand defenceless.[10] 'They cannot represent themselves,' as Marx said of their French counterparts, 'they must be represented.'[11] And this, of course, is where the hero comes in. Moreover, his involvement in the affairs of the community should not be taken as a disinterested pursuit of justice, for the cowboy's interest in law and order is invariably governed by personal considerations. Whether he has lost his 'Maw' or his 'Paw', his kid brother or sister, or whether he has been humiliated or double-crossed in the past, he usually has an axe to grind, a personal stake in the enforcement of law and order. It is those who cramp his style, or impugn his honour, however conceived, who draw his wrath. If the community benefits from the cowboy's actions, this can at the most be attributed to the wonderful operation of Adam Smith's invisible hand, in which private concerns bring about public virtues. This is the reason why the hero seldom settles down in the community; it is merely fortuitous that their interests have tended to coincide in the first place.

It is from this perspective that we should view the cowboy's attitude towards violence and the consolidation of the legal system. As in the case of his individualistic conception of the public interest, the cowboy only agrees to uphold the law on his own terms. If anything prevents the law from representing the interests of the individual, it is centralization and the accumulation of power in the state apparatus. Central government and bureaucracy becomes a law unto itself, leaving the cowboy (in his role as a representative of the smallholder) with no alternative but to short-circuit the due process and take the law into his own hands. It comes as a real disappointment in a western if the desperado is captured and brought to trial, rather than meeting his come-uppance in a shoot-out. There is one important rider to all this, however: only the isolated individual is entitled to resort to violence and circumvent the ordinary course of justice. If there is any basic taboo in the western it is that of mob rule – posses are just about permissible but the lynching party is absolutely out. 'I never hunt in packs,' says Henry Fonda in *The Tin Star* (1957), 'a fellow could get trampled.'

Masterful images: the myth of the west in Irish culture

To turn from the old west of Hollywood to the western world of the Irish Literary Revival is to enter a new moral universe, to pass from a west which was there to be won to a west which was lost and lay waiting to be recovered. In the west of Ireland, Synge, Yeats and other Anglo-Irish figures associated with the Revival found a respite from the very asceticism and self-reliance which characterized the American old west. In Ireland, of course, this killjoy mentality was not so much an expression of the Calvinism of the homesteader, as of his Irish counterpart, the tenant farmer who was the driving force behind what Emmet Larkin calls the 'Devotional Revolution' in post-Famine Ireland.[12] Though the experience of the tenant farmer has been characterized, in terms similar to those of the western, as one of 'paranoiac individualism', the primacy of the family in a rural society circumscribed by Catholic teaching would seem to vitiate this claim.[13] Nevertheless, the rigours of a puritan ideology were no less pronounced, and indeed were inscribed on the very agrarian ideal from which this nation-building class drew imaginative sustenance. Central to this ideal, which attracted Pearse, Eoin

MacNeill and other leading nationalists to the western seaboard, was an image of the west of Ireland, and of the Aran Islands in particular, as a harsh, inhospitable environment, a testimony to the bleak, monastic outlook of its early Christian inhabitants. As Canon Sheehan expressed this moral vision of the west:

> Across that bight of sea sleep the three islands that link us with the past, and whose traditions, were we otherwise, would shame us. They are *Aran-na-Naomh*, Arran of the Saints . . . a place for the hermit and the saint; and mark you . . . the hermit and the saint must again resume their rightful places in the economy of new orders and systems! You cannot do without them. They symbolise . . . comfort without wealth, perfect physical health without passion, love without desire . . . clean bodies, keen minds, pure hearts – what better world can the philosopher construct, or poet dream of?[14]

The kind of rural myth articulated in this passage corresponds to what the art-historian Erwin Panofsky has termed 'hard primitivism', a form of romanticism closely related to the 'production ethic' outlined above, which played such a crucial role in the transition from feudalism to capitalism. The feudal ideal on the other hand, imbued with aristocratic values of leisure and self-indulgence, conforms to an ethic of consumption or 'soft primitivism', evoking a world of recklessness and sensual abandon which stands as a direct antithesis to an ascetic ideology of duty, discipline and self-control.[15] These contrasting images form the basis of Hoch's distinction between the 'puritan' and the 'playboy', and in terms of this opposition, Synge had little difficulty in coming down firmly on the side of the latter. Indeed, in the character of Christy Mahon, he placed him right at the centre of his vision of the western world.

From early childhood, Synge's personal development was a long inventory of emotional crises, brought on for the most part by his zealous, overbearing mother who never tired of preaching the virtues of a strict Evangelical form of Christianity. The chronic sense of isolation and loneliness which Synge experienced throughout these years was reinforced rather than ameliorated by the break with religious fundamentalism occasioned by his reading Darwin at the age of sixteen or seventeen. 'It was a terrible experience,' he remarked ruefully in his 'Autobiography': 'Till I was twenty-three I never met or at least knew a man or woman who shared my opinions.'[16] This morbid individualism and alienation from his own background had a profound effect on Synge: as a result of it, according to G. J. Watson, he felt all 'the more keenly the need to belong to, or give expression to, some kind of communal consciousness'.[17] On the threshold of his literary career, he wrote in one of his notebooks: 'The individual mood is often trivial, perverse, fleeting, [but the] national mood [is] broad, serious, provisionally permanent.' The kind of communal identity he sought could be compared, he suggested, to that achieved by a musician in an orchestra: as he expressed it himself 'the collective passion produced by a band working together with one will and one ideal is unlike any other exaltation'.[18]

On the Aran Islands Synge found the sense of exaltation, the 'collective passion', he so desired. Recreating the islands in the image of an aristocratic social order, he remarked approvingly of the islanders:

> Their way of life has never been acted on by anything more artificial than the nests and burrows of the creatures that live round them, and they seem in a certain sense to approach more nearly to the finer type of our aristocracies – who are bred artificially to a natural ideal – than to the labourer or citizen. (66)[19]

Here was a refuge from the world of 'the greasy till', from the calculating self-advancement of what Synge (283), in a venomous turn of phrase, referred to as the 'ungodly ruck of fat-faced, sweaty-headed swine' who constituted the emergent Catholic bourgeoisie. There was no trace of the inhibited and stunted emotional life eulogized by Canon Sheehan, the clamp on pleasure and sensual enjoyment which retarded Synge's own upbringing, and which left its mark on Irish society in general after the Famine. Synge could only record his astonishment at the vitality and exuberance of the islanders, their perfect candour and lack of self-consciousness in giving expression to their feelings. The total loss of control in ventilating grief at wakes and funerals, and, above all, the complete abandon which accompanied the expression of physical pain or anger must indeed have come as a shock to someone brought up on the tradition of the stiff upper-lip. 'I have sometimes seen a girl writhing and howling with toothache,' he writes, 'while her mother sat at the other side of the fireplace pointing at her and laughing at her as if amused by the sight.' He goes on: 'An old man who was ill in the winter took me out the other day to show me how far down the road they could hear him yelling "the time he had a pain in his head"' (163).

It was the women on Aran, however, who made the greatest impact on Synge. They dressed and undressed in his company, breast-fed their children in front of him, bathed 'half-naked' (as he describes it) in public, sang obscene songs, and entered freely into physical contact with him. He refers to their 'strange beauty', their 'exquisite bright frankness', and their 'complete absence of shyness or self-consciousness'. More often than not, it is the word 'wild' which comes most readily to his mind in describing them. These women were far removed indeed from the Madonna figures in terms of which the Catholic church and Arthur Griffith's Sinn Féin were attempting to cast Irish maidenhood. As Synge himself put it, not without perhaps a little hyperbole: 'The women of this island are before conventionality, and share some of the liberal features that are thought peculiar to the women of Paris and New York' (143).

Synge immersed himself in the ambience of the islands, finding there the loss of self and sense of community which evaded him during his unhappy upbringing. However, it is the nature of his relationship with the community which is of most interest to us here, for Synge notes that while he needed their company and identified with them, the process was not reciprocal: 'On some days I feel this island as a perfect home and resting place; on other days I feel that I am a waif among the people. I can feel more with them than they can feel with me' (113).

It is precisely this theme which informs *The Playboy of the Western World*. The trajectory of the play charts Christy's passage from isolation and loneliness to an act of recognition, and a sense of identification with the community. Christy confesses to Pegeen Mike in Act II that before he met her, 'I was lonesome all times, and born lonesome, I'm thinking, as the moon of dawn.'[20] Whereas the cowboy embraces solitude as the precondition of freedom and independence, Christy's sojourn as a lone ranger traversing the countryside only makes him more aware of his estrangement from the intimacy of others. He tells Pegeen how lonesome it was on his travels to pass through small towns or places 'where you'd hear a voice kissing and talking deep love in every shadow of the ditch'. When Pegeen remarks that she thinks this is odd, Christy replies: 'What would any be but odd men and they living lonesome in the world' (109–10). Christy is eventually accepted by Pegeen and the community at large on the strength of the 'big lie' that he has killed his father, and reaches the height of his popularity when he proves his mettle at the local races. But as soon as the lie is exposed and the gap between imagination and reality revealed, this acceptance turns to rejection and Christy is finally forced out of the community.

There is no question, however, that Christy leaves the settled community to ride off, as it were, alone into the sunset like his American counterpart. On the contrary, Christy's last words indicate that his lonesome days are over:

> Ten thousand blessings upon all that's here, for you've turned me a likely gaffer in the end of all, the way I'll go *romancing* through a romping lifetime from this hour to the dawning of the judgement day. (173, my italics)

It is this parting shot which reveals the crucial difference between the American western and Synge's conception of the western world. In the former, as we have seen, it is the community that needs the individual, the hero; in the latter, the individual needs the community. Synge's playboy is no self-made man; he is in fact made by others, 'created by the collective fancy of a rural community'.[21] The contrast between the two is very well brought out in a perceptive comment by Alan Price, in which he explicitly compares Synge's play to one of the classical Hollywood westerns:

> The play concerns the impact of an outsider on an isolated, closely-knit community. The situation is seen . . . in Westerns such as Schaefer's *Shane* . . . Usually the community is decisively affected, but in *The Playboy* although it is aroused and shown striking potentialities it eventually rejects the outsider and all that he stands for. It is he alone in the end who goes on significantly developed and enriched . . . no opportunity is given similarly to transform the people and their surroundings, and the problem remains.[22]

Christy's inability to strike the pose of the self-made man is seen to greatest effect in his relationship with women. It has been remarked of the American western that 'time after time, one can detach the females without endangering the structures of the main plot. The West is a man's world, and the women are relegated to mere decoration'.[23] This is inconceivable in the case of Irish drama, and particularly where Synge's representation of women is concerned. According to Sean McMahon, Synge 'is pre-eminently a portrayer of women . . . [his] male characters are never as fully palpable or finished as his women'.[24] The traits and characteristics with which he invested his fictional women were precisely those which attracted him to the women on the Aran Islands. As McMahon remarks: 'courage, honesty and frank sensuality were the qualities which Synge found in some Irish women, particularly in the wilder west'. One cannot imagine the impassive western hero losing face by admitting his desire and need for a woman's affection, as does Christy in *The Playboy*:

> What good'd be in my lifetime if I left Pegeen . . . it's Pegeen I'm seeking only, and what'd I care if you brought me a drift of chosen females, standing in their shifts itself, maybe, from this place to the Eastern World. (165–7)

It was this passage which incensed the Abbey audience during the notorious first run of *The Playboy* in 1907. The hostility provoked by the sexual connotations of the word 'shift', however, was merely a symptom of a more general sense of outrage expressed by leading nationalists such as Arthur Griffith and Patrick Pearse at Synge's treatment of women and sexuality.[25] In this respect, one of the most notable features of Synge's representation of women is the lack of reverence towards the virginal mother figure which dominated Catholic devotional practices, and indeed family life itself in post-Famine Ireland. Synge is not content merely to subject the idyllic mother figure to ridicule as when he depicts the unruly Widow Quin poisoning her husband and burying her children – he also redirects his mockery towards the church itself. In a grotesque perversion of the most intimate bond between mother and child, the Widow Quin, we are told, not only suckled a black ram at her breast, but the ram itself ended up on the Bishop's dinner table 'so that the Lord Bishop of Connaught felt the elements of a Christian, and he eating it after in a kidney stew' (89).

In this, Synge was striking at the very foundations of orthodox Catholic nationalism, the tightly knit family unit around which the consolidation of the rural bourgeoisie was based. As early as 1903, in his play *The Shadow of the Glen*, Synge had drawn the wrath of Arthur Griffith by heaping scorn on the 'loveless marriage', the encasing of desire and sexuality in a grid of economic calculation. Synge returned to this theme in *The Playboy* four years later. In attempting to kill his father, Christy is not only escaping the clutches of family life, but is also fleeing from an incestuous marriage with a woman who had breast-fed him as a child. Pegeen herself, as a publican's daughter, is in a similar predicament, seeking to avoid the drudgery of a pre-arranged marriage with the obsequious Shawn Keogh, the representative of the venal, gombeen mentality of the small proprietor so detested by Synge. It is clear, moreover, that Synge had no illusions about the political implications of his work in this regard. Expressing privately his dissatisfaction with a series of articles on rural distress which he wrote for *The Manchester Guardian* in 1905, he remarked:

> There are sides of all that western life, the groggy-patriot-publican-general-shop-man who is married to the priest's half-sister and is second cousin once removed of the dispensary doctor, that are horrible and awful. This is the type that is running the present United Irish League anti-grazier campaign. . . . I sometimes wish to God I hadn't a soul and then I could give myself up to putting those lads on the stage. God, wouldn't they hop![26]

And hop they did, as the uproar during *The Playboy* riots showed.

It is important to note, furthermore, that it was not only Pegeen's smouldering sexuality which aroused the indignation of the middle-class audience during the first run of *The Playboy*, but also her fascination with evil, her complicity with violence. In marked contrast to the female protagonist in the western, who invariably acts as a counterweight to bloodshed, the sexuality of Synge's heroines is inextricably bound up with the darker impulses of cruelty and destruction. The puritan, as Hoch points out, negates sexuality by simply cancelling it out (hence the virginal figure of the western); the playboy, on the other hand, sublimates desire by charging it with terror and violence.[27] In Synge's play, it is the women – whether it be Pegeen, the Widow Quin, or Sara Tansey and her friends – who repeatedly brings out the violence in Christy, forcing him to exaggerate the savagery of the act on each occasion of its retelling. 'It's great luck and company I've won me,' he says, 'two fine women fighting for the likes of me – till I'm thinking this night wasn't I a foolish fellow not to kill my father in the years gone by' (93). The ominous association between violence and sexuality in Synge's writing is at its most apparent in a chilling observation which he makes on the red petticoats worn by the women on Aran:

> What has guided the women of grey-brown western Ireland to clothe them in red? The island without this simple red relief would be a nightmare fit to drive one to murder in order to gloat a while on the fresh red flow of blood.[28]

Synge's preoccupation with lawlessness and violence is central to his overall conception of the western world, for in throwing off the shackles of discipline and constraint, he is undermining one of the main requirements of modernization as exemplified in nineteenth-century Ireland – the centralization of law, ideology and the state apparatus. Throughout his work, therefore, we find Synge celebrating all those attributes – drunkenness, sexuality, lying, violence and mob rule – which threaten the composure of the cowboy or his equally inhibited Irish counterpart. In constructing his wayward and exuberant version of 'soft primitivism', moreover, Synge was not drawing entirely on the resources of his own imagination. He was, rather, reverting to an image (albeit a selective one) of pre-Famine Ireland, when the hegemony of the Ascendancy was still secure, and landlord and peasant, 'noble and beggarman', were interdependent aspects of the same social order. In this world, early and improvident marriages, poteen-making, faction-fighting and communal violence had still not given way to the process of 'disenchantment' which, according to Max Weber, ushers in the legal-rational system of a developing capitalist economy.[29]

This is the background to Daniel Corkery's sustained nationalist critique of *The Playboy* as a 'spirited' rather than a 'spiritual' play, a 'Dionysiac' extravaganza 'drenched in poteen'.[30] It also goes some way towards explaining the intensity of nationalist protests during the first production of *The Playboy* at the manner in which Synge portrayed Irish attitudes towards murder and lawlessness. The evident contempt in which the community holds the law in the play is clear, not only from their sympathizing with a murderer, but also the rough justice they propose to mete out to Christy when they discover that he has not really killed his father. Contravening the primary taboo of the western, they propose to lynch him there and then, with Pegeen burning him on the leg for good measure. It is interesting to note, finally, that in recreating pre-Famine Ireland in this manner, Synge was not simply rewriting history to suit his own wishes. In an extraordinary passage in his book *On Local Disturbances in Ireland*, published in 1836, George Cornewall Lewis noted that a general hatred of law pervaded the Irish countryside and a sympathy with criminals 'so great as to be scarcely credible'. He continues:

> A singular instance of this feeling . . . was the conduct of a labourer in the county of Tipperary, who, unable to obtain employment in his own neighbourhood, changed his abode; and in order to excite the sympathy of the farmers, gave it to be understood that he had quitted his home on account of having committed a murder. This plea was successful, and he received work: but his statement having transpired and reached the ears of the police, he was arrested and examined, when it appeared quite clearly that his story was a pure fiction, and he was accordingly discharged.[31]

One wonders had Synge read Cornewall Lewis before he embarked on his own, not so pure fiction.

2.2   *Dublin Opinion* cartoon

The political controversy surrounding *The Playboy* may be construed, as simply an argument about representations, with the conflicting parties held captive by images but oblivious to the reality which lay beyond them. However, it would be wrong to characterize the clash between Anglo-Irish and orthodox nationalist versions of the west in these terms, as if mere representations of Ireland alone were at stake. For these were, in Yeats' phrase, 'masterful images', and what we find in the confrontation between Synge and his Catholic nationalist opponents is a struggle over access to a dominant ideology, to a controlling vision of Irish life. This is precisely the theme to which *The Playboy* addresses itself, 'the power of the big lie', of images and representations, in transforming society. Yet for all that, it is ironic that while idealizations of the west were a source of major ideological debate, life on the western seaboard was slowly succumbing to a new form of cultural domination. As W. R. Rodgers relates it:

> I recall going to visit a Gaelic story-teller who was reputed to be the only man left in his district who could tell in the traditional manner *The King of Ireland's Son*, a tale that took him two weeks of nights in the telling. He was not at home; I found him in his enemy's house, the local cinema, watching a Wild Western picture.[32]

3.1   *The Quiet Man* (1952)/Collecting Turf from the Bog (John Hinde)

3. BACK PROJECTIONS:
John Hinde and the New Nostalgia

What goes by the name of love is banishment, with now and then a postcard
from the homeland . . .

Samuel Beckett

There is a startling sequence in Muiris Mac Conghail's documentary on the
Blasket Islands, *Oileán Eile*, in which, after a succession of images recalling the
past in black-and-white photographs and archival footage, the islands are sud-
denly illuminated in colour. For a moment, we assume that we are back at reality,
and that the camera has caught up with the present. But as the images unfold, the
bedraggled clothes and the unkempt thatched cottages bring home to us that this
is also archival footage, perhaps some of the earliest colour film of Ireland. The
strangeness comes from viewing the myth itself in colour. It is as if we had
escaped from Plato's cave, and seen a life known previously only through shadows with the heightened perception that belongs to another world.

We tend to associate colour with realism, on the assumption that it cannot but
bring us closer to the truth. What is easily overlooked is that for the first century of
photography, its claims to verisimilitude rested on its black-and-white tones. This
was not due solely to the technical limitations of early photography. Realism as an
aesthetic code was bound up with naturalism, with the moral project of relent-
lessly exposing the dark side of the landscape. Hence, while painters in the Pre-
Raphaelite movement were idealizing a vanished past in effulgent colour, photographers were stalking the back streets of Victorian London, intent on revealing
the grim realities that lay hidden in the shadows. Truth was invariably cast in the
worst possible light, as if the leaden, monotonous seriousness of the world could
only be captured in the monochrome tints of the photograph.

It is striking how this understanding of realism was carried over into the new
medium of cinema. When young female workers were employed by the film pio-
neer Georges Méliès to painstakingly hand-paint every frame of some of his early
forays into science fiction, the lurid colours only added to the extravagance of his
flights of fantasy. Colour in cinema finally came into its own in the 1950s in the
attempt to win back audiences from television. But even then, its appeal for audiences still lay in the opportunity it provided for spectacle and visual pleasure, as
is evident from its key role in the dream worlds of musicals and Hollywood epics.
As late as 1957, a film industry manual could advise prospective film-makers:

3.2

> Musicals and fantasy pictures are open to unlimited opportunities in the creative
> use of colour. Here we are not held down by reality, past or present, and our
> imaginations can soar. Musicals and fantasies are usually designed to provide
> the eye with visual pleasure in the way that music pleases the ear.[1]

Written in 1957, the year in which John Hinde published his first postcards, this
could easily be taken as a manifesto for his highly tinctured vision of Ireland.

The reference to musicals and fantasy provides a useful gloss on the particular
pictorial genre to which postcards belong. To criticize these idealized images for
ignoring the 'real' Ireland, for masking over the squalid social realities of the time,
is to miss the whole point of the genre; it is like taking *The Wizard of Oz* (1939) to
task for failing to make a slice-of-life documentary about Kansas in the Depression
era. (It is no coincidence that in *The Wizard of Oz*, the 'real life' setting at the
beginning of the film is photographed in black-and-white, while Dorothy's entry
in to the dream world of Oz is signalled by a transition to colour.) This does not
mean, of course, that such stylized forms are incapable of yielding some home
truths, or indeed, of making home truths specifically their business. Though the
postcard is conventionally associated with the message '*Wish you were here*', what
in fact it is often trying to say is '*Wish I was home*'. The platitudes about the
weather that pass for experiences of another place are like similar opening gam-
bits in everyday conversation: they are less about the climate, and more about our
desire to establish or maintain social contact, particularly in unfamiliar surroundings. The emotional shorthand relayed by the postcard through gossip, trivia, and
other idle talk was such as to lead to its association with what were perceived as
characteristic female modes of address: 'The Postcard', wrote one portentous

3.3

commentator at the turn of the century, 'has always been a feminine vice. Men do
not write Postcards to each other. When a woman has time to waste, she writes a
letter; when she has no time to waste, she writes a Postcard'.[2]

This identification with the feminine is intrinsically bound up with the nostalgia which suffuses the postcard image. This is not simply an evocation of an
idealized past, but a very distinctive form of longing: *nostos*, to return home, *algos*,
a painful condition – the painful desire to restore the sense of belonging that is
associated with childhood, and the emotional resonance of the maternal. In recent
Hollywood cinema, this theme is taken up in films such as *E.T.* (1982) in which
we encounter a world bounded almost entirely by the horizons of mother,
children, and, of course, home.[3] It is of interest, in passing, to note that E.T.'s
desire to phone home is prompted by a chance encounter on television with no
less an exercise in nostalgia than John Ford's classic film *The Quiet Man* (1952),
and specifically the pathos of the scene in which Sean Thornton returns to his
windswept ancestral cottage for the first time [Fig. 3.1]. This, it could be argued, is
the film which launched a thousand postcards, for John Hinde's photographs owe
more to Ford's Arcadian images than to the black-and-white snapshots in which
most people up to then stored their visual experiences. When colour photographs
first appeared in Irish family albums, they were usually the images left behind by
returned emigrants, and were thus more redolent of memory and desire than of
the grey realities which characterized everyday life in Ireland. In this setting, the
mass-produced postcard became the Irish emigrant's way of phoning home.

Yet there is an important difference between Hollywood nostalgia, and its Irish
counterpart. E.T. actually managed to fulfil his yearning to return home, but in

3.4

John Hinde's Irish postcards, there is an uneasy feeling that we are getting a last glimpse of a world that is lost. It is as if the emigrant's break with the past has been internalized *within* Irish culture, forming its popular images of itself. Thus in many of the landscapes, there is usually a visual barrier – a row of foxgloves, a border of foliage, or in some cases, a female figure – in the foreground, which frames and distances an imaginary vista. In one image, a mother and child on an escarpment look down wistfully on the beach at Lahinch, as if it is a back-projection belonging to an entirely different pictorial plane [Fig. 3.2]. On a postcard of Tramore beach, women and children again dominate the foreground, and such men as are visible are reduced to the status of children, whether in pictorial size or at the level of activities (playing games, etc.). The image operates almost as a flashback on another possible world, as if expressing the spectator's aspiration: 'Wish I was there'. The attempt to recover the innocence of a receding past is crystallized in the archetypal image of the thatched cottage from which a mother emerges to welcome her two children approaching with donkeys and creels [Fig. 3.3]. This could be the homecoming of the two tousled children loading turf on a donkey in what is perhaps the most emblematic of all John Hinde images [Fig. 3.1]. Unlike the prodigal son, however, the prodigal colour and total artifice of these narratives suggest that there is no real prospect of returning home. It is worthwhile recalling Freud's observation on the male desire to recapture an imaginary self-sufficiency associated with nature, childhood and the maternal: 'It is as if we envied them [women, children, animals] their power of retaining a blissful state of mind – an unassailable libido-position which we ourselves have long since abandoned.'[4]

3.5

The relative lack of males in prominent positions in these images suggests not so much their absence as their presence *behind* the camera, irrevocably cut off from the field of vision. Notwithstanding the actual employment of female photographers, the camera is invariably equated with a male point of view, as in the case of the suburban Adonis, complete with camera, who gazes at a reclining, bikini-clad Aphrodite on Skerries beach, or elsewhere, the two male photographers who seemingly impale a woman under the Blarney Stone. For the most part, however, the male disappears behind the lens. In one image of Butlins at Ayr, a cable car containing a mother and her children soars, Peter Pan fashion, into the sky, the family waving goodbye to the absent figure taking the photograph [Fig. 3.5]. In another postcard of Butlins, we are actually presented with a Peter Pan railway carrying its passengers back into childhood, while a primitive, foetus-like totem appears in the top left-hand corner. In a strange adjoining image of the indoor heated pool at Ayr, it would seem that full regression has taken place: a blurred father-figure hovers behind the transparent walls of the pool as if at last returning to the womb with a view [Fig. 3.6]. The irony is that by virtue of his life-size aperture, he is as much cut off from the mother and child in the foreground as is the photographer – or, for that matter, the spectator holding the postcard.

The identification of the male with the visual technology of the camera signals another difference between the lost plenitude of John Hinde's Ireland and Hollywood nostalgia. In films such as *E.T.*, the reassuring comfort of home is menaced by a (male) public sphere in which state agencies (the police, etc.) and technology acquire a sinister, threatening profile. One of the most surprising aspects of the earliest John Hinde images, by contrast, is the

3.6

apparently benign view of modernization, as exemplified by the city, airports, modern transport, etc. In one image of London, traffic stops in the background (with a bus enjoining us to go to the cinema), while the state intervenes in the foreground, in the form of a Dixon of Dock Green-type bobby, to allow women and children safe passage across the street. Even government is imbued with a romantic aura, as in the golden sunset which presides over the Houses of Parliament in London. This celebration of the modern state is bound up with an important aspect of the development of postcards: their connection with prestigious, state-building projects such as World Fairs and Expositions at the turn of the century. The popularization of the French postcard for example is attributed to the centennial 1889 Exhibition in Paris, just as the World Columbian Exposition in Chicago, 1893, ushered in its American equivalent. Hence the seemingly paradoxical homage in postcards to state-of-the-art technology (particularly air travel) and the primitivist appeal of a vanishing past. John Hinde's framing of a native Kenyan decked out in tribal costume with spear, beside a modern light aircraft, could have come straight from one of these Expositions [Fig. 3.6]. However, as the consigning of native culture to the built-in obsolescence of the primitive indicates, it is no longer a living concern, and owes what little vitality it retains to the courtesy of the state (or its tourist board). The lion may lie down with a Mini-Minor, as the postcard of the wildlife sanctuary at Longleat in Wiltshire indicates, but such a reconciliation of opposites is only possible in nature reserves, or their pictorial equivalents.

This is the context which allows evocations of thatched cottages to lie alongside futuristic images of Dublin Airport, framed again by the female body [Fig.

3.7

3.7]. It is not just that they connect different facets of the emigrant's or tourist's experience; it is also that they reveal the antinomies of state-building in a late developing economy. The severance from the past which once characterized the emigrant's experience becomes a general cultural condition in a modernizing society. Traditional or vernacular culture is relegated, quite literally, to the level of a cottage industry, to pave the way for industrialization and progress. The difficulty with nostalgia in these circumstances is not that it turns its back on the modern, but that it is part of it, if by that we mean a particular view of social change which embalms rather than actively renegotiates the past.

Such are the vagaries of history, however, that while nostalgia during the first life-cycle of these postcards was directed towards the rural idylls they depicted, now it is directed at the postcards themselves, and the optimism of the halcyon days of modernization in which such images were possible. If current debates over the future of the national airline service are anything to go by, the image of the air hostess standing proudly in front of a new airport terminal may soon be as quaint and as anachronistic as a shawled woman in front of a thatched cottage. The unexpected afterlife bestowed on these images by re-situating them in the Irish Museum of Modern Art for the 'Hindesight' exhibition points to a new nostalgia, recalling the optimism of an era in which full employment was considered possible, and indeed in which even emigration would come to an end. For these postcards, it is not the past but modernization itself which has become imbued with longing.

4. FROM KITCHEN SINK TO SOAP: Drama and the Serial Form on Irish Television

Are we not going to descend to the kitchen sink? Are we not going to scrape the bottom of the barrel? It would be a disaster for drama to be overplayed . . .

Rev. Luke Faupel, at Knights of Columbanus Conference, Dublin 1964

When Telefís Éireann opened on New Year's Eve 1961, Eamonn Andrews, Chairman of the recently appointed Radio Éireann Authority, noted that in the eyes of many people, Ireland was entering a new era: 'Cathleen Ní Houlihan . . . was in danger of becoming Cathode Ní Houlihan.'[1] The whole way of life embodied in the resonant image of Cathleen Ní Houlihan – the nationalist tradition, the cultural heritage, the primacy of rural values, the repression of sexuality – was about to meet its most serious challenge since the founding of the state. Dire warnings were sounded from all quarters, with the leaders of both church and state attaching particular gravity to the occasion. Cardinal D'Alton advised Telefís Éireann to adhere to the high ideals of Irish life and warned of the dangers of TV addiction. President de Valera took this a stage further by depicting television as the cultural equivalent of atomic energy in terms of the devastation it could wreak on traditional values: 'It can be used for incalculable good,' he pointed out, 'but it can also do irreparable harm . . . it can lead to decadence and dissolution.'[2] Television, he hoped, would devote itself to the expression of the true, the good, and the beautiful, categories not always distinguishable in some of his more romantic evocations of Irish life.

There is little doubt that, in the intervening years, television hardly lived up to the elevated role bestowed on it by de Valera. It is possible, in fact, to see in its subsequent operation a parting of ways between the ideals and realities of Irish life which had merged imperceptibly to form some of the most powerful images of Ireland bequeathed by the Literary Revival. Yet one of the most interesting features of the early years of Irish television is that it was not so much an emphasis on 'the true' – if by that we mean current affairs and documentary – which posed the greatest challenge to traditional cultural norms, but rather developments in such marginal areas as light entertainment (as in the case of *The Late Late Show*), and in some of the less prestigious forms of television drama. From the outset, current affairs was very much at a disadvantage in that politicians were either not available for television discussion – in which case they were replaced by political journalists or specialist commentators – or else their appearance was tightly

44

controlled by party whips, giving programmes such as *The Politicians* the air of a party political broadcast.[3] With current affairs in what was effectively a political quarantine, it is not surprising that other ostensibly less informative and 'serious' television forms stepped into the breach.

There is reason to believe, moreover, that even had current affairs enjoyed a high profile in the opening years of Telefís Éireann, it would still have met with considerable difficulties in broaching some of the more sensitive and contro-versial aspects of Irish society, particularly in relation to family issues and sexual morality. A market research survey undertaken in June 1983 reported that while Irish people were willing to look to television, and to a lesser extent, radio and the press as primary sources of information about politics and current affairs, this deference to the media was less forthcoming in the case of personal or sexual morality.[4] This was not because these areas were considered 'private', but rather because they fell within a different public domain, one which looked to the Catholic Church as a source of guidance and authority. It is to be expected then that when television sought to address itself to these issues, the most innovative coverage was not to be found in the tightly controlled formats of cur-rent affairs or documentary programmes, but in the more flexible and respon-sive genres of the live talk-show and the television serial, which were more open-ended and less susceptible to the array of political and legal controls which pervaded Irish television from the outset.[5]

From the single play to the serial: the development of drama on Irish television

Notwithstanding the particular features of the Irish situation, it would be mislead-ing to suggest that the prominent role accorded to television drama in opening up debates on controversial social issues was unique to Ireland. It is almost common-place by now to point to the extraordinary impact made by single television plays such as *Cathy Come Home* and *Edna the Inebriate Woman* on British public opinion in the 1960s and early 1970s.[6] Many reasons have been adduced to explain how British television drama found itself in this privileged position, acting, in John Caughie's words, 'as some kind of cutting edge, working to extend television's social or sexual discourse'.[7] In the first place, as Caughie points out, the single television play has traded on the great tradition of high seriousness and creative freedom which has governed thinking about artistic practices in western societies since the Renaissance. This provided a degree of insulation from commercial pres-sures and managerial intrusion, thus giving television drama a level of prestige and autonomy which is exceptional in terms of the marketing outlooks and vertical power structures that characterize broadcasting organizations. Crucial to the flexi-bility and oppositional stance of the television play, moreover, is the fact that it is script-centred, in that the once-off play is seen as the product of a *writer* existing *outside* the institutional structures of the station, as against the director or producer who work within the confines of the organization.[8]

This tendency to consider the television play as the work of an author or playwright derives, of course, from the stage or mainstream theatre, and this points to a second reason why British television drama made such effective inroads on social and political orthodoxies, particularly in the 1960s. To a greater extent than its American counterpart, which operated in what was largely a cinematic or Hollywood context, the British television play was able to draw on developments in theatre, precisely at a time when British drama was undergoing a radical reorientation towards working-class life and related social and political issues.[9] The 'theatre of protest' ushered in by the 1956 production of John Osborne's *Look Back in Anger*, and developed subsequently in the work of playwrights such as Arnold Wesker, John Arden and Harold Pinter, was part of a general cultural recovery of working-class existence and a questioning of the political consensus that took place in the late 1950s.[10] Underpinned at a critical level by the writings of Raymond Williams and Richard Hoggart, it provided an important thematic focus not only for theatre but also for the novel, cinema and, ultimately, television. Though the connection with high culture is often considered a major restraint on the emergence of popular cultural forms,[11] it is clear that in the particular conjuncture of post-Suez Britain, the ability of television drama to take its terms of reference from radical currents in mainstream theatre worked decidedly to television's advantage, and was at least partially responsible for the success (or notoriety) which it enjoyed during its heyday.

This discussion of British television drama has a direct bearing on the Irish situation, for the emphasis on the more squalid and unpalatable aspects of 'low' life, and the dissenting voices implicit in many of the plays, did not go unnoticed in discussions of Irish television policy during its formative years. Thus, in a seminar on Social Communications convened by the Knights of Columbanus in Dublin, June 1964, it is not surprising to find television drama singled out for special attention during the group discussions. As the report of the seminar group on this topic expressed it:

> There was general agreement that drama had a very definite place in television and that it was desirable to have considerably more drama on television with, however, certain provisos. We felt that we would not like to see a recurrence of what did for a while occur, at least, on the Independent Television programme in England, an excess of drama devoted to the kitchen sink school, in which the sordid and immoral seemed to be the only things which could be found worthy of the pen of the playwright.[12]

Commenting on this, the Rev. Luke Faupel, a Catholic communications expert from London, expressed certain reservations even about these qualified recommendations:

I am slightly worried at the idea that we should have more drama. I am not at all conversant with the amount of drama that you have, but in England, we have a surfeit of drama. . . . Five plays a week on BBC television and five plays on commercial television, amounts to nearly five hundred plays a year. Are there five hundred playwrights [in Ireland]? Are we not going to descend to the kitchen sink? Are we not going to scrape the bottom of the barrel? It would be a disaster for drama to be overplayed.[13]

As a counterweight to what he perceived as the excessive realism of British television drama, Fr. Faupel looked to the edifying idealism of the Irish dramatic tradition, discerning in it a model for the future course of Irish television drama:

I am sure that in this country there must be people – you have a heritage, a dramatic heritage – that can present the concept of the Christian life with all its values, its virtues, its wholesomeness in dramatic form. . . . I am sure you should be very conscious of the dramatic output of a Catholic country like Ireland. I was hoping that you would see a way in which you could support perhaps young script writers . . . especially those people who are content to see virtue in the normal. We have been told that people are disedified with the concentration of [sic] the normalities of our society. . . . Why can't we present the ideal in dramatic form. . . . [14]

There is a certain irony in the fact that the very strength of the Irish dramatic heritage is invoked in this passage as a means of curtailing the growth of a socially committed dramatic movement, whether it be in theatre or on television. By the 1950s, theatre in Ireland was still languishing in the doldrums of the Literary Revival, and, with the exception of the experimental work of the Pike Theatre and a number of fringe companies, was far removed from the political environment which revitalized British drama.[15] Depictions of Irish life were for the most part confined to an endless treadmill of kitchen comedies and second-rate 'peasant' plays, despite the efforts of playwrights such as Maura Laverty, M. J. Molloy, Brendan Behan, Gerard Healy and Seamus Byrne to introduce more controversial subjects into the dramatic canon. With the appointment of Hilton Edwards, one of the most distinguished figures in the Irish theatre world, as the first head of television drama in Telefís Éireann in 1961, it was evident that the television play was not going to be a vehicle of radical or even muted social comment. Though by no means unadventurous in his projects – staging among other things an ambitious studio-bound version of *Moby Dick* – Edwards' tendency to think of television drama predominantly in studio terms, and his reluctance to use video for editing purposes or for outdoor locations, prevented him from fully utilizing the possibilities of the new medium.[16] In a revealing comment some years after leaving RTE, Edwards explained how television's unique ability to bring live coverage of events onto the screen convinced him of the need to clearly demarcate between theatre proper, and socially committed drama which really belonged to the newsroom or the current affairs programme:

> There is nowadays, caused by the confusion of television, which is also a news medium, a kind of feeling that the drama in the theatre has got to be a kind of newspaper. A lot of people at the Gate are saying to me, why aren't you doing a play about the troubles in Belfast? . . . I'm afraid that, dramatically, I'm a romantic and an escapist. . . . I think fine plays will be written, but a certain removal in time may be necessary if they are not to be the sort of reportage that I always notice as being the weakness of an O'Casey play.[17]

Edwards' comments are an important corrective to the view, often found in RTE's Annual Reports in its early years, that financial constraints were the main reason for its poor record in producing television plays.[18] Though the high costs incurred in staging once-off productions were undoubtedly a major contributory factor, an equally important area of resistance would appear to have been the ideological climate (which presided, for example, over the Knights of Columbanus conference quoted above), as well as the undue reliance placed on a moribund, if overpowering, dramatic tradition which felt it had nothing to gain from the new medium. Some measure of the stagnation and complacency which had set into Irish theatre is indicated by the supercilious manner in which one writer, John O'Donovan, dismissed television drama in the course of a survey of nine playwrights conducted by the *RTV Guide* in 1962:

> Television isn't going to make any radical change in the art of playwriting, and those who pretend that it will are phonies and fakers. Television is a method of presentation, nothing more, nothing less. It presents no challenges in dramatic techniques that have not already been presented by the stage and the cinema . . . . The important thing is *what* you present, not *how* you present it, and no amount of lighting effects, camera gimmickry and hopping from one lens to another will turn a bad play into a good one.[19]

Of the dramatists questioned, only one, Gerard Healy, seemed fully aware of the wide-ranging possibilities afforded by television to break from the deadening influence of mainstream theatre, and to explore new areas of experience in dramatic form.[20] In these circumstances, it is not surprising to find that, by the end of 1964, the paucity of original television drama had begun to provoke a response from some of the more critical members of the audience. As one viewer commented in a letter to the *RTV Guide* in November of that year:

> It is very disappointing to note that in its nearly four years of existence, Telefís Éireann has failed to discover even one Irish playwright of note who writes solely for television. The drama department has been relying regularly on either adaptations of stage plays or imports from the BBC. With rare exceptions it is a proven fact that stage plays are not suitable for TV. . . . Is any effort being made to discover a television playwright, as distinct from a refugee from the stage?[21]

In her reply to these charges, Chloe Gibson, Head of Drama at Telefís Éireann, pointed out that this outright dismissal of the station's efforts to attract new talent was somewhat unjust, since by then Eugene McCabe, James Douglas and Michael Judge had begun to contribute new original television plays to the station. Nevertheless, the reduction of television to the status of a mere audio-visual aid for existing theatre is evident from the subsequent explanation given for the preponderance of stage adaptations on Telefís Éireann: 'These were transmitted', she writes, 'in response to widespread demand, particularly from people outside Dublin, who normally have no opportunity of seeing plays produced in the Dublin theatres.'[22]

From this remark, it is clear that while some money and energy could be found for television plays, it did not make its way into the commissioning of new material. As the experience of British television showed, such a departure was likely to bring about a rupture with the conservative values which pervaded Irish theatre, opening up new, controversial areas of society to dramatic scrutiny. It was this power of television to focus on contemporary reality, and to probe the darker recesses of social life which, more than anything, alarmed the earliest critics of television in Ireland. In 1961, even before Telefís Éireann opened, the Ninth Annual Summer School of the Social Study Conference was devoted to 'The Challenge of Television' in Ireland. At this conference, reservations were expressed about the possible impact of television on two crucial components of Irish life: the family and the farming community. In a memorandum sent to the Minister for Posts and Telegraphs, and to Radio Éireann, the conference noted that while television cannot be expected to 'hold itself aloof from contemporary problems such as emigration and immigration from rural areas, the relatively depressed state of agriculture and the lack of an image of farming as a "good life"', nevertheless, it

> was particularly concerned that the overall impact of the programmes on Irish television should not be such as to convey the image of urban or city life as the only desirable one, and that any tendency towards associating an excess of sordid themes with rural life should be avoided.[23]

The conference accordingly expressed the hope that 'most' of the programmes on the new television service 'including news films would have a rural bias',[24] an aspiration which was clearly aimed at reinforcing and consolidating the affirmative images of rural life which informed Catholic ideology since the founding of the state. Of particular interest, in view of the subsequent development of Irish television drama, is the fact that the new station was enjoined to make programmes which would 'underline the importance of the family unit farm'.[25] The centrality of the family in agricultural production meant that the position of women received special attention in this regard, particularly in relation to the need to defend traditional ideals of marriage and motherhood against the incursions of British television drama:

> Programmes on married life, which would stress the vocation of motherhood, its satisfactions and trials were, they felt, particularly necessary as an antidote to the constant repetitions in films and plays from BBC and UTV of the theme of broken marriages and delinquent children. The group also asked that some attempt should be made to provide on the feminine side the equivalent to the various heroes for boys which abound on television screens, such as the Lone Ranger, Maverick, etc. A feminine ideal is a necessity for young girls and the absence of any regular 'heroines' on television screens was stated to be injurious to young girls, particularly teenagers. Serial features on women heroines such as Elizabeth Fry, Edel Quinn, the Angel of Dien Bien Phu, or some of the valiant women of the Old Testament could be attractively presented and should contain enough drama to satisfy even male as well as female viewers.[26]

The most perceptive commentators at the social study conference, however, were not content to direct their criticisms solely at the subject matter or thematic concerns of future programmes, but also turned their attention to the operation of television as a cultural *form*, and particularly to its unrivalled ability to impart knowledge, attitudes and values through the gilded pill of entertainment. In a paper delivered at the conference, and subsequently published as a pamphlet, James J. Campbell pointed out that though the primary aim of television is 'to entertain and not to convert' or instruct, nevertheless 'television is the most influential factor in education today' in the sense that

> the effective vehicle of propaganda [i.e. education] . . . is drama, dramatic representation, which, as every schoolboy and girl knows, poses a problem, sets a conflict and gives us all a thrill (it is hoped) in the working out of the problem.[27]

This corresponds, of course, to the classic definition of narrative, according to which dramatic action takes the form of a movement from order (the beginning), through disorder (the middle) and back to order again (the end) with the resolution of the problem or enigma which impeded the flow of the narrative. This kind of ending or closure brings with it a note of uplift or optimism, and works to best advantage in the single play or self-contained programme. However, the difficulty with television, as Campbell sees it, is that it does not work by instant conversions, but is characterized rather by a 'drip effect' which builds up a 'composite picture' over a period of time: 'The impact,' he writes, 'is consistent and repeated. It is not a question of a single programme, it is a question of trends and emphases.'[28] This makes for a much more diffuse and indeterminate outlook on life, the absence of an affirmative or clear-cut ending tending to leave difficulties and problems unresolved. Hence we have

> an attitude to grown-up life which is very disturbing, especially among girls for whom there are, as has been said, few positive models on television: we have fear, worry and anxiety about grown-up life and marriage. Young people need reassurance, something positive. What do they get? Uncertainty, fear, anxiety and, of course, no spiritual values, utter materialism.[29]

Though few examples are cited of programmes with such demoralizing tendencies, it is noticeable that the *serial* form is singled out for special mention, 'in particular those referring to health and social problems' on UTV or BBC.[30] This concern with the corrosive effects of the serial form is taken up again in another document which emerged from the conference, a fifteen-point memorandum to the Pilkington Committee on Broadcasting which was then sitting in the United Kingdom. In recommending the establishment of a statutory advisory council to monitor broadcasting output, the memorandum goes on:

> We think that in particular the terms of reference of such a council should include a special mention of the effect of dramatic programmes . . . especially those in serial form . . . we are emphasizing . . . that the main impact of television on values and attitudes derives from such programmes.[31]

It is difficult reading these forecasts of impending doom and dissipation to avoid feeling that they are in some sense self-fulfilling prophecies, the very appropriateness of the fears giving rise to their own realization. The misgivings about drama, and the identification of the serial as the trojan horse of Irish television smuggling in alien attitudes and values, the apprehension about the demise of positive images of the family unit farm, and of traditional female roles, all seem to point towards the inevitable introduction of a farming serial such as *The Riordans*. The wonder is not that the fears and the realities coincided as they did, but that they took so long to do so.

Tolka Row, family life and the urban serial

One of the most remarkable features of Irish television is that in a country with such a distinguished dramatic tradition, the single play should have been superceded as a critical force in television drama by the much despised serial form. As early as 1968, Tom O'Dea could enquire in his television column in the *Irish Press*:

> When has RTE's Drama Section broadcast a play that reproduces the attitudes and present temperature of Irish life or a section of it? Now and then *The Riordans* takes up something like the shenanigans that accompany the dismissal of a teacher, or *Tolka Row* tries to dramatize Irish attitudes to the tinkers; but the formal, full-length plays, in which the contemporary, questioning, sometimes dissenting Irishman may be viewed in some depth, are just not there. The most recent Irishman that spoke through RTE's Drama Section was Bernard Shaw . . . his Ireland is a half-century old.[32]

It is interesting to note, moreover, that while the critical edge of the serial was readily apparent to those commentators who looked at the new television service from the outside, its full potential in this regard did not impress itself on those working within the station for quite some time. The successes and

shortcomings of once-off dramatic productions, for instance, figured prominently in the Annual Reports during the earliest years of Telefís Éireann, but it
was not until 1966, when *Tolka Row* was already three years old and *The
Riordans* well under way, that the serial received its first honorary mention –
being described, somewhat tersely, as the 'most popular form of television
entertainment'. Even Christopher FitzSimon, who perhaps more than any
other producer was responsible for the impact made by the serial on Irish
television, could still refer to it in 1966 as 'the woman's weekly stories of TV',
fulfilling their function 'which is to provide light dramatic entertainment'.[33]

Over the years, and particularly since the growth of American soap operas
such as *Dallas* and *Dynasty* in the early 1980s, the serial has existed in a kind
of critical limbo, its success with audiences being only paralleled by the
studied contempt meted out to it in popular television criticism. While much
of the animus directed at the serial may be attributed to the elitist values of the
'quality' press, or to the influence of outdated critical precepts derived from
high culture, some of the more considered estimates have dismissed the serial
as being either a vehicle for a displaced urban nostalgia (as in the case of a
naturalistic serial such as *Coronation Street*), or else as a celebration of American
capitalism in its most crass, consumerist form.[34] Both of these strictures are
related, and may be seen as part of a wider general response to the serial, and
indeed to all popular or romantic fiction, which finds it wanting on at least
two fundamental grounds:

(i) The first is that regardless of its surface attention to detail, and its
carefully contrived semblance of reality, the serial manages to obscure and
conceal the most important areas of society, in particular the relations of work
and production. *Dallas* is ostensibly about oil and economic power, but we
seldom see the workforce which allows the Ewings to live a life of endless, if
not always carefree, consumption. In this, the occupants of Southfork are no
different from other participants in prime-time pastorals as described by
Dennis Porter:

> It should not necessarily surprise if the inhabitants of the land of soap are never
> observed sleeping, washing, commuting, jogging . . . writing, or even work-
> ing, and if the closest housewives come to cooking is to pour out a cup of coffee
> . . . soap opera is . . . a country without history, politics or religion, poverty,
> unemployment, recession or inflation, and with only minimal references to class
> and ethnicity.[35]

While this elision of labour and production, and of political and economic
structures is hardly surprising in the heightened melodrama of *Dallas* and
Dynasty, one would not expect to find it in the documentary-style naturalism
of *Coronation Street*. Yet as many commentators have pointed out, industrial
labour for the most part is conspicuous by its absence in this purportedly

working-class community.[36] Working-class existence is defined not in terms of the factory floor, but in relation to the domestic environment of the home, or the communal retreat of the Rover's Return. This brings us to the second major objection which is levelled at the ideological basis of the serial.

(ii) One of the key characteristics of the television serial is the central importance accorded to the family, and by extension, to personal and domestic problems over and against the larger social conflicts which dominate the public arena. This may give rise to a situation in which complex political or economic relations are not so much rendered invisible, as shifted onto a different plane where they are re-routed through an intricate network of emotional or personal entanglements. The private arena, according to Charlotte Brunsdon, 'colonizes the public, masculine sphere, representing it from the point of view of the personal'.[37] Thus in *Dallas* it would appear that whole economic empires can change hands overnight, and the oil industry brought to its knees, so that JR can settle an old score with his rival Cliff Barnes, or assert once more his faltering authority over the wayward and refractory members of the Ewing household.

It is this tendency to explain away the social in terms of the personal which constitutes the basic contradiction of the serial in the eyes of its critics, for in the very process of reducing complex political and economic questions to personal or family dilemmas, we are thereby prevented from understanding their real nature, let alone acting upon them. In modern industrial capitalism, the family is at one remove from the process of production, and is therefore in no position to resolve, of its own accord, the various social and economic problems which arise in the wider community. It was precisely for this reason that RTE's first important serial *Tolka Row* (1964–1968) came to grief. Based on the day-to-day activities of the Nolan family, who had just moved up in the world from tenement rooms in the Liberties to a new corporation estate, it tended to present the family, not only as the main focus of dramatic interest, but also as the centre of power relations in the community, the place to which everyone turns in the event of personal or social upheavals. 'Life in Tolka Row never runs on an even tenor,' an article in the *RTV Guide* informs us in 1965, 'it is a battlefield "of crabbed youth and age", of boy breaks with girl, of all hands on deck, lads, the family ship is going on the rocks.'[38]

The extent to which the family in *Tolka Row* is bound up with the general concerns of the community is clearly evident in its relationship to the workplace. Jack Nolan works as a foreman in a garage, and in the course of his work is brought into contact with an older workmate, Gabby Doyle. As the story unfolds, Gabby is gradually brought within the ambit of the Nolan household, eventually marrying Statia, Jack's 'spinster' sister, who is living with them in Tolka Row. No sooner has the workplace been reclaimed by the family home in this manner than Sean, the Nolan's modish teenage son, returns from England (to which he had gone after a row with his father) and takes up an apprenticeship in the garage. It is obvious in these circumstances that the workplace is not functioning as an economic unit but rather as a foil for the various liaisons and conflicts entered into by the Nolan family.

This pattern recurs in the work experience of the other members of the family. When Peggy, the Nolans' daughter, is widowed after a brief marriage to Mossy Walker, she takes up a job in the Royal Tara Hotel, and strikes up a friendship with Joan Broderick, a young woman on the hotel staff. Joan immediately finds herself drawn into the Nolan circuit, attracting romantic advances not only from Sean but also from his friend Michael Carney. A similar fate befalls Maggie Bonar, a friend of Gabby Doyle's from his homeland in Donegal, who comes on the scene much to the displeasure of the envious and insecure Statia. This rivalry is resolved, or is rather redirected, when Statia and Maggie agree to go into business by forming a domestic employment agency. The very centrality of Statia in the narrative structure, moreover, points to another important aspect of the Nolan household, namely, that it is an extended family catering for relatives and dependants as well as its immediate kin. Aunt Statia lives with the Nolan family, as do the financially independent daughter and sons, and in the original stage play as conceived by Maura Laverty, Rita Nolan's father, Dan Dempsey, was also part of the household.[39] The family, in other words, not only infiltrates the workplace but also becomes, as Martin McLoone points out, a kind of surrogate welfare state, a point of intersection for the various affective and social ties which bind the community.[40] At the heart of this notion of the family, of course, is the mother in the personage of Rita Nolan. As an article in the *RTV Guide* in 1965 expresses it:

> The focal point of *Tolka Row* is Rita Nolan. Rita, who as mother and wife rules the Nolan household, is the peacemaker in times of strife, the source of comfort in times of trouble, and a loyal friend to her relations in Ballyderrig.[41]

The article goes on to relate that Jack Nolan is about to face a crisis – losing his job as it turns out – which will test his strength and 'tax both his common sense and his sense of security. In which case we can rely on Rita to give him support.' The fact that in the final episode of the serial Jack Nolan's main activity is washing the dishes after meals is a testimony to the assertion of the family – and Rita's – values over those of the workplace and the outside community. But it also reveals what was perhaps the underlying structural weakness of *Tolka Row* as a television serial.

In the *post mortems* which took place after the termination of the serial was announced in March 1968, many explanations were offered for the demise of the programme. Some viewers saw the deterioration setting in after the death of Maura Laverty in 1966, while others, including Carolyn Swift, the script editor, pointed to the inordinately high turnover in the members of the cast.[42] In this respect, the serial was perhaps dealt a mortal blow in 1967 when Iris

Lawlor, who played Statia, left the cast to be replaced by another actress. (So irrevocable was the audience's identification of Iris Lawlor with the character of Statia that the waggish TV critic of *The Munster Express* refused to accept the 'new' Statia, contending that *Tolka Row* had gone to the dogs since Gabby Doyle had started sleeping around 'with a strange woman passing herself off as Anastatia'!)[43] These setbacks undoubtedly helped to expedite the end of the serial but perhaps the most decisive factor in bringing about its disappearance from the television screens concerned its production context, and in particular the immense strain placed on resources by maintaining two serials (*The Riordans* having started in 1965, one year after *Tolka Row*).

From the outset, *Tolka Row* was greatly hampered by the fact that it was predominantly a studio-bound drama, a limitation which may be attributed not only to the new station's scarce resources, but also to its derivation from a successful stage and television play. Outdoor locations were entirely absent until the second year, but even then they were very infrequent, the action being invariably drawn almost by a gravitational pull back to the Nolan household. (One particular point of frustration for viewers was the inability to peer inside Mrs. Feeney's home next door to the Nolans, and to see the nine 'chislers' she was always complaining about!) The restricted use of sets not only made for a certain amount of visual tedium, but also meant that one of the basic dramatic devices of the serial was absent, a communal meeting place such as the Rover's Return in *Coronation Street* or Johnny Mac's in *The Riordans*. As Christine Geraghty points out, such institutions form the basis of the strong sense of community which exists in the serial, providing a kind of common ground where characters can come into spontaneous or accidental contact, and from which innumerable sub-plots (and gossip) may emanate.[44] In *Tolka Row*, however, Keogh's Pub figured at the very margins of the action, frequented only by the likes of Mrs. 'Queenie' Butler – the official community troublemaker – or Oliver Feeney, Mrs. Feeney's layabout husband.

The lack of a suitable source of common ground or collective meeting place had far-reaching implications for *Tolka Row*, since it entailed the virtual absence of any wider communal or social dimension to the action. As a result, the various social problems thrown up in the course of the story (unemployment, housing and welfare issues, alcoholism, etc.) were invariably relocated and displaced onto a family context. 'Before the Nolans took their annual leave,' wrote Brian Devenney, the *Irish Independent* TV critic, in 1967, 'the serial was living off cups of tea and whatever minor excitements could be reported (not shown) within the claustrophic confines of the Nolan family circle and the studio sets available.'[45] When the serial returned for the final time in October of that year, it attempted belatedly to adopt a social conscience, addressing itself to controversial issues such as the intolerance shown to travellers. Far from revitalizing the flagging serial, however, this episode and other forays into the darker sides of urban experience – crime, gambling, etc. – only helped to alienate it further from the audience, giving rise to charges that it was unduly preoccupied with the more unsavoury and squalid aspects of working-class life. In reply to these objections, Carolyn Swift pointed out that the 'passionate belief in the reality of *Tolka Row*' meant that it had a responsibility 'not only to amuse and entertain, but also not to mislead'.

> No one feels that *Tolka Row* should become a documentary about Dublin housing estates. Yet equally it would be wrong to suggest that life in Ballyfermot or Drimnagh or Finglas or Walkinstown presents no problems that cannot be wound up within half-an-hour in a happy ending. No one wishes to introduce the sordid or the vulgar, but we feel we have a duty not to shirk reality, and the truth is that problems in life can be grim at times and are endured with courageous, down-to-earth humour. . . .[46]

The fatalistic implication in this remark that problems are to be endured rather than tackled, and the desocialized character of what is considered an adequate response to urban problems, is hardly surprising, since the attenuated nature of the wider community outside Tolka Row ruled out any possibility of concerted social action. As Peter Cleary noted pithily in one of the obituaries which marked the passing of the serial, though it drew attention to a number of social problems '*Tolka Row* never stepped on anybody's toes.'[47]

It is difficult to avoid the conclusion that the family in *Tolka Row* represents not so much the new working class, but an urban residue of a rural family structure.[48] This is apparent not only in the extended nature of the Nolan household but also, as we have seen, in its tendency to derogate wider social functions (having to do, for example, with work or welfare) onto itself, thus giving rise to a misplaced confidence in its own ability to withstand the harsh realities of social and economic change. The existence of a rural backdrop was evident in Maura Laverty's own conception of the serial, and particularly in her characterization of female roles; while living in Fitzwilliam Street, we are told, she 'came to know the horror and warmth of the nearby slums. She found the women there more akin to the countrywomen she had grown up with than anything she found among the city's bourgeoisie.'[49] It would seem, moreover, that in the original scenario for the serial, Maura Laverty intended to locate the source of disruption and conflict in the external community, the 'menacing' character of Mrs. 'Queenie' Butler ('a holy terror' in the author's eyes) acting as a counterpoint to the more sentimental Mrs. Nolan and Mrs. Feeney.[50] As the narrative developed, however, the character of Mrs. Butler was 'softened' and conflict and tension came to reside within the confines of the home, precipitated not only by Statia and the other temperamental members of the Nolan household, but also by the production context which put 'the studio-bound *Tolka Row* into a sordid, bickering second best' to *The Riordans*.[51]

According to Wesley Burrowes, who worked as script editor on *Tolka Row* at the height of its popularity, it was this family squabbling and tension which eventually killed the programme.[52] It was time to look elsewhere for a dramatic serial which was more outgoing and less restricted in the range of its concerns. The growing success of *The Riordans* ensured that RTE's Drama Department did not have far to look.

The Riordans: narrative, family and community

The Riordans occupies a central place in the development of Irish television, equalled in importance only by *The Late Late Show* and, to a lesser extent, the *Seven Days* current affairs programmes of the late 1960s, and the acutely observed *Hall's Pictorial Weekly* satirical programmes of the mid-1970s. It shared with *The Late Late Show* an ability to combine a consistently high level of popularity with an innovative, indeed a pioneering, approach to television production, its outdoor location work in particular attracting interest from television stations all over the world. It is easy to see in retrospect how *The Riordans* was unusually well placed to exploit in full the narrative possibilities of the television serial, but at the time the launching of a popular rural drama involved a number of considerable risks. Not least of these was the likelihood that the serial would be recuperated back into the idyllic versions of Irish life which had dominated traditional representations of the countryside, and which, as we have seen, loomed large in the thinking of the earliest critics of Irish television. *The Riordans* not only managed to steer clear of this romantic ideology, but, in divesting rural experience of many of the myths which had surrounded it, made the first major break at a popular level with both the visual and the dramatic legacy of the Cultural Revival.

One basic point of departure, not only from the romantic image of Ireland but also from some of the standard conventions of soap opera, lay in the unprecedented emphasis which *The Riordans* placed on work practices, and on the day-to-day routines of farm production. This derived not from any high-minded attempt to bring about a 'realist revolution' in Irish visual culture, such as Courbet and Millet had effected in French painting in the previous century, but from the rather mundane circumstances which gave rise to the serial in the first place. Initially, *The Riordans* was conceived as a didactic agricultural programme, as a vehicle for imparting, if not smuggling in, the latest information on farm modernization and machinery. As Gunnar Ruggheimer, the Controller of Programmes responsible for the serial, expressed it, the aim of *The Riordans* was

> to get across *surreptitiously* ideas about good farm management and farm practices . . . and to make certain that the actual manipulation of farm equipment is in accordance with normal practice . . . the whole validity of the

series, which of course is built on its verisimilitude to a real solution, depends on the actors acting like farmers in every last detail. [my italics][53]

It was this recurrent need for authentic outdoor farm locations which led to the introduction of what was then a completely new concept in television drama, the use of an Outside Broadcast Unit for fictional purposes. This equipment, normally used for televising sporting fixtures and other live events, was unwieldy and cumbersome in the extreme, but by bringing the action out into the open, it dispensed with the convention whereby television drama was incarcerated within a claustrophobic studio setting. By the same token it allowed for different approaches to lighting and editing, but above all, it facilitated a more improvised acting style which helped to break with the Hollywood/Abbey Theatre axis which had up to then monopolized pictorial representation of Ireland.[54] It is not without interest, in this respect, that the basic core of *The Riordans* acting personnel was either new to drama, or else was recruited, not from the Abbey or Gate Theatres, but from the small touring companies which travelled Ireland in the post-war years and which knew at close-quarters the concerns of rural audiences.

So successful was *The Riordans* in its instructional role that it almost contributed to its own redundancy by paving the way for a regular programme, *Telefís Feirme*, which addressed itself directly to farming matters. By releasing farmers from an unquestioning reliance on time-honoured farming methods – usually underpinned by little more than the authority which the father exercised over the son – *The Riordans* had brought about a situation in which a rural audience was more receptive to social change, and more open to criticizing traditional norms. Having set a precedent, therefore, in using the serial as a didactic vehicle, the question arose: where was it to turn next? It would appear that Wesley Burrowes, the writer and editor of the serial, did not need any prompting on this score:

> It seemed to me that we could now begin to use the agricultural themes as a backdrop to the human and social aspects of rural life. My plan, if it could be called that, was to go on chronicling human relations. But if in the lives of the same people, something of wider social significance were to crop up, then we would prefer to plunge into the heart of the issue rather than skirt round its edges. . . . Already, with . . . episodes . . . about attitudes to the Travelling people, and to a lesser extent in the scenes about coursing, we had gone a little distance in that direction. With that decision, I suppose inevitably, came the beginning of my experience of censorship.[55]

So a pattern evolved in which the programme began to switch its attention to controversial moral and social issues, but with the same lack of deference to authority and to traditional pieties which characterized its approach to farming matters. It is important to bear in mind, however, that this shift in emphasis did not mean relegating agricultural or economic affairs to a backstage role. Though it maintained the serial's characteristic concern with family life and personal issues, *The Riordans* was also able to relate these directly to wider social and economic questions because, uniquely, it afforded the prospect of a world in which personal and familial considerations are intrinsically bound up with the very nature of production.[56] This arose from the fact that it dealt with life on a *family farm*, the basic economic unit of Irish agriculture. The interdependence of home and production on the family farm enabled *The Riordans* to explore complex social and economic problems in the very process of delineating personal and emotional relationships, and without violating the specific character of each domain. It is not surprising in view of its strategic location in the ideological structure of Irish society, that the need for an affirmative image of the family farm was placed so high on the agenda of the earliest critics of Irish television.

The contrast between the favourable social environment of the family farm, and the impersonal nature of industrial work which removes production entirely from the domestic sphere, formed a key element in the defence of rural values which dominated traditional Catholic social teaching, acquiring particular urgency in the changing economic climate of the 1950s. Writing on the rural family in 1952, the Rev. H. Murphy argued strongly against the 'individualism' of city life on the grounds that it 'destroys the unity of family life and weakens the marriage bond'. This situation arises, he contends, when the husband works away from home, but is particularly aggravated by the participation of married women in the workforce, 'for then husband and wife are leading to a great extent separate lives: their work, instead of binding them together, separates them'. As against this trend, however,

> rural life . . . exercises a much more favourable influence on the family . . . [the] sharing in the occupational activities of the farm binds husband and wife more closely together, for they are linked not only in a domestic but also in a business partnership.[57]

This fusion between 'domestic' and 'business' interests had a considerable bearing on the dramatic economy of *The Riordans*, for it entailed that, in effect, the personal is divested of its purely private connotations and is inserted instead into a network of economic and communal relations. In such a public arena, some of the basic set-pieces of the serial form are given a new lease of life: gossip, communal rituals, and the tension between individual freedom and social conformity. In a characteristic scene from one of the earliest surviving episodes of *The Riordans* (10 June 1973), Benjy sets aside his sheep-shearing in the farmyard to tell Fr. Sheehy the news of his engagement to Maggie. On being offered Fr. Sheehy's congratulations, Benjy cautiously refuses to shake hands in case anyone is looking and the game is given away. Fr.

Sheehy has to assure him that only the sheep can see them, before Benjy stops looking nervously around and agrees to stamp this sharing of confidence with the seal of an everyday ritual.

That there are in fact few secrets in Leestown is borne out in the next scene in which we see Benjy, his brother Michael, the local publican Johnny Mac and a number of others standing around in a group after Mass, discussing the forthcoming party to be held in the Riordans' house. Johnny proclaims grandiloquently that 'there is a theory gaining currency that the purpose of the exercise is the announcement of your own impending nuptials' – though mistakenly he thinks it is Michael who is getting married, not Benjy. As if to correct this error, Benjy takes Julia Mac, Johnny's wife, aside in their lounge bar in the next episode, and lets her in on the 'secret' – which in the circumstances is the next best thing to broadcasting it. As Fr. Murphy reminded his readers in his *Christus Rex* article of 1952, in the days before the lounge bar rivalled the church as the main focal point of the community:

> In a rural community . . . all know the difficulties and troubles of each other. . . . The centre of the community is, happily, the parish church and . . . the recurring attendance of the same congregation in the same church fosters fidelity to religious and moral duties. The black sheep is very conspicuous in the country.[38]

The ultimate triumph of community over privacy occurs some episodes later when Benjy and Maggie's idyllic honeymoon in Lahinch is interrupted by the appearance on the scene of Tom and Mary Riordan, Benjy's father and mother, followed by Batty Brennan, the Riordans' aged farm labourer, and his wife Minnie, the local gossip – all converging 'by coincidence' at the holiday resort! It is no wonder Maggie's exasperation shows when she asks Benjy, while they are both lying by the swimming pool: 'What are you thinking about?' 'Bovine Tuberculosis' comes the reply. Even the memories of the wedding night are not immune from the imperatives of farm production.

This casual exchange is not without significance in the overall context of *The Riordans*, for it draws attention to what is perhaps the most important site of identification between 'domestic' and 'business' interests in a farming community. This concerns the question of property, and the role of marriage in transferring the family farm to the favoured son who remained at home (often referred to as a 'young boy' well beyond his fortieth year).[59] The need to keep the heir apparent or the favoured son on the straight and narrow path, free from the predatory designs of young unattached females, fell to the protective influence of the mother, and was a frequent theme in kitchen comedies such as George Shiels' *The New Gossoon* (1930) or Lennox Robinson's *The White-headed Boy* (1916) which formed part of the repertoire of touring companies before the advent of television.

This fundamental bond between mother and son, in many ways the emotional basis of the family unit farm, received a formidable challenge from

The Riordans. From the outset, it seemed to set itself the task of replacing this overpowering mother/son relationship by a liaison between the son and an emotional peer of his choice – even if, as in the case of Maggie in *The Riordans*, the girl in question was devoid of economic prospects, having come from an orphanage to work as a barmaid in Johnny Mac's. As Wesley Burrowes describes this conflict of loyalties: 'If drama depends on tensions, then the relationship between Maggie and her mother-in-law is the stuff of tension'.[60] The cause of the tension, he goes on to point out, is 'the fact that they [both] were rivals for Benjy'. Yet as Burrowes contends, if one of Maggie's great achievements in the programme was 'to have been accepted by the public as the rightful and natural contender for Benjy's hand', it is clear that this was far from being an inevitable outcome. It came at the end of no less than eight separate engagements on Benjy's part, not all of them with Maggie but all of them to no avail since, as Burrowes remarks of the various candidates for Benjy's affections:

> The viewers did not accept them as suitable for Benjy, any more than Mary Riordan did. . . . In the case of Benjy, the mothers of Ireland have to some extent looked on him as a foster-son. And like Mary, they think nobody is good enough for him.[61]

So desperate was Burrowes to get Benjy married off that at one stage he had Maggie 'displaying symptoms which the most sheltered of viewers could hardly mistake'. The authorities at RTE felt that this was forcing the issue somewhat, and asked him to drop this interesting line of approach. Burrowes had to consult a doctor to find some alternative explanation for Maggie's symptoms – though the viewers had to wait for three months before the final verdict was delivered.

One might have expected the eventual marriage of Maggie and Benjy to have marked the end of *The Riordans*, and this would undoubtedly have been the case had it been other than a television serial. One of the basic areas of dramatic interest in the serial, however, is that it presents a diffuse, open-ended narrative as distinct from the once-off play or television series which turn for the most part on single, self-contained episodes.[62] Because of the need to establish continuity of action, and not just character (as in the series), the serial was prevented from having the kind of *closure* or final *resolution* which brings about the termination of action in a conventional, linear narrative. This absence of an ending, still less of a happy ending, was of considerable importance in a serial such as *The Riordans* which was intent on addressing itself, as we have seen, to social issues. It meant that while there was a continual tendency to open up social problems, and to foreground controversial areas of Irish society, no means were provided of solving them. Not surprisingly, marriage, and issues relating to sexual morality in general, were at the receiving end of this narrative strategy, the serial bringing to the surface with almost relentless zeal every possible transgression of the traditional Irish family enshrined in the 1937 Constitution.

First to emerge in late 1966 was the issue of illegitimacy, although at this early stage Burrowes was careful to ensure that the unmarried mother was a conspicuous outsider, being introduced into the proceedings as the young English niece of Miss Nesbitt, the upper class Protestant in the serial. Miss Nesbitt's status as an outsider, however, was diminished to some extent by another development taking place at the time. Early in the season, she had accepted (the Catholic) Dr. Howard's proposal of marriage, thus giving rise to a protracted series of negotiations between the various parties, including Fr. Sheehy and Canon Browne (the Protestant vicar), on the implications of a mixed marriage in terms of Catholic teaching. Canon Browne reluctantly conceded to the wedding's taking place in a Catholic church, but expressed his regret that marriage, ostensibly a means of bringing people together, should be used to keep them apart by institutionalizing some of the more entrenched religious divisions in society. This problem received a final twist some years later when the Howards initiated steps to adopt a child, only to discover that they were prevented as partners in a mixed marriage from doing so, under the Adoption Act of 1952. In the circumstances, they had to fall back on fostering a child, a decision which was itself to have unhappy consequences when the natural mother returned some time later looking for her son.

In the meantime, the more unacceptable side of Irish family life had invaded the Riordans' household, with the break-up of Jude Riordan's marriage to the agricultural instructor, Jim Hyland. (It is said that this forced Derek Young, the actor who played the part of Jim Hyland, to leave the serial, since in his acting roles outside *The Riordans* he was frequently berated with calls of 'Get back to Jude!') Had Jude suffered the ignominy of a marriage separation in isolation, the issue would perhaps have been laid to rest, but there was a widespread angry reaction from viewers when she started keeping company with a divorced Canadian mining executive who was surveying mineral deposits in the Leestown area. On this matter, the viewers were simply re-echoing Mary Riordan's incomprehension at the very prospect that a marriage could break down irretrievably. In an interesting exchange from the episode of 10 June 1973, which deals with the preparation for Benjy's (as yet unannounced) engagement party, Fr. Sheehy attempts to bring this problem out into the open with an air of feigned innocence, while Mary is serving the ubiquitous cup of tea:

Fr. Sheehy:	Have you seen Jude lately?
Mary:	Seen Jude? Of course I have Father.
Fr. Sheehy:	How are things?
Mary:	How are things . . .?
Fr. Sheehy:	Just things generally . . .
Mary:	Indeed, I don't know what you're talking about Father. There's never anything between Jude and myself that we can't sort out over (looking at her cup and saucer) – over a cup of tea.

In the following episode, Michael attempts once more to probe this raw nerve, forcing Mary to *think through* the problem rather than simply acquiescing to authority and tradition in the search for a clear-cut answer. When Mary expresses her concern that Jude is going from bad to worse by taking up Bridge and 'this annulment nonsense', Michael's reply to his mother is that she will have to get used to it:

Mary:	I never will.
Michael:	Ma, listen. You're against her because it goes against everything you ever believed in, right?
Mary:	That's exactly the reason, Michael.
Michael:	In other words, its against what the church taught you –
Mary:	Yes it is –
Michael:	But all she's doing is asking the church to decide. She's not against them, its just the opposite – she's going to obey their ruling.

When Mary responds that there is only one ruling the church can make, Michael asks her how would she feel if it came to the worst, and the church annulled the marriage?

Mary:	I would feel let down.
Michael:	You wouldn't agree with the decision?
Mary:	No, I certainly would not.
Michael:	But don't you see, then, your argument wouldn't be with Jude, it would be with the church?
Mary:	Ah! – You're only trying to confuse me with all this smart talk. It's not right, Michael, and it never will be.

Characteristically, the argument is designed to raise questions rather than provide answers, and the problem is left unresolved as the action shifts in the next scene to the more congenial topic of Benjy's forthcoming marriage. As Michael says to Benjy: 'When she hears your news, it might take her mind off the Jude business.' Mary's respite was to prove temporary, however.

On different occasions, the exploration of other sensitive issues – for instance, the prevalence of sexual ignorance (as in Eamonn Maher's famous question to his wife Eily: 'Do you think are we doing it right?') or the problem of 'living in sin' and the 'kept woman' (as in Paddy Gorey's unwelcome return to Leestown) – helped to dispel the idea that marriages were made in heaven, even if their material purpose was to facilitate the inheritance of various tracts of earth. It was not until difficulties began to surface in Benjy and Maggie's marriage, however, that it became clear that the age of innocence had finally passed in representations of family and rural life in Ireland. The 1974 season revolved around the contentious theme of contraception, precipitated by Maggie's decision to go on the Pill following the complications which attended the birth of her first child. When Maggie turned to Fr. Sheehy for advice on the rights and wrongs of the issue, she was told that there were no pat answers to what was in the last resort a matter of an informed, personal conscience: 'I wish I could give you a direct Yes or No, Maggie. But I can't. Simply because I'm not you. . . . I can't even mediate for you, in the real sense.'[63] By its very non-committal nature, Fr. Sheehy's answer was undercutting a deeply ingrained tendency in Irish Catholicism, evident in the 'question box' or problem pages of popular religious periodicals and Sunday newspapers, to consider complex personal dilemmas as some kind of abstract moral theorems to be solved by having recourse to the appropriate religious 'experts' or authorities.

As the strain began to tell on Benjy's and Maggie's marriage, this non-directive approach was carried over into the treatment of marital infidelity, whether it took the form of Benjy's notorious 'affair in the bushes' with Colette Comerford, or Maggie's more desperate relationship with Pat Barry, played by the handsome newcomer in front of the camera, Gabriel Byrne, who came originally as a farm labourer to replace Benjy on the farm but found himself combining 'business' and 'domestic' interests in a rather unorthodox manner. Throughout the duration of the serial, it was this tendency to open up moral and social issues without closing them off which drew the most opprobrium, not only from the general audience but also from such forums of liberal opinion as the *Irish Times*. In his TV column in the *Irish Times*, Ken Gray admonished the serial on the grounds that it 'constantly throws up contentious and controversial issues and then neatly sidesteps the implications':

> Many themes with potential for development in the way of social content have been raised, tossed around like a hot potato for a week or two, and quietly dropped.[64]

In his reply to this criticism, Wesley Burrowes argued that the lack of moral uplift or affirmative endings in the programme arose from its verisimilitude and its ability to reflect life as it is actually lived in the real world: 'I believe that real life provides very few neat wrap-up solutions such as those we are accustomed to in *Kojak* and *The Waltons*.'[65] Ironically, however, *The Riordans'* critical edge derived not so much from its transparent rendering of the actual world but from its relationship to *Kojak* and *The Waltons*, that is, from its status *as* a television serial. It was precisely the manner in which it *constructed* its raw material, processing it through generic conventions such as an open-ended narrative, and through a production context which exempted it from the constraints of Irish theatre and studio drama, which was responsible for the structured ambivalence which lay at the heart of the serial.

The operation of the dramatic conventions of the serial can be seen to telling effect in the deployment of another formal device which, in a sense, acted as a bridgehead between family and domestic issues and problems having wider social and political import. Much of the documentary feel of a 'realist' continuous serial comes from its use of 'naturalistic time', according to which time in the fictional world of the narrative appears generally to coincide with time in the 'real' world. Thus when it is Christmas time in the outside world, it is also time for seasonal cheer in Coronation Street or Brookside or Leestown. However, this device acquired an extra degree of authenticity in *The Riordans* on account of the need to impart agricultural advice which was both accurate and relevant at the time the farming community was viewing the serial. This made for an unusually close correlation between life in Leestown and the everyday concerns of life outside the serial, which in turn opened up a valuable space for allowing debates to develop on topical issues almost as soon as they happened. A case in point would be Jude's unhappy experience on moving into a flat in Kilkenny which was subsequently bought by an unscrupulous landlord. This episode represented another setback in Jude's attempt to organize her life after her broken marriage, but was taken out of its domestic setting and invested with direct political significance by virtue of the fact that it coincided with an actual campaign which was being waged in Kilkenny at the time, as part of a concerted national drive against the exploitation of flatdwellers.[66]

This was just one of many forays into controversial, and at times volatile areas of society, made by *The Riordans* in the course of its fifteen years on Irish television. Among the issues which it tackled with varying degrees of conviction were travellers, wages and conditions of farm labourers (both recurrent concerns because of the presence of Eamonn Maher, Batty Brennan and Pat Barry on Tom Riordan's farm), mental illness, church control of schools, ecumenism, custodial care of children, gambling, coursing, alcoholism, addiction to tranquillizers – as well as an extensive range of agricultural matters such as farming co-operatives, farm retirement schemes, conflicts over right-of-way, mining rights, etc. At times the sense of immediacy in its treatment of events was such that it was expected to have an almost journalistic topicality, as when on one occasion viewers complained about Tom Riordan's absence from the protests which took place during a national farmers' strike. Indeed, such was its record at intervening in social issues that at times it set the agenda for various public debates. Hardly had Johnny Mac declared war on the rounds system in his pub than this initiative was commended by President Childers, who began his own campaign to beat the rounds system. At a more serious level, the Minister for Lands, Tom Fitzpatrick, had occasion to cite Benjy's protracted struggle to gain majority shareholding on the family farm as an argument for early farm retirement to facilitate progressive young farmers.[67]

It is perhaps in the general area of family politics, rather than in its treatment of any one particular issue, that *The Riordans* made its most valuable contribution to Irish society. By disengaging the rural family from the cycle of inhibition, authority and conservatism in which it had been traditionally enclosed, it made deep inroads on a dominant ideology which looked to the family – and indeed the family farm – as the basic unit of Irish society.[68] Unlike the conventional soap opera (or for that matter *Tolka Row*) which runs the risk of mystifying and desocializing power structures by reducing social and economic relations to the vicissitudes of personal life, *The Riordans'* concern with the rural family brought it out of the individual private arena and into a wider social domain.

Yet it is important to point out that despite the centrifugal movement away from the family,[69] one of the striking features of *The Riordans* was the relative absence of forms of collective action that transcend familial or affective ties. Though Jude's dispute with the rackrenting landlord coincided with the activities of an organized flatdwellers' campaign in the 'outside' world, it was not approached from this angle within the story but rather mediated through Tom Riordan's intervention, both in his role as father and as an independent County Councillor. In the episode of 10 June 1973 adverted to above, a related housing issue (in this case the shortage of homes for old people) is taken out of the sphere of impersonal confrontation when Fr. Sheehy seeks to persuade Michael Riordan to establish a voluntary housing co-operative venture along the lines of the Christian Community Action group which was operating successfully elsewhere in the country.

It is difficult to escape the conclusion that while solidarity or collective effort is easily mobilized around consensual or communal issues, it is less forthcoming at an adversary level, or in the case of social divisions or conflict. It is instructive, for example, that while the community rallies around Batty Brennan, the Riordan's aged farm labourer, in his hour of need when he hears the news of his wife's relapse in hospital, this occurs in Johnny Mac's pub, at the level of consumption, one might say, rather than production. When problems arise relating to his – or more particularly Eamonn Maher's – status as a farm labourer, this collective support is less visible. Though Eamonn has recourse to the rulings of the Agricultural Wages Board in his numerous rows with Tom Riordan over wages and conditions, his response usually takes the form not of union activity but of the ineffectual 'expressions of annoyance, boredom and chafing against restraint' which vitiate social conflict in Arensberg and Kimball's description of the Irish rural community.[70] In the long term, Eamonn overcomes the problem by securing his own farm, thus exemplifying the pattern noted by David Fitzpatrick whereby 'social mobility is hostile to class-collective action [in the rural community], since it encourages queue-jumping rather than conspiracy among frustrated queuers to take over the bus'.[71] As Miley Byrne says to the disgruntled Pat Barry in *The Riordans'* successor *Bracken*, who, having just made the transition from farm labourer to smallholder, complains about the fact that seventy per cent of the land of Ireland is owned by five per cent of the people: 'Do you know all this thing about the five per cent – the rich men, the Dalys. You don't want all that money and wealth shared out. You just want them to move over, to make room for yourself.' Indeed, such is Eamonn Maher's ability to make room for himself that from his initial position as a traveller, he ends up in a protracted relationship with Colette Comerford, the daughter of the wealthiest farmer in the district.

Personal relationships also provide Batty Brennan with a means of escape from the confines of his class position – in this case his marriage to Minnie, owner of Leestown's Home Bakery 'with Select Accommodation above'. Yet while class tensions are blurred and defused in this manner, the whole narrative thrust of *The Riordans*, at another level, is to close off this escape route by undermining at every turn the central role of marriage as a force of reconciliation in the community. It is revealing that in the case of Jude and Paddy Gorey, for whom marriage is ruled out as an option, their inability to negotiate this terrain is accompanied by a descent in social status and esteem. For similar reasons, characters like Michael Riordan and Willie Mahoney, for whom marriage is an external possibility rather than a practical reality, move around in a kind of social cul-de-sac, always promising but never delivering. In all of these situations, problems are thrown up which, with the disintegration of familial structures, call for forms of resistance or concerted action that confront adversity or conflict at a more engaged, organized level. The need for campaigns around issues such as divorce, contraception, and unemployment is frequently alluded to, but is never fully developed. Collective responses of this kind resemble those characters who, though temporarily removed from the serial, always maintain, in Jean O'Halloran's words, 'a peripheral presence',[72] hovering at the edges of the action even when they do not directly manifest themselves.

Bracken: melodrama and the disintegration of family and community

By the time *The Riordans* was taken off the television screens in 1979, the image of the Irish rural family had travelled a long way from the sentimental conceptions of family and community which informed the earliest critical appraisals of Irish television. Almost every variation on the theme of the happy Irish home had been given an airing, to the extent that when *The Riordans* was replaced in 1980 by a new serial, *Bracken* (1980–1), all but the faintest traces of the family unit farm were excised from view. In *Bracken*, the brooding figure of Pat Barry returns from his job as a labourer on Tom Riordan's farm to take over the diminutive holding left to him and his emigrant brother on his father's death. Though we are led to believe that only the mountain of Slieve Bracken separates Leestown from the townland of Bracken, to pass from one community into another is, in effect, to enter a new moral continent. In *Bracken*, there is a narrative shift from a naturalistic to a melodramatic genre, albeit in a less-heightened, restrained form. The family, where it is present at all, is a site of internecine struggle and personal intrigue, and its internal divisions are no longer inscribed on the wider social and ideological conflicts taking place in the community. By the same token, the idea of community is itself attenuated, and recedes into the background as a menacing presence, an aggregation of glancing looks and mumbled conversation which only impinges on the action in the form of collective violence.

Bracken in a sense takes up where *The Riordans* and *Tolka Row* leave off. The conflict between Pat Barry and Daly, the rancher farmer manipulating the community for his own ends, is not mediated by family ties or domestic considerations, except insofar as Louise, Daly's daughter, is a pawn in his calculations. For this reason, it is not surprising that in *Bracken* there is a complete eclipse of the mother figure, the most powerful source of cohesion in the community. The only approximation to the mother role is the insipid Jill Daly, Louise's mother, but she is merely a cipher for her husband's opinions, is inefficient as a wife and as a protector of her daughter's interests, and in the end throws off the last vestiges of the virgin-mother ideal when Daly abandons her and she has an affair with Pat Barry.

Just as Jill is an affront to the role of mother as represented by Mary Riordan (or Rita Nolan), likewise her daughter Louise is far removed from the homely and unaffected Maggie in *The Riordans*. Louise's presence invariably emits an erotic charge which seems totally at odds with the maternal instincts which come so naturally to Maggie. To a certain extent, this sexual profile is imposed on Louise in that, as a daughter rather than a son, she is not directly entrusted with responsibility for producing the heir to the Daly estate. As such, her sexuality, like that of Peggy in *Tolka Row*, is less defined by the procreative role which circumscribed Maggie's behaviour in *The Riordans* – or at least did until Pat Barry came on the scene.

Pat Barry, with little to worry him by way of property except an impoverished sheep farm, is not unduly burdened either by the task of securing his line of succession – nor is it likely that others will be attracted to him because of his wealth and material possessions. Marriage for him is merely a form of social mobility, a means of advancing his own interests by what he sees as the only route open to the man of no property. His sexual appeal, understated at first, proves to be his passport to the big house, bringing about an affair not only with Louise, but also with her mother and, for good measure, Louise's best friend, the appropriately named Eve, who momentarily diverts Pat from his more profitable emotional engagements.

Insofar as marriage and the family manifest themselves at all in *Bracken*, it is in the form of patriarchal relations. However, father figures, far from being centres of authority and action, are repeatedly brought down in the world and reduced to a state of abjection and powerlessness. It was Pat Barry's neglect of his own father, through his departure for Leestown, which led to his father's loss of interest in life and to his eventual death. A similar fate befalls the unctuous Dinny Byrne whose son Miley leaves him at one point to go to England on finding out about his underhand dealings with Ned Daly. Daly's own fortunes take a dramatic downturn as he becomes increasingly isolated from his wife and daughter, and returns to his old haunts in England in an attempt to recover the self-respect he once enjoyed. In a dingy pub on a backstreet, his path crosses that of the hapless Dinny, aimlessly searching for his missing son. *Bracken*, clearly, is no country for old men.

It is interesting to revisit Bracken, Leestown and Tolka Row in the light of the renewed assaults which have been levelled at imported melodramatic serials such as *Dallas* and *Dynasty* for corrupting the moral fibre of the Irish nation. These charges seem to have gained impetus from the 1983 constitutional referendum on abortion, and have been a regular feature of popular analyses of the drift away from traditional Irish attitudes towards sexuality. As Frances O'Rourke puts it in the course of a discussion on the causes of teenage pregnancies in Ireland:

> If kids are sex mad, look at TV ads, look at *Dallas*, look at our place in western pop culture and at human nature for some reasons why.[73]

As in the case for the argument that the demand for abortion in Ireland was being imposed from abroad on an unsuspecting Irish public, likewise 'bed-hopping soaps' (to quote Frances O'Rourke's graphic phrase) are singled out as the source of the irremovable stains which have tarnished images of family and community in Ireland. It is difficult to escape the conclusion that commentators here are searching in vain abroad for what they can readily find at home. In an astute observation in an issue of the Dublin *Northside Express*, the television critic relates how he listened to a letter from 'an outraged licence-holder' on the RTE programme *Mailbag* who

> complained that RTE should screen more home-produced goodies like *Glenroe* and *The Riordans*. 'Programmes like *Dallas*,' he complained 'are destroying the moral fibre of the country.' While I sympathize with him about *Dallas*, we would like to point out that between *Glenroe*, *The Riordans* and *Bracken*, every form of vice reasonably imaginable has been screened. We've had extra-marital sex, adultery, drunkenness, pub brawls; hardly the sort of stuff to improve the moral fibre.[74]

5. FROM MEGALITH TO MEGASTORE: Broadcasting and Irish Culture

What more natural play for the lusty son of the caveman than to kick with his foot any spherical fruit or semi-round planthead that lay in his hunting path! He learnt the rudiments – toe down, drive with the instep!

'Carbery' (P.D. Mehigan) on the origins of Gaelic football

The development of the media in Ireland has been constrained from the outset by the competing forces of the *nation* and the *state*, the pleasure principle and the reality principle in Irish politics. Since the opening of 2RN, the first radio service, in 1926, the statutory legislation governing broadcasting has stressed the importance of maintaining and consolidating national identity, but the day-to-day policies of successive governments have worked almost as consistently to undermine these ideals. The media are often portrayed as modernizing agencies, releasing society from the weight of tradition. Yet while television in Ireland did much to alter what are considered traditional values and other aspects of 'national life', there was nothing inevitable about this. One has only to look at the role of the media in perpetuating the cult of the monarchy in Britain to see that popular cultural forms, even television, have no difficulty in propping up, still less inventing, even the most venerable 'national traditions'.

It is tempting to suggest that the media only reinforce those 'traditions' which emanate from the heartlands of the culture industry, particularly those within the Anglo-American power bloc. But this does not happen as a matter of course. If we attend to the specific example of the monarchy and the media, it is clear that its integrative function in British society is closely bound up with the public service ideal of broadcasting as it evolved under Lord Reith, the first director-general of the BBC. The 'high culture' aspirations of public service broadcasting made no secret of the fact that they were in the business of *establishing* a national consensus and projecting a symbolic image of the nation. There was no illusion that the cultural brief of British broadcasting was to give the people back their own self-image: indeed with its emphasis on 'excellence' and 'high-seriousness', it was designed to combat the everyday culture of the masses and expose them to the 'higher self' of the nation. In the United States, faced with the problem of unifying a vast population of immigrants and different ethnic groups, there was even less pretence about *constructing* the nation. As Alistair Cooke has put it, 'America didn't inherit a nation: it invented one and boasted it would be better than everything that had gone before'.

"Ðí ꝼeꝺꝶ ꞟnn ꝼꝺꝺó ꝺꝘuꞟ ꝼꝺꝺó ꝺ ðí——will ye listen to me?"

5.1 *Dublin Opinion* cartoon

Nothing could be further from the situation in Ireland. From the beginning, policy formation in Irish broadcasting operated under the assumption that the *nation* was already in place: only the *state* awaited completion as part of the unfinished business of securing a coherent Irish identity. The state derived its legitimacy from the existence of an antecedent nation, and thus the function of broadcasting was not to establish but to revitalize this nation, releasing the cultural energies which, it was believed, had accumulated over centuries. It was the state, in fact, which needed building, given the fragility of the political settlement after the Civil War. To this end, broadcasting was brought under the direct control of the central administration, functioning as an extension of the civil service until 1953. Under direct state control, there was general agreement that the new radio service could hardly fail to preserve a distinguished national heritage, bringing it to wider audiences than ever before. As Dr. Douglas Hyde stated in his speech at the opening of the station, underlining the difference between the cultural pedigree of the nation, and the artificial, political character of the state:

> A nation cannot be made by Act of Parliament; no, not even by a Treaty. A nation is made from inside itself; it is made first of all by its language, if it has one; by its music, songs, games, and customs. . . . So, while not forgetting what is best in what other countries have to offer us, we desire to especially emphasize what we have derived from our Gaelic ancestors – from one of the oldest civilizations in Europe, the heritage of the Os and Macs who still make up the bulk of our country.[1]

Initially this faith in the medium did not appear to be misplaced. The appointment of Seamus Clandillon, an ardent revivalist and music enthusiast, as director of the new station ensured that the Irish language and wider cultural concerns received comprehensive coverage. As a well-known traditional musician, Clandillon himself had no reservations about doubling up as a performer on his own station. In the area of Gaelic games, the station made broadcasting history by carrying the first live transmission of a sporting event in Europe when it covered the All-Ireland hurling semi-final in 1926. From the 1930s the voice of the sports commentator, Michael Ó Hehir, became synonymous with Gaelic games and so close was the affinity between the new service and official culture that a Dáil deputy in the early 1940s could welcome the appointment of a new director, Seamus Brennan, in the following convivial terms: 'I should like to make a few suggestions to the Minister in this connection. I congratulate him on the appointment of Mr. Brennan as director of Radio Éireann. Mr. Brennan is a good friend of mine and was one of the best Gaelic footballers and step-dancers in the country.' All this is consistent with the earliest stages in the development of a new medium. As Bertolt Brecht has pointed out, radio did not come into the world with its own readymade subject matter but had to look to pre-existing cultural forms for its 'raw material':

> [Radio] looked around to discover where something was being said to someone and attempted to muscle in. . . . That was radio in its first phase as a substitute. As a substitute for the theatre, for the opera, for concerts, for lectures, for café music, for the local columns of the press and so on.[2]

Radio, in other words, had to adjust itself to the prevailing cultural dynamic, and in Ireland this was closely identified with nationalism. It would be mistaken, however, to conclude that in drawing on Irish culture in this way, radio was merely popularizing a long-established native heritage. The idea that the media could act as an electronic museum, bringing the wisdom of ancient traditions to mass audiences, may have proved attractive to cultural revivalists such as Douglas Hyde but seriously overlooked the fact that the media are themselves cultural *agencies*, actively shaping and reconstituting the material which passes through them.

The extent to which the media do not simply *transmit* but actively *transform* their content was a major preoccupation of the German critic, Walter Benjamin. In his influential essay 'The Work of Art in the Age of Mechanical Reproduction', published in 1936, Benjamin argued that the first casualty of the new media technology was precisely *tradition*, the shared experience of a continuous past. The endless proliferation of copies facilitated by mass production dispels any trace of 'authenticity', the 'aura' of the original, which is central to the concept of tradition. To compensate for this liquidation of tradition, the media offers a new form of public identity, the sense of belonging which comes from being a member of a mass audience experiencing a national (or even an international) media event.[3] In the case of media coverage of Gaelic games in the 1930s, for example, what is often interpreted as the 'handing down' of a sporting tradition from time immemorial was in fact a fundamental restructuring of the whole basis of Gaelic games. So, far from passively relaying the activities of a thriving sporting body to an already captive audience, both radio and the press contributed substantially to creating a *nationwide* audience for Gaelic games, thus establishing the Gaelic Athletic Association as a truly *national* organization. Radio broadcasts were augmented by the blanket coverage of Gaelic games in the *Irish Press*, the first daily newspaper adequately to represent nationalist public opinion. Within a year of its founding in 1931, no less than six correspondents were assigned to Gaelic games, and the *Irish Independent* had to increase its coverage tenfold to keep up with its rival. The GAA capitalized on its new national profile through the efforts of its dynamic General Secretary, Padraig Ó Caoimh (appointed in 1931), and by the end of the 1930s it had secured its reputation as Ireland's leading cultural organization.[4]

A similar situation obtained in the case of Irish music. While Radio Éireann's far-seeing archival policy saved whole repertoires of traditional music from extinction, it is again mistaken to construe this as preserving the native heritage in an unmodified form. The cultivation of a nationwide audience for traditional music did much to 'flatten out' variations in regional styles, and there is even a sense in which broadcasting may have invented a key element in the traditional canon. According to some authorities, the ceili band, which was regarded as the distinctive sound of Irish music in the 1950s, was not an 'organic' development but was actually devised by Seamus Clandillon during the period when he was appointed the first director of the new radio service. Whatever about the origins, there is little doubt that this collective approach to the performance of Irish music owed its popular currency to the 'alien' institutions of the electronic media and the dance-hall. It would seem, then, that the changes visited upon traditional culture by the media were not acknowledged as such but were considered to have maintained and even reinforced cultural continuity. Transformations and innovations, even of a substantial kind, are silently assimilated and accepted as indigenous once they make a positive contribution to an established tradition. It was easy for cultural revivalists to portray the media as exponents of some type of Socratic method, releasing the inner cultural resources of the hidden Ireland, while masking over the radical discontinuities involved in such exercises in retrieval. The role of the state, accordingly, was merely to provide a supportive environment for this form of national renewal.

State versus nation in Irish broadcasting

The first rift between broadcasting and its designated cultural role occurred in 1932–3 when the new Fianna Fáil government indicated that its main political priority was to strengthen the state, if need be at the expense of the more intangible nation. One of the anomalies in the financial structure of the new station –

and one of the features which distinguished it from the BBC – was that even though it was under direct state control, the state sought to reduce its financial liability for the service, insisting that it be self-supporting as far as possible. Thus it was expected to live up to the ideals of public service broadcasting in an Irish context while maintaining its commercial viability at the same time. It was accepted in Britain that since the Reithian conception of public service broadcasting drew its bearings from high culture, this would not be commercially viable and hence would have to be funded like other uplifting areas of life from the public exchequer. In Ireland, however, the equation of public service broadcasting with cultural nationalism gave rise to the illusion that the media were simply giving the nation back its own birthright, promoting cultural values the population at large could readily identify with. If native culture was truly organic and 'of the people', there was no reason why it should not be commercially viable. The nation could look after itself: it was the state which was in urgent need of additional revenue and popular support.

In its initial phase, 2RN (as the station was called until the name Radio Éireann gained currency in 1937) derived its revenue from three sources: import duties on radios; licence fees; and advertising. Of these, import duties contributed by far the greatest portion to the station's finances. The number of radio licences increased from 2,805 in 1925 to 33,083 in 1933, and the import duties on these radios accounted for almost two-thirds of total revenue, thereby acting as an efficient buffer between the station's public service remit and the commercial vagaries of the market. The prospects of a lucrative windfall, however, proved too attractive to the Department of Finance, and in 1933 the Minister, Sean MacEntee, directed that in future the revenue from import duties would accrue to the central exchequer. 'By this decision,' Maurice Gorham writes, 'the government had at a stroke deprived the broadcasting service of one of its chief sources of income. . . . But it still clung to the other half of the formula – that broadcasting should pay for itself and not get any help from the proceeds of general taxation.'[5] As a result of this shortsighted measure, the station was compelled to fall back on advertising as a vital source of revenue, the immediate effects of which can be seen from the fact that whereas in 1932 advertising accounted for a meagre £220 in income, by 1933 it had increased dramatically to £22,827.

The new Fianna Fáil government saw no inconsistency between this reliance on advertising and the cultural objectives of the station: indeed, by stipulating that only native Irish companies were eligible to advertise, they were able to convince themselves that it was a positive advance on previous policy. However, the logic of the market was moving in a different direction, and the state's economic and political requirements began to diverge sharply from the path of cultural nationalism. Advertisers were extremely reluctant to sponsor programmes which catered for 'minority' interests such as classical music and the Irish language, and looked instead to a popular formula of jazz, tin-pan alley and swing music to sell their wares. As Fr. R. S. Devane wrote of the changing fortunes of the Gaelic revival in the first decade of the century:

> The soul of the nation was then deeply stirred by it. A mystic idealism spread throughout the land. A national messianism, the feeling that the nation had a secret mission, took possession of the people . . . It is now sad to look back on those halcyon days . . . Gone is the idealism; gone the mysticism; gone the messianism. They have been replaced by cynicism, fatalism and pessimism. Native music and song have given way to jazz, crooning, and the dances of African primitives.[6]

In the early 1940s, the Minister for Posts and Telegraphs sought belatedly to reverse this trend by banning 'jazz and crooning' from the airwaves, as if it was only the false allure of popular music which was preventing Irish people from appreciating their true heritage. This crude protectionist measure was not accompanied by any change in the financial structure of broadcasting. The 'preservation' of national culture only proved attractive, it seems, when it added to the state's coffers. In 1932–3, for example, at the same time that the radio service was being deprived of import duties, a similar tax was imposed on 'alien' newspapers which netted the exchequer a substantial sum of £140,000. Patrick Pearse's famous dictum, that Ireland should be not merely Gaelic but free as well, was given a new commercial meaning when it came to the question of funding Irish culture.

The increasing popularity of Anglo-American mass culture made it difficult to sustain the belief that the official national culture was a spontaneous effusion of the people. Accordingly, it is not surprising that the middle-class basis of official cultural nationalism was thrown into sharp relief, and the centre of gravity in Irish culture shifted from a folk/cultural model towards a *rapprochement* with high culture. Thus, in the case of Irish music, the 1940s and 1950s witnessed what Seán Mac Réamoinn has referred to as 'the "waiting for our Dvorak" school' which entreated the Irish people to cherish their 'rich heritage of native melody and keep it safe for the great composer who, one day, will come along and make of it something which will take its place among the musical masterpieces of the world'.[7] With the appointment of Dr. T. J. Kiernan as director in 1935, Irish music on radio began to progress in an upwardly mobile direction from the Ceili House to the Concert Hall, and in the early 1940s a Light Orchestra was established to confer respectability on this and other forms of music.

This adoption of a high-minded Reithian outlook in Irish broadcasting was a major setback for cultural nationalism, for Irish culture on the radio began to shed whatever populist appeal it may have had in the past. Actors, readers, and presenters in the Irish language were recruited from a small coterie of teachers and civil servants, and the lack of diversity eventually took its toll. In 1949, Seamus Brennan (the well-known 'Gaelic footballer and step-dancer') could write more in sorrow than in anger of the failure of the station to inject new life into Irish culture during his tenure of office as director (Brennan, it is worth noting, was recruited to the station from a post as Secretary to the Commission on Irish in the civil service):

> To me, I think the most disappointing aspect of broadcasting in Irish was the apparently complete lack of interest, the indifference, the apathy – call it what you will – of the listeners, so much so that I often wondered whether anyone listened to Irish . . . let the programmes be very good, indifferent or bad . . . there was complete silence. . . . A remark Dr. Kiernan once passed to me will illustrate the position, viz. 'You could get away with murder in Irish on radio'.[8]

Brennan's suspicions about the decline, if not disappearance, of an audience for Irish language programmes were borne out by an analysis of radio listenership figures in the late 1950s by Garret FitzGerald. This showed that while Radio Éireann had a virtual monopoly of airwaves during news, popular variety and sponsored programmes (comprising over 80 per cent of the listeners), the figures plummeted drastically when it came to Irish language content. Only 1 per cent listened to the news in Irish at 6.00 p.m. (as against 41 per cent to the 6.30 English language news) while less than 0.5 per cent tuned in to the 7.30–8.30 slot in which a play in the Irish language was broadcast. The fact that 'Irish people seem to listen voraciously to variety and popular music', FitzGerald added in a revealing comment, should not be taken as a reflection 'either on Radio Éireann or on the Irish language [but] might, perhaps, be taken as reflecting on the Irish people'.[9] Not for the first time the people were blamed for the parsimony and the ineptitude of government policy.

FitzGerald's analysis of radio listenership is of interest, as it proves an important corrective to the popular myth that it was television which brought about the demise of the cultural nationalist dream. Television is an obvious scapegoat for, as we shall see, it has been unduly reliant on imported products for its programming schedules. Yet it is clear that the problem long predates the advent of television. In the conclusion to his article, Garret FitzGerald warned that the crisis in Irish language programming on radio was a portent of what would happen if any attempt were made to combine commercial viability with a public service mandate in the new television service. His warning went unheeded and in both the establishing legislation for the television service and in subsequent policy formation, the rigid emphasis on balancing the books was accompanied by ritualistic incantations of the need to make programmes which 'would reflect traditional Irish values' (Radio Éireann, *Annual Report*, 1960–61), and promote 'a deeper appreciation of the intrinsic value of Irish language, history and tradition, [and] the development of a better public consciousness of national identity' (*A View of Irish Broadcasting*, RTE Authority, 1971). In the meantime, as Seamus Brennan had observed as early as 1949, the subservience of broadcasting to the state was becoming more apparent, with the added proviso that the interests of the state were conveniently interpreted as coinciding with those of the government of the day:

There is nothing the average Irishman loves more than a real live argument or discussion. My experience was that we had to be so careful for fear of offending anyone, or of allowing anyone to use the *Government radio* for the purpose of criticising a Government Department or Government policy of any kind that we had substantially to avoid open discussion. [my italics][10]

Television and cultural identity

The inauguration of the new television service on 31 December 1961 took place against a backdrop of immense social change in Ireland. The First Programme for Economic Expansion, devised by T. K. Whittaker in 1958 and implemented by Sean Lemass, opened up the economy to foreign investment; and membership of the United Nations (1956), the application for membership of the EEC (1961), and the reforms of the Second Vatican Council (1962–5) were seen by many as ushering in a welcome, outward-looking attitude in Irish life. Television played a major part in bringing the effects of these 'global' initiatives into the living rooms of Irish people, thus clearing away many of the cultural cobwebs which had accumulated since the founding of the state. Nor was television alone in this, for the appointment of Douglas Gageby to the *Irish Times* in 1964, and the facility with which both the *Irish Press* and new radio programmes addressed issues raised by the women's movement, also helped to redefine the relationship of the media to Irish society.

It is significant, however, that the liberalizing trends promoted by the media were confined for the most part in areas outside the political and economic domain, and were most evident in precisely the realm of 'traditional values' that broadcasting was enjoined to protect in official policy statements. In the case of television, deference towards religious authority, the conservative sexual morality of the post-Famine era, the bias against urban life and many other conventional pieties came under critical scrutiny from programmes such as *The Late Late Show* (1962–), once-off plays such as *A Week in the Life of Martin Cluxton* (1971) and *Hatchet* (1974), and drama serials such as *Tolka Row* (1964–8), *The Riordans* (1965–79), *Bracken* (1980–1), the six-part *Strumpet City* (1980) and *Glenroe* (1983–). The most striking feature of Irish television is that it was *home-produced* programmes, not imported products, which posed the greatest challenge to traditional cultural values.

Of course there is a sense in which, notwithstanding their native origins, the formats or 'genres' of many of these programmes (the 'talk show', the 'continuous serial', the 'slice-of-life' television drama) are of Anglo-American origin, and thus in the eyes of some critics represent a more insidious form of cultural domination. As Herbert Schiller expresses it, with regard to the influence of Anglo-American programmes on indigenous production:

Imitations of that material may appear when and if the indigenous broadcast/ film/print industries demand a share in their home market. Directly or indirectly, the outcome is the same. The content and style of the programming, *however adapted to local conditions,* bear the ideological imprint of the main centres of the capitalist world economy.[11]

The problem with this formulation is that *any* kind of influence from the metropolitan centres is evidence of cultural imperialism. On this reckoning, much of what is already taken to be traditional in Ireland – ceili music, Seán Ó Riada's adoption of jazz and classical formats during the folk revival in the 1960s, the foundation of Gaelic games (an adaptation to Irish circumstances of the sports revolution which swept Victorian Britain), even cultural nationalism itself (which was, after all, greatly influenced by German romanticism) – all of these can be dismissed as examples of foreign cultural penetration. The interaction between dominant and subaltern cultures is considered entirely in terms of one-way flow, as if cultures on the periphery have no power to resist or assimilate external influences in ways which may prove positively beneficial.

The resilience of Irish television in the face of the Anglo-American culture industry is clearly evident in programmes such as *The Late Late Show* and *The Riordans,* perhaps the two most successful home productions. Both the critical impact and popular appeal of these programmes derived from the manner in which they broke the conventions of their original models, reworking them in terms of local cultural idioms. The long-running serial, *The Riordans,* pioneered the use of outside broadcast cameras for television drama, an exigency which arose from its origins in a failed outside broadcast series on an Irish village. This innovation contributed a type of documentary realism to the action which helped it to investigate topical social issues, releasing television drama from the studio-bound approach which had dominated it up to then. The impact of the serial on Irish life was such that Raymond Williams was able to cite *The Riordans* in support of his argument that, in some cases, the despised serial form could engage in a more subtle form of social criticism than the more prestigious once-off play. (Williams' article, written in 1969, appears to have been the first significant appraisal of the television serial as a dramatic genre.)[12]

The Late Late Show, compèred by Gay Byrne, also brought the American-style talk show out of the realms of light entertainment by using its open-ended format to probe and question some of the most entrenched conservative values. As if bearing in mind Seamus Brennan's statement, quoted above, that the Irish love nothing better 'than a real live argument or discussion', the show went out live (uniquely for a talk show at the time) and this, coupled with the active participation of an audience which frequently upstaged both the panel and the presenter, seemed to invite controversy from the outset. The apparently unscripted nature of the show, which moved abruptly from levity to gravity, from frivolous items to major social issues, without any advance warning, made it compulsive viewing for audiences. The paradoxical manner with which the programme combined a home-spun intimacy with 'Brechtian' television techniques (displaying studio technology, the presenter himself calling the shots at times, including the show's catch phrase 'Roll it there, Colette') gave it a place in Irish life not unlike that of the provincial newspaper: people watched it if only because they were afraid they might miss out on something.

Yet the show's penchant for controversy had limits, and these became obvious when it made incursions into politics and the area of current affairs. While it made deep inroads on what might be understood as 'the nation', it met an immovable object when it confronted the state. A turning-point came in 1983 when it was prevented, on the direct instructions of the chairman of the govern-ment-appointed RTE Authority, from devoting a special episode of the show to a discussion of the constitutional referendum on abortion. Three years later, it did present a studio debate on the pros and cons of the divorce referendum but the discussion was virtually neutralized by adopting the stilted, legal format of a simulated courtroom. Open discussion is given free rein on television so long as it does not concern itself directly with politics. Affairs of state for the most part are confined to the tightly structured formats of current affairs programmes which leave little room for questioning the dominant political consensus.

The consolidation of the state's control of broadcasting was secured by a special provision, Section 31 of the 1960 Broadcasting Act. It was never invoked in the 1960s, as government ministers felt free to interfere at will in the day-to-day operations of the station. The position was summed up in 1966 by the then Taoiseach (Prime Minister) Sean Lemass when, in a statement to the Dáil, he declared that RTE 'was an instrument of public policy and as such is responsible to the government':

> The government reject the view that Radio Telefís Éireann should be, either generally or in regards to its current affairs and news programmes, completely independent of government supervision.[13]

Section 31 was not enforced until the escalation of the northern 'troubles' and from the early 1970s it has been used primarily to silence the voice of radical or para-military nationalist groups. The full rigours of censorship were first experienced in November 1972 when the RTE Authority was sacked by the Minister for Posts and Telegraphs for an alleged breach of Section 31. Following the appointment of Conor Cruise O'Brien as Minister in 1973, the provision of the section was refined by specifying the groups which were prohibited from the airwaves. The most prominent of these were the Provisional IRA and Provisional Sinn Féin, but the remit was extended to include any organization proscribed by the *British* govern-ment in Northern Ireland. The gap between the state and the nation in Ireland could not be greater, for at the same time as he was implementing these new direc-tives, Dr. O'Brien was proposing to use the new television channel, RTE2, to relay the BBC signal to the entire country. The fact that the BBC did *not* prohibit inter-views with paramilitary organizations at the time apparently did not trouble him.

The attempt to place an Irish television channel at the disposal of a foreign television network highlighted a serious problem which had been developing for some time in Irish broadcasting. In the early years of RTE, approximately two-thirds of television programmes were home produced. By the late 1970s this proportion was reversed, and in 1980 almost 70 per cent of all programmes were imported, thus putting RTE into a 'Third World' category in terms of cultural dependency. The reason for this marked imbalance was not the lack of interest in home-produced programmes: on the contrary, they dominated the TAM (Television Audience Measurement) ratings throughout this period. The problem was the same as that which beset radio broadcasting: the stipulation that the television service had to be self-financing forced it to rely on cheaper imported products rather than more expensive home-produced quality material.

The solution to this is not to revert to a form of cultural insularity which seeks to defend a 'pure' native culture against foreign contamination. One does not counteract the one-way flow of cultural imperialism by closing the ports and placing an embargo on all imported products. The dramatic revival of interest in the Welsh language in recent years is a standing rejoinder to such acts of cultural enclosure. Thus while Irish language activists such as Maolsheachlainn Ó Caollaí were pointing out the corrosive effects of 'alien' genres such as soap opera or the television serial on Irish culture, their Welsh counterparts were noting their potential for attracting popular audiences to Welsh language programmes. As Harri Pritchard Jones expressed it, ironically citing an Irish example to drive home his point:

> One thing we must make sure of is that the native language channel does not become a Ghetto. One certainly does not want a channel for penillion singing, rural crafts and customs and the problems of rural decline. One must produce a balanced diet of news and current affairs . . . a lot of sport and serial plays of the type of the O'Riordans [sic] . . . and a great deal of popular entertainment.[14]

The strength of an indigenous culture does not lie in its ability to avoid contact with the dominant forces in the culture industry, but in the manner in which it *appropriates* the forms and products of the metropolitan centre for its own ends. In the case of film, for example, the French 'new wave' and recent German cinema have shown how Hollywood genres such as the thriller and family melodrama can be reworked and turned against the American culture that produced them. At their most astringent (for example, the films of Godard or Fassbinder) such cross-cultural offensives are no less critical of their own native culture, using the universal thrust of international culture to expand what are often constricting local horizons.

The dynamism of these cultural initiatives does not derive from any 'national mystique' or ancient heritage but from the more mundane prerequisite of a secure *production base*, geared towards an indigenous film or television culture. It is precisely the lack of commitment by successive governments to establish the most basic resources in this area that has prevented Irish culture from making a sustained, creative engagement with popular culture. The insistence that culture is simply 'part of what we are', something handed down in tablets of stone from a prehistoric past, has helped the state to perpetuate the delusion that culture does not need 'artificial', i.e. material, support. The myth of a homogeneous, continuous nation is also partly responsible for the state's hostility to *internal* criticism, to any form of cultural activity which explores the social divisions and contradictions concealed by the mists of the Celtic Twilight.

Since 1986, a new administration in Irish television has attempted to redress the imbalance between imported and home-produced programmes, making greater resources available for programmes aimed solely at Irish audiences. In line with this, negotiations were opened with independent film makers to break the monopoly of in-house production in RTE, and bring a greater diversity in approaches to home production. However, no sooner had this discussion begun than the Fianna Fáil government under Charles Haughey abolished the Irish Film Board in 1987, thus undermining the production base of the fledgling Irish film industry. At the same time, developments were taking place in Irish radio broadcasting aimed at deregulating the airwaves, thus paving the way for the proliferation of commercial stations dominated by play-listed, middle-of-the-road pop music. Once again, the state seems willing to leave cultural policy to unbridled market forces, as if the megastore is the custodian of a megalithic past. Writing about the decline of the Gaelic revival after the founding of the state, the historian George Boyce has observed:

> The state was, in this most central aspect of Irish nationalism, modifying the nature of the ideology that inspired its birth. The very establishment of an Irish state created the widespread belief that such an act, by itself, ensured the preservation of the Gaelic League idea. . . . The task was, by implication, completed now that the state was a reality. And the Gaelic League, that most effective pressure group, was the victim of its own political influence: by helping to inspire political freedom it left the state with no really effective critic.[15]

From its inception, the state has tended to blame outside forces – Hollywood, Anglicization, mid-Atlantic culture – for the erosion of Irish culture. Perhaps, like de Valera, it should look into its own heart to see the real source of the problem.

6. COMING OUT OF HIBERNATION?
The Myth of Modernization in Irish Culture

History has stopped, one is in a kind of post-history which is without meaning.

Jean Baudrillard

There is a well-known story which relates how de Valera was captured during the Civil War while making a speech at Ennis. A year later he returned to the same spot, cleared his throat, and began: 'As I was saying before I was interrupted . . .' A week may be a long time in English politics but in Ireland a year is merely a pause for breath in the middle of a sentence.

The historian Oliver MacDonagh has argued that the 'contemporaneity of the past', the tendency to collapse the past into an ever-receding present, is one of the distinguishing features of Irish political culture.[1] 'The memory of the dead' certainly played a key role in the nationalist call to arms, and more than one commentator has pointed out how the opening paragraph of the 1916 Proclamation looks to the past rather than the present for its political mandate: 'Irishmen and Irishwomen: In the name of God and of the dead generations from which she receives her old tradition of nationhood, Ireland, through us, summons her children to her flag and strikes for her freedom.' As nationhood belonged to the cultural as much as to the political domain, what Frank O'Connor referred to as 'the backward look' also fixed literature and the arts within its controlling vision. While T. S. Eliot was trying earnestly to renew contact with a literary heritage in his famous essay 'Tradition and the Individual Talent', Irish writers such as James Joyce and Seán Ó Faoláin were attempting to escape the nightmare of history.

It is generally held that Irish society had to await the end of the de Valera era to awake from its nostalgic slumbers. With revisionist hindsight, 1959 is taken as the *annus mirabilis* of modern Ireland, the year in which God said 'Let Lemass be!' – and there was light, dispelling the mists of traditionalism which had obscured the path to progress and industrialization. The appointment of Sean Lemass as Taoiseach paved the way for the First Programme for Economic Expansion, a major initiative inspired by a senior civil servant, T. K. Whittaker, which broke with the protectionist policies of the previous generation and extended an open welcome to foreign investment and multinational capital. The subsequent exposure of Irish society to the ways of the world on the crest of a post-World War II boom is familiar to students of recent Irish history. In 1961 Ireland applied for membership of the EEC and finally gained admittance in 1973. In 1962, it took its place in the global village of mass communications with the opening of Telefís Éireann. In the same year, the hardened arteries of Irish Catholicism were revitalized by the Second Vatican Council (1962–5) which brought an infusion of new ideas and values into the rigorist moral regime of the post-Famine era. This change was echoed in the educational arena by the publication of the 1965 report *Investment in Education*, which set out to remove the school from the sacristy, and place it in line with the need for greater technological change in Irish society. These developments took place against a wider economic backdrop which saw a shift from agriculture to industry as the mainstay of the Irish economy: in the period 1961 to 1980, employment in the agricultural sector fell from one-third to one-fifth of the workforce, while those working in industry increased from 16 to 30 per cent.

In political circles, it was widely expected that the new sweeping changes would break the old moulds, and bring an end to civil war politics. The historic meeting in 1965 between Sean Lemass and Terence O'Neill, the recently appointed Prime Minister of Northern Ireland, was considered an important breakthrough in this regard, as was the Anglo-Irish free-trade pact agreed at the end of the same year. Many on the left had equal cause to welcome the demise of nationalism. Writing in 1980, Paul Bew, Peter Gibbon and Henry Patterson could state confidently that 'urbanization and industrialization have relegated the national question to the margin of Irish politics',[2] thus clearing the way for a realignment in politics along class lines, or on a left/right division, as in other advanced European countries. Nationalism, it seemed, was obsolete in the new international order. Much was made of the fact that half of the population was not only under the age of twenty-five but, as the Industrial Development Authority (IDA) billboards proudly proclaimed, was not merely young but European as well. The land of eternal youth had turned out to be a land without frontiers.

The screening of the award-winning drama *The Ballroom of Romance* in 1982 provided a focus for the reassuring belief that the fifties were no longer with us. Here was a world that seemed as remote from contemporary Ireland as did the glamour of Brideshead from Thatcherite England in the 1980s. Viewers could confront the harsh realities of poverty, emigration, sexual repression and the enforced domestication of women, secure in the knowledge that 'The factory was coming to town' – a recurrent topic in conversations between characters in the play – which would make all these features of the old social order redundant. Such optimism, however, seems strangely at odds with the subsequent unfolding of events in the mid- and late-1980s. The chronic unemployment, the Granard tragedy, the Kerry babies controversy, the demoralization in the aftermath of the abortion and divorce referenda, the growth of a new underclass, the reappearance of full-scale emigration, the new censorship mentality and, not least, the moving statues, constituted a return of the repressed for those intent on bringing Ireland into the modern world. If a Rip Van Winkle fell asleep in the 1950s and woke up in 1988, he could be forgiven for thinking that nothing had changed in between. Even the Brylcreem look and baggy trousers were back in vogue, thanks to the influence of 'retro-chic' fashion. In the political arena, the resurgence of nationalism following the hunger strikes in 1981 was a stark reminder to those revisionist critics, whether on the right or left, who had written it off as a historical anachronism. The equation of urbanization and industrial development with enlightenment values of progress, secularization and cosmopolitanism proved no longer viable in the austere cultural climate of the 1980s.

For some commentators, the collapse of the social and economic policies of the 1960s and 70s was sufficient to throw into question the whole project of modernization as it applied to a newly industrialized country such as Ireland. Others, however, preferred a different explanation, concentrating on what they perceived to be the native obstacles to progress and development. Primary among these was the persistence of *tradition*, the tenacity of rural values in the face of social change. 'For all our urbanization,' wrote John Healy, 'we are still a people of the land with the old value system of the land.'[3] The argument that the time-warp of tradition was never really dislodged in Irish society, and that rural values were the main factor retarding the forces of progress, was thrown into bold relief in a newspaper headline, following the abortion referendum in 1983: 'TWO NATIONS!' proclaimed the *Irish Independent*, as if henceforth the main division in Irish society was not between the North and the South, or even labour and capital, but that which existed between the country and the city.

In this new version of the battle between the ancients and the moderns, it is not as if the urban/rural divide is so pronounced that the city is left to its own devices as an agency of modernization, while the countryside holds on to the detritus of de Valera's Ireland. Part of the animus against the enduring influence of traditional values is that they are not simply confined to the rural hinterland but have allegedly distorted, if not prevented, the development of a genuine urban identity in Irish cities. An Irish sociologist was once quoted as saying that Dublin was the largest village in the world, with Belfast coming a close second. In a vigorous polemic against sentimentalists who advocate a return to rural values as a panacea for Ireland's social problems, Declan Kiberd has argued that many of the social problems themselves derive from the lingering malaise of rural ideology. The corrosive effects of urban crime, inner city decay, inept planning, and the educational fallout of the dole-queues, is attributed by Kiberd to the fact that decision makers have invariably come from a rural background. Pointing out that it was a Donegal man, Neil Blaney, who planned and promoted the tower blocks of Ballymun, Kiberd goes on to quote a leading architect, John Meagher, on the reasons for the destruction of the social fabric of the city: 'This city is run by road engineers who are all first generation country people and have no idea how cities should be designed.'[4] Contrary to Brendan Behan's wisecrack, the culchies no longer end where the tram tracks begin. The city in Ireland is simply the country at one remove.

The problem with this analysis is that it assumes that the rural ideology which presided over the national revival was a genuine expression of country life, as if the plain people of Ireland had only to look into their hearts to see what de Valera was thinking. It ignores the extent to which idealizations of rural existence, the longing for community and primitive simplicity, are the product of an *urban* sensibility, and are cultural fictions imposed on the lives of those they purport to represent. In the United States, for example, it was not cowboys who sang the praises of the Old West but rather writers and ideologues from the East, intent on establishing a mythology of the last frontier. By the same token, it was urban-based writers, intellectuals and political leaders who created romantic Ireland, and perpetrated the myth that the further west you go, the more you come into contact with the real Ireland.

In a critical discussion on the abiding influence of rural ideology on Irish literature, Fintan O'Toole takes account of the fact that 'the notion of the peasant and of the country which the peasant embodied was not a reflection of Irish reality but an artificial literary creation, largely made in Dublin, for Dubliners'. However, he manages to exonerate the metropolitan centre from ultimate responsibility for this imaginary Ireland by arguing that the appeal of 'the myth of the West' for the Dublin audience derived largely from the fact that they were of rural extraction, and since they were 'often no more than a generation removed from the country-side a visit to the Abbey was a travelogue into its collective past'.[5] The hankering for a return to nature and the simple life, therefore, is a form of nostalgia for a world which was lost, and is simply an attempt to restore to the countryside an ideology which was taken from it in the first place. This view of rural nostalgia accords with Raymond Williams' definition of 'residual ideology', that is, a value system which outlives its own era and survives in a new social order.[6]

The difficulty with this argument lies in its assumption that the rural myths cultivated during the revival conformed in an earlier period to the actual experience of life in the countryside: an assumption which O'Toole appears to reject above and which, in any case, is clearly at odds with the harsh realities of agrarian society in nineteenth-century Ireland. There would in fact have been no need to leave the countryside and go further afield if life was an idyllic affair of cosy homesteads and comely maidens dancing on the village green. As Kerby Miller has pointed out in his study of Irish emigration, the backward look towards a peasant arcadia does not represent a form of *continuity* with the rural past of the emigrant, but a *break* with it. The shock of the city and the new world resulted in a dislocation rather than a continuation of the emigrant's previous rural experience. The precipitating factor in the construction of romantic Ireland, then, was the metropolitan centre, and by extension the social upheavals wrought by the modernization process. As Miller puts it: 'those very innovations, so pregnant with social disruption and demoralization, themselves encouraged greater popular reliance on traditional outlooks and "explanations" which could relieve the tensions consequent on rapid transition'.[7]

It is often forgotten that what are now taken as traditional values – myths of community, the sanctity of the family, devotion to faith and fatherland – are not a residue from an old Gaelic order but are of quite recent vintage, dating in fact from what Emmet Larkin has called 'the devotional revolution' in post-Famine Ireland.

As such they were part of the first phase of modernization rather than an obstacle to it. The 'traditionalism' and religious conservatism associated with the west of Ireland, for example, so evident in the results of the abortion and divorce referenda, is a comparatively late development, given that in the early nineteenth century Connacht was the region with the least, not the highest, Mass attendance, with figures in some places falling as low as 20 per cent. What happened in between to alter this situation? The centralization of church control under Cardinal Cullen in the post-Famine era brought the more dissolute forms of popular belief – 'genuine' traditional practices, if you like – into line with mainstream Roman Catholicism. This devotional revolution was part of an overall modernizing thrust which included the resolution of the land question and the national revival, all of which were a response to the pressures placed on Irish society by its gradual, direct integration into the capitalist world economy. As Miller again expresses it, those 'in the forefront of capitalist development . . . found it most expedient and essential to explain or justify their innovations and consequent dominance in traditional categories which could inhibit resentment and resistance from those who were or felt disadvantaged by the resultant discontinuities'.[8] Tradition, therefore, unlike Topsy, did not just grow and grow: to a considerable extent it was fabricated in the rural hinterland by the metropolitan centre.

In an interview in 1980, the artist Robert Ballagh suggested that those who judge Ireland by its promotional images abroad must risk a certain cultural schizophrenia: 'You have the IDA out in the US selling Ireland as a modern progressive go-ahead capitalist society. Invest in Ireland and make a profit. And you have Bord Fáilte eulogizing roads where you won't see a car from one end of the day to the other: it's almost as if they're advertising a country nobody lives in.'[9] The implication here is that the dynamic image of Ireland as a high-tech paradise projected by the IDA is somehow incompatible with the image of Ireland as an unspoiled romantic paradise promoted by Bord Fáilte. Certainly tourist literature is not known for its emphasis on the economic realities of Ireland – the dole queues, the multinational corporations, the fact that more people are employed in industry than agriculture, the rise of agri-business and the extinction of the small farmer. To this extent, the dream Ireland of Bord Fáilte obscures the technocratic world of the IDA. But the exclusion is not mutual. The most striking feature of IDA promotional material is that it does not simply acknowledge but actively perpetuates the myth of romantic Ireland, incorporating both modernity and tradition within its frame of reference. The shamrock not only acquires a new biochemical identity [Fig. 6.1] but the great antinomies of romantic ideology, nature and industry, landscape and technology, are magically reconciled within the terms of the formula 'IRELAND: The Most Profitable Industrial Location in the EEC . . . is also . . . in one of the most beautiful' [Figs. 6.2, 6.3]. As the IDA brochure from which this cover is taken expresses it:

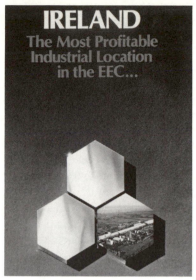

6.1

6.2

6.3

A relative latecomer to industrialization, Ireland has been able to avoid the excesses of the original industrial revolution. The factories and the bustling towns and cities exist in harmony with the Ireland the tourists flock to see, a land of unsurpassed natural beauty.

The location of advanced technological factories in remote, often spectacular, settings was motivated, not by a love of the picturesque as the IDA's own copy would have us believe, but by the more prosaic imperatives of a regional policy which guided the IDA's industrial strategy until the early 1980s. This policy could be described as industrialization without urbanization. Part of the attraction of outlying rural areas for industrial investment was that they lacked the strong traditions of trade union militancy which are characteristic of the urban working class. By the end of the 1970s, only one-quarter of new industrial employment was generated in the east of the country: the west and midlands were the main target areas of the new industrial policy, with the north-west receiving particular attention. To this extent, then, the images of the old and the new co-existing side by side [Fig. 6.4] make sense and it was perhaps this phenomenon which renewed interest in the 'residual ideology' thesis, reinforcing the argument that traditional rural values were displacing urbanization as the underlying rationale of economic development.

Yet, while recognizing the failure of modernization, these accounts of arrested development convey the impression that the pull of the past is due solely to the

6.4

traditional sector, as if the metropolitan centre, by contrast, could only impel à society towards the future. What is not acknowledged is the possibility that it is the modernization process itself, or rather the mutant which passes for modernization in Ireland, which is the source of the social and cultural 'backlash' of the 1980s. In 1983, the IDA undertook a fundamental reappraisal of its industrial strategy, shifting the emphasis from employment towards *wealth* creation. Given the inexorable flow of wealth from the periphery towards the centre, this reformulation of policy in effect consigned the outlying regions to economic stagnation.[10] We might expect then that having been freed from the obligation to accommodate itself to tradition, a more clear-cut emphasis on progress and cosmopolitanism – the cultural dynamic conventionally associated with the centre – would ensue. In fact, the opposite happened. The invocation of the past grew even more pronounced in IDA promotional literature, as the subject matter of the images retreated in time towards the nineteenth century (decked out in medieval or neo-Gothic form) [Fig. 6.5], to the island of saints and scholars [Fig. 6.6] and eventually towards remote antiquity in the form of Newgrange [Fig. 6.7]. The more intangible the connection with the present, the more likely it was to appear in an image. Newgrange surfaced not only in IDA brochures but also in the Bank of Ireland's publicity material. Dolmens proved particularly attractive to the new pre- (or rather post-) history, appearing in advertisements for Guinness, Digital computers, and, again, the Bank of Ireland. The appeal of remote antiquity to today's information society is spelled out in the copy accompanying the Bank of Ireland's celebration of the dolmen in its calendar for 1987:

> Our modern world owes much to our remote ancestors, unknown men and women who were no less intelligent and inventive than the scientists and technologists of our times. We thought that, in plotting your course through 1987, you might draw encouragement and inspiration from these twelve illustrations of prehistoric planning.

This is not a reassertion of vestigial ideology, as if 'prehistoric planning' was part of an ancient cultural legacy which survived into the contemporary world. It is instead an invented tradition, a recourse to the past which exceeds even the most imaginative flights of nationalist history in its desire to confer an aura of permanence on the new information order. The facility with which distant aeons are collapsed into the present has more in common with the ersatz history of American wax museums than with the lingering traces of rural values.[11] Traditionalism looks to history for continuity: neo-traditionalism abolishes not only continuity but history itself.

It is no coincidence that neo-traditionalism, a fabricated relationship to the past, appears in conjunction with the new information technologies. Part of the driving force of the Industrial Revolution in its western capitalist phase was that it acted as an engine of the Enlightenment, carrying liberal ideals of reason,

IN A 16TH CENTURY IRISH UNIVERSITY:
21ST CENTURY KNOWLEDGE.

6.5

progress and universal values in its train. This is the blueprint which dominated theories of modernization as late as the 1960s, and it advocated full integration into the 'free world' economy as a means of breaking down the 'Chinese walls' of obscurantism which impeded development in traditional societies. With the emergence of transnational corporations and a new international division of labour in the aftermath of the World War II, it became clear that modernization, in this sense, had less to do with development than with *under*development, i.e. with systematically increasing the dependency of peripheral countries on the economic power of the metropolitan centre. When rapid industrialization did take place, moreover, as in the Far East and particularly Japan, it did not follow the western route but appeared to negotiate its own distinctive path to development. A heavy emphasis on micro-electronics, communications and computer industries is partly responsible for the sudden elevation of these economic regions to the ranks of advanced capitalist economies. What is more interesting for our present purposes is that industrial policies based on the new information technologies need no longer replace tradition, but may actively refashion and intensify its grip on society. Instead of retarding economic growth, Chinese walls, or their national equivalents, may often accelerate it.

The Japanese case is particularly instructive, given the tendency of recent initiatives at a policy level in Ireland to circumvent the Anglo-American axis and look to Japan as a model for economic development.[12] Many commentators have drawn attention to the manner in which pre-industrial values of familialism, group loyalty, deference to authority and, indeed, weak trade union organization, have presided

THE CASTLES, AND THE KINGS

We Irish may take a romantic view of the past, but our feet are set firmly in today.

We are a pragmatic people. We recognise that knowledge and specialist skills are crucial to success, and we have invested heavily in them. Which is why more than 850 international companies have invested heavily in us, including the leading U.S. hi-tech and international services companies.

These companies work with people who are better educated and more technically literate than any other workforce in Europe. In a country more sympathetic to business. More committed to its interests.

The Irish. We appreciate the past. We don't live in it.

IDA Ireland ♣
INDUSTRIAL DEVELOPMENT AUTHORITY

The Irish government's industrial development agency has offices in Dublin (Head Office) Tel. (01) 686633, New York (212) 972 1000, London (01) 689 5941. Offices also in 18 other cities worldwide.

REPUBLIC OF IRELAND

"WE'RE THE YOUNG EUROPEANS."

6.6

over the Japanese economic miracle, instead of the individualism and liberal humanism associated with modernization in the west. It is as if, in an eastern setting, Adam Smith's invisible hand had brought about a mysterious fusion of tradition and modernity rather than a convergence between private and public interests. While nativist apologists within Japan have been eager to proclaim this as a vindication of the Japanese way of life, and its veneration of the past, a more accurate appraisal would see it not as a conservation but as a *restoration* of aspects of tradition that lend themselves to social control from a distinctively contemporary standpoint. As Johann Arnason has written of the 'Janus-faced' nature of Japanese modernization: 'it combined an exceptionally thorough effort to assimilate the achievements of a more advanced civilization . . . with the reappropriation and revalorization of a tradition that had previously been marginalized or at least divorced from the real centres of power for a long time'.[13] There is no genuine recrudescence of traditional values: rather 'traditions' are manipulated and selected from the past in order to establish new hierarchies in the present. The clock may be turned back at a cultural or even social level, but industrialization proceeds apace. Hence the phenomenon of 'regressive modernization', a form of advanced industrial development which, unlike the initial Industrial Revolution, has no commitment to social, political or cultural modernization. It is from this perspective that we should view the IDA's slogan: 'Missing the Industrial Revolution was the best thing that ever happened to the Irish.'

This is saying, in effect, that a 'post-industrial' revolution in an electronic age need no longer be encumbered by a vision of social progress. Applied to

6.7

Ireland in the 1980s, this means that the 'conservative backlash', or the reversion to traditional values of family, faith and fatherhood, may not be an aberration but may even be a logical extension of the modernization policies pursued by successive governments and development agencies. On 20 March 1979, almost one million PAYE workers took to the streets of Dublin in a protest march against the punitive tax regime in the Republic. This was seen by many contemporary observers as the coming of age of the Irish working class, the culmination of the modernization process. Within a few months, a million people had again gathered in Dublin, but this time it was in the Phoenix Park to greet Pope John Paul II. This was taken by the same commentators as a throwback to a previous era, but in fact it was this gathering, rather than the PAYE march, which was a portent of things to come. The Phoenix Park was an appropriate setting for confessional Ireland to emerge from the ashes.

The idea that modernization is helping Ireland to 'catch up' with its advanced industrial neighbours is no longer tenable. If there is any convergence between European nations, it involves a form of liberalization designed to create new inequalities, endemic unemployment and an enlightenment without hope for the casualties of this upwardly mobile form of modernity. As Edward Said has pointed out, those who equate fundamentalism and revivalism with pre-modern societies such as Iran often forget that the heartlands of fundamentalism are in the West, in the 'Victorian values' of Thatcherite Britain or in Ronald Reagan's call for a 'return to the range' in the United States.[14] The bogey of traditionalism and rural

MISSING THE INDUSTRIAL REVOLUTION WAS
THE BEST THING THAT EVER HAPPENED TO THE IRISH.

You won't find many smoke-stacks, crumbling kilns or
abandoned cotton-mills in Ireland—or the negative
industrial attitudes that went with them.

Our industrial revolution coincided with the electronic age.
Today, Ireland is the European base for leading companies
in hi-tech and international services industries—
thanks to the innovative skills and progressive
attitudes of its people.

Ireland. Home of the Irish. The young Europeans.

IDA Ireland ♣
INDUSTRIAL DEVELOPMENT AUTHORITY

The Irish government's industrial development agency has offices in DUBLIN (Head Office),
Tel: (71) 686633, LONDON (01) 629 5941, TOKYO (03) 582 7921, HONG KONG (5) 267304,
SYDNEY (02) 633 5999. Offices also in Cologne, Stuttgart, Munich, Paris, Amsterdam,
Stockholm, Copenhagen, Milan, New York, Chicago, Houston, Los Angeles, Cleveland,
Menlo Park, Calif., Boston, Atlanta.

REPUBLIC OF
IRELAND

"WE'RE THE
YOUNG EUROPEANS."

6.8

values can no longer be used in Ireland as a scapegoat for a regressive politics that
emanates from the metropolitan centre. As Declan O'Connell has acutely
observed: 'The romantic idealist ideology that dominated Irish political debate for
so long and [is] traced to western small farmers' "remote economic situation" and
"shelter from worldly pressures" might also be understood more fully as a
consequence of capitalist underdevelopment.'[15] The IDA image of Ireland as the
silicon valley of Europe may not be so far removed after all from the valley of the
squinting windows.

7.1 James Gralton (courtesy Pat Feeley)

7. LABOUR AND LOCAL HISTORY:
The Case of Jim Gralton, 1886–1945

The Gralton case is the very essence of the battle now raging between the worker and farmer masses and the capitalists of whom the Fianna Fáil government is the representative . . .

Workers' Voice (1933)

Socialism does not easily lend itself to local history. Universal schemes of human emancipation are concerned with social change on a grand scale, and are bound to feel constrained by the narrow horizons of local experience. As Raymond Williams put it: 'The key argument in Marxism was always whether the proletariat would be a universal class – whether the bonds it forged from a common exploitation would be perceived as primary, and eventually supercede the more local bonds of region or nation or religion.'[1]

This version of Marxism has proved very attractive to those on the left in Ireland who see nationalism as the cause of all current discontents, and look to internationalism (not necessarily international socialism) as the way forward in politics. It is considered progressive to extend an uncritical welcome to multinational investment as a positive step in helping people to think in global terms, and socialists have been among the most vocal supporters of calls to become post-national 'Young Europeans'. 'Modernization' is the key concept here and the integration of the economy into that of the advanced industrial nations, and the absorption of Irish culture into a more cosmopolitan, universal culture, are both deemed necessary to liberate Irish society from the shibboleths of the past.

Yet it is far from clear that this respectable form of progress has much to offer Marxists in less-developed or peripheral countries. It was Gramsci, grappling with the problem of accommodating Marxism to traditional agrarian societies, who pointed out that this kind of universality is a caricature of socialism 'and has more to do with bourgeois cosmopolitanism than with proletarian internationalism'. Like Esperanto, the dream of a single universal language, it 'is nothing but a vain idea, an illusion of cosmopolitan, humanitarian democratic mentalities which have not yet been made fertile and been shaken by *historical critical* thinking'.[2] The equation of universality with standardization and uniformity is, in fact, a capitalist idea, and has more in common with the 'Big Mac' philosophy of McDonalds than with Marx.[3]

It is partly in recognition of this that some socialists have become less enamoured with a vision of the socialist future that seems indistinguishable from the global anonymity of late capitalism. Two areas in particular have come in for re-appraisal, that of the relationship *to the past*, and the role of cultural or *regional* difference in international socialism. The old platitudes that history and cultural diversity are nightmares from which socialists are trying to awake seem increas-ingly hollow in a world where capitalism is liquidating any genuine sense of the specific, whether it be in terms of time or place.[4] It is the Anglo-American culture industry, the ideological arm of multinational corporations, which seeks to annihilate history, turning the past itself into a commodity to be consumed in wax museums, cultural Disneylands or other neo-traditional extensions of an imaginary Brideshead. By the same token, the relentless centralization of power, whether it be at a state or corporate level, is part of a process which seeks to exert control over the most peripheral regions of the world economy, and even the most elusive aspects of everyday life.

Faced with this spectre of a totalizing global order, some socialists are understandably drawn towards 'the local', towards a small-scale scheme of things which restores the lived texture of human relations. This is not without its problems, however, for the difficulty here is how to avoid relapsing into a mys-tification of local experience, construing it as a repository of the kind of communal 'face to face' society which, in the last resort, invalidates all forms of social division or class conflict. This is precisely part of the attraction of local history for a new wave of social historians represented by the 'Leicester School' of English local history. By setting us 'face to face with flesh and blood', one of its key exponents, H. P. R. Finberg, tells us, 'local history puts a curb on those abstract hatreds which can so easily turn the heart to stone'.[5] Yet far from curbing abstract hatreds (shorthand, we may presume, for nationalism), this idealist view of local history is, in fact, one of the foundation stones of nationalist sentiment. From the point of view of cultural nationalism, at least in its German romantic variant, the nation is simply the parish writ large, transferring onto a wider political plane the alleged cohesion and consensus of the smaller social unit. As Raymond Williams again expresses it: 'the real and powerful feelings of a native place and a native formation have been pressed and incorporated into an essentially political and administrative organization, which has grown from quite different roots'.[6]

This conscription of the local into an avowed nationalist project is so pervasive as to suggest that the attribution of harmony and simplicity to small rural com-munities is partly a retrospective invention of idealist forms of nationalism, a construction imposed on the periphery as a foundation myth for the centre. In a recent valuable reassessment of the role of local studies in historical research, Raymond Gillespie and Gerard Moran point out that the growth of popular loyalty to the parish or county in Ireland is often a nineteenth-century develop-ment, owing more to the voting register, the reorganization of the Catholic Church, the Gaelic Athletic Association and even provincial newspapers, than to primordial ancestral ties.[7] It is in this nation-building context that the myth of an organic, homogeneous community arose, an imaginary source for the agrarian values that were later to be enshrined in official nationalist ideology. When writers and intellectuals took to the countryside then, to remote parishes or isolated communities on the western seaboard, it was to recreate them in the image of an imaginary Ireland, a microcosm of the indestructible nation. Thus, for example, the enthusiasm of Aodh de Blacam, one of the most influential nationalist propagandists in the early decades of the century, on arriving in the Donegal Gaeltacht around 1920:

> It is, indeed, a wonderful experience. It is like plunging back through the centuries and awaking in the Ireland of Hugh O'Neill – heroic, Gaelic, unsubdued Ireland. The musical, racy Irish speech on every side of you brings to your mind a thrilling sense of the reality of Irish nationality, such as the dweller in the cities amid English speech and English papers, never feels.[8]

The irony in such sentimental accounts of local allegiance to the nation is that the nation-state was often the farthest thing from the minds of those supposedly responsible for its preservation. Indeed, an unintentional consequence of the search for cultural purity was precisely to cut off the supposed custodians of the national heritage from the rest, the vast majority, of the Irish people. In a shrewd comment on the enlisting of the Blasket Islands in the cause of cultural nationalism in the 1930s, D. A. Binchy remarked:

> I have often wondered about the nature of the difference, at once so subtle and so infinite, between the people of the Gaoltacht [sic] and the bulk of their compatriots whose mother tongue is English . . . in reality they belong to quite a different world. Tralee, Cork and Dublin are almost as 'foreign' to the Blasket Islander as London or Glasgow. Indeed, by a curious irony of circumstance, they are much more remote from him than Springfield, Mass., where so many of his kith and kin are congregated. In a sense he is a stranger in his own land, singularly indifferent to the questions which agitate his English-speaking countrymen. He knows little of the wrangles of our politicians (each group of whom vies with exalting him to the skies), almost as little as he knows of that political nationalism which owes its introduction to the descendants of English colonists and its progress to the spread of the English tongue.[9]

By a curious inversion of logic, the parish, idealized by both political and religious ideologues, is closer to the United States, to an international frame, than to the capital city, or even the hinterland, of the nation which it purportedly represents. The peremptory deportation of the socialist Jim Gralton from the small townland of Effernagh in County Leitrim to New York, around the time D. A. Binchy was writing, testifies to this strange convergence between the local and the universal. Characteristically, he did not go through Dublin but on his arrest was shipped directly via Cobh, without being given the time even to pack a suitcase.

Gralton's arrival in New York after his deportation in August 1933 left one lasting image with those who were there to greet him: that of a lonely bespectacled man walking down the gangplank, carrying nothing but an overcoat draped over his arm. It was as if he left home intending to walk to the nearest village but ended up in New York. It was not Gralton's first time to undergo the alienation of exile, but on this occasion it was different. Historians have debated whether 'push or pull' factors, economic circumstances or the bright lights of the city, were predominant in Irish emigration, but in Gralton's case there is no mistaking the push factor. He enjoys the unique, if invidious, distinction of being the only emigrant who was forced to leave Ireland at the direct behest of the Irish government.

The historical experience of emigration overshadowed Gralton's upbringing in Leitrim. While agriculture underwent an intensive process of 'modernization' in the post-Famine period, it did not hold out much promise for the rural poor. In 1841, the population of Leitrim was 155,297. By 1911, four years after Gralton first emigrated to the United States, it was 63,582. In the intervening sixty years, no less than 82,629 persons had emigrated from the county. The role of emigration as a safety valve for economic unrest, dissipating the energies and frustrations of the rural poor, can hardly be overestimated. The blocking-off of emigration outlets during World War I was one of the major factors in the 'conacre war' and land agitation which galvanized the countryside into an unprecedented level of class consciousness.[10] In 1916 there were only 5,000 members in the Irish Transport and General Workers' Union (ITGWU): by 1919, there were over 30,000 agricultural labourers alone, the largest single category in the union.

The North Roscommon/South Leitrim area was a flashpoint of social unrest, partly due to the prominent role of the radical republican priest, Father Michael

7.2   Gralton after arrival in New York

O'Flanagan, in organizing social and political agitation in the area. In February 1917, O'Flanagan masterminded the first republican election victory after the Easter Rising in North Roscommon, often mistakenly referred to subsequently as the 'Sinn Féin by-election'. The myth of continuity in the campaign waged by Sinn Féin before and after the Easter Rising was largely the creation of Arthur Griffith's newspaper, *Nationality*, and came in for harsh criticism from O'Flanagan:

> Anyone who depends upon *Nationality* for the history of the next few months [early 1917] will know next to nothing of how a new republican organization came into existence. He will not know the history of the absorption of the old Sinn Féin, of the Liberty Clubs and of the Nation League, or how the released prisoners came to be represented on the provisional committee. He will be left under the impression that the old Sinn Féin suddenly grew into a great national organization.[11]

The illusion of continuity in what was still a fragmented national movement belies the specific material issues around which republicanism mobilized at a local level. Primary among those was the question of land agitation and re-distribution. Organized land-seizures took place in Crossna, County Roscommon, O'Flanagan's own parish, and in the nearby coal mining district of Arigna where 100 acres of the best land in the area owned by Lord Kingston were seized from a local big farmer by 300 people under the leadership of the local Volunteers.[12] In August 1918, Arigna miners joined the ITGWU, and in the course of a strike in the mines, John Lynch, the ITGWU organizer in the area, was sentenced to three months' hard labour as a self-styled 'soldier of the Irish Republic'. In May 1921 the 'Arigna Soviet' took place, though the term 'soviet' does not appear to have been used by the ITGWU members who commandeered two pits owned by the Arigna Mining Company. Notwithstanding the limited objectives of the miners themselves, resisting a wage decrease and the closure of mines, Thomas Foran, ITGWU President, considered the action of the miners, and of the workers who took over Knocklong Creamery, County Limerick, in 1920, to be 'the most inspiring business before the Congress' in 1921. Thomas Johnson added his weight to these sentiments, stating that the action of the workers in Knocklong and Arigna 'is the most important question that could be raised in the Labour movement or in Social Economy . . . It is a challenge – and let us make no mistake about it – to the rights of property'.[13]

This was the social ferment into which Jim Gralton stepped when he returned from New York to Leitrim for the first time in June 1921. He threw himself into the local Direct Action Committee which organized land seizures and was so effective in re-allocating land that he was accorded the dubious honour of having one of his settlements upheld in a Free State court.[14] Pat Feeley, in the course of his discussion of this land agitation, draws attention to the fact that some of those involved 'were "respectable" Catholic farmers intent on increasing their holdings at the expense of their Protestant neighbours . . . because of their traditional unionism and loyalty to the British connection'.[15] This is undoubtedly true in some cases, but it is less than the full story: the Arigna land seizures, for instance, were directed *against* a big Catholic farmer, who had taken the land from Lord Kingston, and who identified with the more conservative elements in the Nationalist Party. This has an important bearing on the Gralton story for it helps to explain how, after an initial semblance of unity, Gralton gradually found himself on a collision course with the most powerful interests in rural society. Gralton's activities, both in the 1920s and on his return in 1932–3, had laid bare the nerve centres of power in the local community, and for this he came up against an array of opposition, ranging from the Free State Army to the IRA, from local landlords to parish priests and cautious nationalist politicians, all of whom attempted to turn him into an exile even in his own locality. That they did not succeed in this, and had to resort to physically deporting him from the country, points to the existence of another, almost clandestine, hidden Ireland that eludes Daniel Corkery's nets of land, nationality and religion.

The unremitting hostility which Gralton met from the Catholic Church arose not just from his personal views or even his uncompromising attitude towards land agitation, but rather from the fact that through the establishment of a dance-hall, the Pearse-Connolly hall built at Gowel in 1922, he posed an *institutional* challenge to the church's determination to secure its position as the sole focal point for communal organization in the locality. In retrospect, it is difficult to grasp the intensity of the opposition to dance-halls mounted by moral crusaders as diverse as the *Irish Times* and the Catholic hierarchy and more work needs to be done to sketch in the volatile cultural climate of the period to account for such moral panics. The dance-hall was singled out on several occasions by the hierarchy as the most dangerous source of corruption in the community. In 1925, the Bishops issued a major statement on the evils of dancing, with express instructions that it be read quarterly in the churches of the country. Dance-halls were blamed for the increase in alcoholism, unmarried mothers, and the wave of infanticide which was so widespread as to constitute 'a national industry', in the words of one District Justice.[16] Significantly, it was small rural dance-halls in isolated areas which came in for the most opprobrium, and the tone of the animosity Gralton had to face is well captured in a Lenten Pastoral by Bishop Morrisroe in the nearby diocese of Achonry in 1929, which could almost have been written with Gralton in mind:

> There is one agency, which Satan has set up here and there in recent years, that does incalculably more harm than all the others we have mentioned. It deserves to be called after his name, for he seems to preside at some of the dark rites enacted there. We have in mind the rural dance-hall, owned by a private individual . . . conducted with no sort of responsible supervision, a cause of ruin to many innocent girls . . . One need not have a lively imagination to realize the possibilities arising from promiscuous mingling of the sexes under conditions so favourable for the machinations of wily corrupters from far and near, who swoop down on their innocent prey with the greedy rapacity of Harpies.[17]

It was this kind of moral foreboding which lay behind the whispering campaign that Gralton was running a den of prostitution in his hall, and rumours that people dressed up as nuns frequented his dances and were seen driving around the countryside with Gralton and a local Protestant in a taxi. (The irony here is that the latter rumours were probably true since it is likely that they referred to Gralton's sister who actually was a nun and who was home from America in 1932!)[18]

For the most part the clerical campaign against dance-halls had no direct political connotations, but, unfortunately for Gralton, this was not the case in County Leitrim. Under the stewardship of a redoubtable local priest, Father Peter Conefrey, Leitrim in the 1930s became the centre of operations for a concerted offensive against dance-halls and jazz, on the express grounds that as cosmopolitan influences, they were a smokescreen for international communism. As Fr. Conefrey himself put it, writing in the *Catholic Pictorial* in 1926:

> Jazz is an African word meaning the activity in public of something of which St. Paul said 'Let it not be so much as named among you'. The dance and music with its abominable rhythm was borrowed from Central Africa by a gang of wealthy Bolshevists in the USA to strike at Church civilization throughout the world.[19]

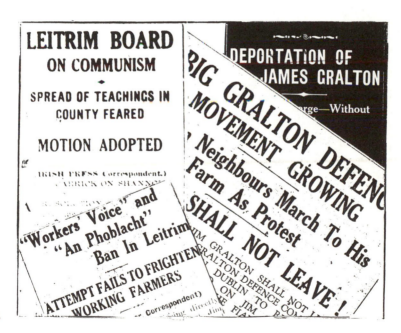

7.3

At the time the deportation order was served on Gralton, Conefrey was transferred to Cloone, less than ten miles away. There he initiated a campaign
against 'the devil's music' that was to culminate in a mass demonstration
against jazz in Mohill, January 1934, which over 3,000 people attended. The
rally was of nationwide interest, attracting messages of support from Cardinal
McRory, President de Valera and the local Bishop McNamee.

The success of Conefrey's campaign suggests that Gralton's hall would have
encountered substantial opposition on cultural and moral grounds even if he were
not a communist. It was his political affiliations, however, which were to prove his
ultimate downfall, particularly when he cut across not just the local religious and
cultural consensus but when he threatened the highly unstable balance of forces in
local politics. The situation during the Civil War speaks for itself, and by 1921 the
material issues around which republicans had organized – trade union militancy,
land-seizures, the outbreak of soviets – were something of an embarrassment to the
national leadership. In a pamphlet *Constructive Work of Dáil Éireann*, Austin Stack,
then Minister for Home Affairs, warned of the possibility that agrarian agitation
might subvert patriotic opinion, and praised the activities of the republican courts
for dampening revolutionary ardour. In the early thirties during Gralton's second
visit home (he returned to Effernagh in March 1932) it might have been expected,
as Feeley suggests,[20] that some kind of 'normalcy' would be restored in Leitrim but,
if anything, the reverse was the case.

On Christmas Day 1931, a well-known local republican, James Vaugh, died
after a short period of detention in the police barracks at Ballinamore. The
inquest on Vaugh opened in Drumshanbo in January 1932 and was attended by
such prominent republican figures as Maud Gonne MacBride and Dorothy
Macardle.[21] One of the detectives accused of ill-treating Vaugh in custody was
Patrick McGeehan, but the accusations of brutality were countered by evidence
from, among others, Patrick Reynolds, an ex-Cumann na nGaedheal TD, who
claimed that he overheard Vaugh thanking the policemen when he was being
discharged. On 14 February, while the inquest was still sitting, both Reynolds
and McGeehan were shot dead by a police pensioner in a dispute over canvassing
in the General Election which had just taken place. The shooting would appear
to have had no direct connection with the Vaugh case, but it added considerably
to what was already a highly charged political atmosphere in South Leitrim.[22]

It was against this turbulent backdrop that Gralton embarked once more on
the dangerous undertaking of pushing local radicalism to its limits. The manner
in which the various militant undercurrents circulating in the area since the War
of Independence intersect in the Gralton affair can be seen from a page in the
Workers' Voice, 27 August 1932. One article carries a report from Packie Gralton,
Jim Gralton's young nephew, on the plight of rural labourers, linking the political
crisis in South Leitrim with the death 'of the latest victim of British imperialism,
Seamus Vaugh of the IRA'. The seizure of Lord Kingston's land in Arigna in 1918
is echoed in an adjoining report of a successful attempt by Gralton to
reinstate an evicted tenant at the gate lodge of the Earl's estate at Kilronan,

North Roscommon. Jim Gralton had in fact joined forces with the local IRA in this action. Arigna itself is the subject of a third story, which carries a trenchant statement from the Arigna Fianna Fáil Cumann proclaiming: 'We call upon the [Fianna Fáil] government to secure fair wages and better conditions of employment in all classes of industry, as we consider the workers have been exploited too long for private gain'. This statement was made in the context of another major strike in the Arigna coal mines in which miners were locked out for refusing to take a drastic cut in their wages.

The fact that Fianna Fáil branches in the area could issue such radical pronouncements partly helps to explain why Gralton, as a communist, could join Fianna Fáil for a brief period in 1932, but it also throws into relief the reasons why a Fianna Fáil government deported him less than a year later. If developments in local power structures, land ownership, nationalism, the Catholic Church, and cultural politics, militated strongly against Gralton's small branch of the Revolutionary Workers' Group gaining popular support, so also did the outcome of events at a national level. The years 1932–4 proved to be a turning point in republican politics. With its accession to government in 1932, Fianna Fáil came in from the cold, both where the Constitution and the Catholic Church were concerned. In June 1932, de Valera officiated at the Eucharistic Congress which was attended by over one million Catholics, thus healing the rift between the republican movement and the Catholic Church which had opened up in the War of Independence. Though de Valera had actually pledged his allegiance on one occasion to the social policies of James Connolly[23] and had even hinted that he would take his political methods once more outside the existing system,[24] the accession to power brought with it an urgent realization of the need to shake off Fianna Fáil's 'slightly constitutional' tag. In the transition to government, Fianna Fáil's political orientation had shifted from the *nation* to the *state*, from a politics based, as we have seen, on a romantic ideal of the small community to a more bureaucratic, centralized system of power. The drift towards centralization in Fianna Fáil's policies is evident in Seán T. O'Kelly's dismissal of those delegates who persisted in calling for a break-up of big ranches, and a dissolution of the Special Branch in the police force, at the Fianna Fáil Ard Fheis in 1932. Referring to the 'squeaks' emanating from the rank and file on the floor, O'Kelly commented: 'You are too provincial, narrow and small-minded to see the big thing that has grown upon you. National Ireland has reawakened and restored the national spirit . . .'[25] The mask temporarily slipped on this occasion but, for the most part, the rhetoric of 'the nation', based on ideals of an organic, small community, continued to be pressed into service to conceal the gap between the periphery and the centre, the parish and the state, in republican politics. The idealization of an agrarian order of smallholders increased in proportion as its practical implementation receded from view, receiving its best-known formulation in de Valera's 'cosy homesteads' broadcast on St. Patrick's Day 1943.

It was this comforting image of a cohesive small community that Gralton, above all, shattered. As such he struck at the very foundations of the ideology which was required to establish a new respectable national consensus under Fianna Fáil. The implications of this were apparent not only to constitutional republicans but also to the militarist wing of the republican movement, the IRA. Though James Hogan could write at the time in his tendentious tract *Could Ireland Become Communist?* that 'Like litmus paper in a chemical experiment the IRA under the acid test of the Gralton case is seen to turn red', in fact the Gralton affair precipitated a parting of ways between the traditionalist leadership of the IRA, and radical activists within the movement.[26] It was the IRA in South Leitrim who, without noticing the irony, fired shots into the Pearse-Connolly Hall and was probably responsible for burning the hall to the ground in December 1932. The taint of communism also brought out a conservative reflex at a national level. One of the most committed and uncompromising republicans, Máire MacSwiney, was to the fore in undermining support for Gralton, using the columns of the *Irish Independent* to attack soviet infiltration of the IRA. The loss of nerve in the leadership of the republican movement is best seen in the failure to send official representatives to a public meeting organized by the Gralton Defence Committee at the Rotunda in Dublin.[27] The fact that prominent writers and intellectuals such as Frank O'Connor, Francis Stuart, F. R. Higgins, Peadar O'Donnell, Denis Johnston and Lyle Donaghy pledged their support for Gralton highlighted the conservative about-turn by the IRA Army Council. The *Workers' Voice*, in a scathing article on the IRA's stand on the issue, argued that the Gralton affair was a test case for the radical credentials of both Fianna Fáil and the IRA, and the article is worth quoting at some length:

> It [i.e. the Gralton affair] is the most damning exposure of the anti-working class character of the Fianna Fáil government, and its playing with republican phrases. But the Right Wing of the republican leadership has no enthusiasm for the fight on Gralton. The first week of the struggle it was silent. Perhaps, there is here the justification that the full facts had to be verified on the spot. But last week's article approached the question in literal fear and trembling. Gralton is introduced to republican readers as a good harmless boy whom any respectable country lady or gentleman need have no fear of supporting. 'It is now alleged by a Fianna Fáil TD that Gralton taught subversive doctrines. We have made careful enquiries. There is no evidence that the hall was used to preach such doctrines. Gralton has been condemned without being given a hearing.' So runs *An Phoblacht's* story . . . Such an attitude to the question simply strips the Gralton fight of all political meaning, representing Gralton as a political nonentity and the government as a stupid fool making trouble for themselves and everybody else over nothing. But the Gralton case is the very essence of the battle now raging between the worker and farmer masses and the capitalists of whom the Fianna Fáil government is the representative.[28]

Hogan's remark that the IRA would turn red in a litmus test of the Gralton affair can be explained simply: litmus paper does not register green.

Though essentially a local conflict, the Gralton episode raises many wider questions for socialist strategy. One of the central, yet inexplicably neglected, problems facing Marxism as a social philosophy is to what extent its universal approach to economic and political questions needs to take stock of the particularities of a regional or a national culture. Though Lenin was an Enlightenment figure to the point of basing all criteria of social progress on the standards of West European civilization, he nevertheless introduced a crucial caveat for those who would take Marxism as a rigid, inflexible system, to be applied to a specific culture regardless of its distinctive historical circumstances:

> We do not regard Marx's theory as something completed and inviolable; on the contrary, we are convinced that it has only laid the foundation stone of the science which socialists *must* develop in all directions if they are to keep pace with life. We think that an *independent* elaboration of Marx's theory is especially essential for Russian socialists; for this theory provides only general *guiding* principles, which, *in particular*, are applied to England differently than in France, in France differently than in Germany, and in Germany differently than in Russia.[29]

Lenin's remarks raise the possibility that the true romantics in Marxist theory are those who look forward to a universal or global civilization, bereft of all cultural differences, in the new socialist order. For what is this kind of monochrome vision, with its emphasis on harmony and cultural uniformity, but the parish writ large, projected onto a *world* plane rather than the more familiar parameters of the nation-state? At its most insidious, as in the Second International, this form of 'post-nationalism' provided a pretext for socialists in the revisionist camp to support imperialist policies in the interests of extending 'world civilization' or breaking down allegedly anachronistic or primitive cultures. As Eduard Bernstein put it, 'to support savages and barbarians who resist the penetration of capitalistic civilization would be romantic', sentiments shared by the Fabian imperialist Sidney Webb, who poured scorn on 'that Fenian abstraction, the "principle of nationality"', and added 'What in the name of common sense have we to do with obsolete hypocrisies about "peoples rightly struggling to be free".'[30]

The mentality which seeks to abolish differences abroad is not likely to recognize them at home either. Hence the contemporary phenomenon of Tory 'little Englander' nationalism whose shrillness increases in proportion as it tramples on those at the receiving end of the cleavages – regional, ethnic, even national – opened up by monetarist economic policies. This xenophobia is perfectly consistent with total acquiescence in the face of American foreign policy (it may even be a consolation for it). By the same token, it was precisely those forms of nationalism which most insisted on cultural exclusivity and racial purity in Ireland which opened the door for new forms of post-colonial domination: the Arthur Griffith who shouted down Synge's *Playboy* in 1907, and who stated that no excuse is 'needed for an Irish nationalist declining to hold the negro his peer', is also the Arthur Griffith who pushed through the Treaty in 1922. Nationalism of this kind offered no resistance to imperialism: it was, in fact, an *extension* of it by other means. When Griffith wrote that 'the right of the Irish to political independence never was, is not, and never can be dependent upon the admission of equal right in all other peoples',[31] he was in effect echoing Sidney Webb's attack on 'that Fenian abstraction, the *principle* of nationality'.

What is striking about Griffith's formulation is its close affinities to the most parochial varieties of localism, and indeed it is no coincidence that it models itself on the 'organic' cohesion of the small community. The Gralton affair was a pre-emptive strike against this rhetoric of an imaginary community. By disrupting the fragile balance of forces between the various conflicting interests in his own locality, Gralton touched a raw nerve in the connective tissue of both Catholic and nationalist ideology. But this is not to say that his legacy was entirely destructive, for underneath the official community was an alternative form of solidarity, a clandestine network which eluded the forces of both church and state and supported Gralton on the run for more than five months. This counter community owed nothing to the simplicity of the folk ideal but was the result of concerted action, an 'artificial' construct held together (as befitted its support for Gralton) by deep-seated principles of justice and freedom, drawing on long-standing traditions of popular agrarian protest.[32] Griffith's imagined community was interested in nothing outside itself: hence its aversion to ideals that embraced other nationalities. A socialist future which looks to a universal civilization, or cultural uniformity, as a precondition of human emancipation is simply an amplified version of Griffith's nationalism. It is precisely an awareness of 'otherness', an ability to identify with others who do not share one's own cultural or social backgrounds, which constitutes the basis of a genuine internationalism – and, in a reciprocal movement, it is the quality of interaction with other cultures which gives each community its own distinctiveness. Local and regional identity, and the cultural differences that go with it, are therefore ineradicable features of genuine international socialism. At one point during the anti-deportation campaign, the Gralton Defence Committee drew the support of Mr. I. K. Yajnik of the Indian Independence League, who compared the severity of Gralton's treatment to a crackdown on trade unionists in India which led to the jailing of the remarkable Irish feminist, Margaret Cousins.[33] There is a fitting irony in the fact that Margaret Cousins, jailed in India, was brought up in Boyle, Co. Roscommon, barely ten miles from Gralton's own locality. It is this ability to fuse the local and the international, to merge events in the Irish countryside with struggles in India six thousand miles away, which is perhaps Gralton's most enduring legacy.

8. THE POLITICS OF SILENCE:
Anne Devlin, Women and Irish Cinema

> Silence can be a play
> rigorously executed . . .
>
> It is a presence
> it has a history, a form.
>
> Do not confuse it
> with any kind of absence.

Adrienne Rich, *Cartographies of Silence*

At a key point in James Joyce's early novel *Stephen Hero*, the young Stephen expresses his disenchantment with a nationalist movement which had lost its political bearings, pursuing an ideal which in his eyes was little more than a charade, 'a liberty of costume and vocabulary'. Attention to regalia and the dramatic gesture, and command of rhetoric, had become the hallmarks of an insurrectionary movement emptied of any material content. When, in *A Portrait of the Artist*, Joyce rebels against this concern with the plumage of patriotism, it is significant that he looks to *silence* – along with exile and cunning – as part of his strategic armoury. For Joyce, it need hardly be added, silence was not an absence of meaning, a space outside language, but an act of defiance, a stress point *within* a linguistic system.[1] Liberation, for Joyce, had to come from within in order to give effect to an external intervention, no matter how well-meaning.[1]

It is a version of this enigmatic silence which presides over Pat Murphy's film, *Anne Devlin* (1984). Anne Devlin is celebrated in popular Irish history as the woman who refused to speak, the faithful servant of Robert Emmet who, despite protracted torture and maltreatment at the hands of her British captors, would not betray her master or the nationalist cause to which he was devoted. It is not surprising that this example of courage and self-sacrifice should find its way into folk memory, even if it has proved an embarrassment to more sober-minded historians intent on rescuing Irish history from any kind of visionary aberrations.[2]

Yet this popular veneration is not without its complications for, characteristically, the received image of Anne Devlin has depicted her as the silent, passive foil to the dashing, melodramatic Emmet, the selfless shadow behind the heroic man of substance. Anne Devlin's virtues of loyalty, fortitude and forbearance, combined with an unlimited capacity to endure suffering, are all too easily reconciled with the domestic ideals of womanhood fostered by the 'devotional revolution' in post-Famine Irish Catholicism – ideals which, in effect, helped to disenfranchise women from participating in public affairs.[3] In this social climate, Mary, the virgin mother, became the model which Irish women were urged to emulate, and it is striking that in its most influential manifestation, that of the Apparition at Knock in 1879, *silence* was a central attribute of this ideal. As Marina Warner puts it, noting that the mute stillness of the Virgin at Knock sets it apart from similar apparitions elsewhere:

> The Virgin at Knock is silent, so the message is interpreted that a good woman is a woman of few words, submissive, obedient and resigned; the Mother set forth as the ideal woman works in the kitchen and is idealized as saintly by her children. But the credit for 'planning' and 'striving' goes to Father . . . Beyond 'Mother' no other woman exists at Knock: it sees no further than biological destiny . . .[4]

It is in the light of this dichotomy between passivity and action, suffering and 'planning', that Anne Devlin lived on in popular memory. Indeed, it may be surmised that at one crucial juncture, these opposing images intervened directly to give shape to the incipient revolutionary consciousness that was to culminate in the Easter Rising of 1916. On moving his school, St. Enda's, in 1910 to the Hermitage at Rathfarnham beside the former home of Sarah Curran, Robert Emmet's sweetheart, Patrick Pearse's volatile imagination was taken over more and more by the figure of Emmet, whose presence he seemed to sense at every turn in the grounds of the new school. In a series of prophetic speeches in 1914, we find Pearse looking to Emmet as an example of 'the dreamer' who awoke 'a man of action', all the more to contrast him with the patient, maternal resourcefulness of Anne Devlin:

> Wherever Emmet is commemorated let Anne Devlin not be forgotten . . . You know how she kept vigil there [in Emmet's house] on the night of the Rising. When all was lost and Emmet came out in his hurried retreat through Rathfarnham . . . she would have tended him like a mother could he have tarried there, but his path lay to Kilmashogue, and hers was to be a harder duty . . .[5]

It is not too difficult to see in this passage a prefiguring of the 'mater dolorosa' theme, with its attendant myth of sacrificial redemption, which was to exert such a decisive influence on Pearse's subsequent political development.

In view of the almost archetypical resonance of the character of Anne Devlin, it would seem that any attempt to reclaim her for feminist politics, for a project which seeks to insert women back into the historical process as agents, faces formidable problems from the very outset. Yet if we compare the film version of Anne to the avowed feminist protagonist of Pat Murphy's earlier film *Maeve* (1981), who demands the right to stand back from what she sees as a male-dominated republican tradition, it is clear that for all her apparent passivity, Anne

8.1

is an *active participant* in the nationalist struggle, representing the critical view from within rather than the position of the detached, ambivalent outsider. She chooses consciously and deliberately to get involved in Emmet's insurrectionary plans, though such is the nature of her commitment that towards the end of the film, during her incarceration in Kilmainham Jail, she appears to lose sight of this initial act of will. When Mrs. Dunn, the jailer's wife, remarks to Anne that they both share the misfortune of living in a prison, Anne responds: 'Except you live here by choice.' Anne seems unaware that she has only to change her mind about informing on Emmet to walk free from the prison. Yet to her this is no choice at all, for freedom, as she sees it, is not a matter of release but of resistance. As Emmet says at one stage, quoting the words of Tom Paine whom Anne is reading: 'the harder the conflict, the more glorious the triumph. What we obtain too cheap, we estimate too lightly.'

The opening sequence of *Anne Devlin* evokes in a series of concentrated images the task which the film sets itself. We see Anne and a number of other women exhuming the body of a murdered United Irishman, and breaking through a cordon of redcoats in order to give him a proper burial – just as, in the future, Anne's own body would have to be rescued from the anonymity of a pauper's grave in 1851 by the historian of the United Irishmen, R. R. Madden. In a sense, Pat Murphy's film is a similar exercise in retrieval. It is as if the film succeeds where Major Sirr fails in his interrogation of Anne, that is, in 'revealing the plot' and 'piecing together an ancient story, like fragments of a mosaic' (to appropriate Major Sirr's own description of his activity).

In restoring a lost fragment of the past, however, no attempt is made to place Anne at the centre of the action, as in the kind of patriotic melodramas which tended to portray Anne (or Sarah Curran) as a latter-day Cathleen Ní Houlihan to Emmet's swashbuckling interpretation of history.[6] Emmet still occupies centre stage, but what we get instead is the view from the wings, the view, incidentally, which exposes the artifice of spectacle, the contrived nature of dramatic action. In the pivotal scene in which Anne first comes to Emmet's house in Butterfield Lane, Emmet assures Anne that she is 'nobody's servant', that her role is simply to *act* like a servant, to 'behave like a housekeeper – even though there is no house to keep'. No sooner has Anne received this assurance than Thomas Russell, one of Emmet's co-conspirators, comes across Anne in an upstairs corridor. 'Who are you?' he asks. 'Anne Devlin, Sir.' 'Oh, well, fetch me some hot water, will you? And a dry towel as well, please.' The house at Butterfield Lane comes to resemble the scene of a subversive masque, where insurgents weave plots, and come and go in all kinds of deceptive guises. Yet it is not only the British who are misled by appearances: the conspirators themselves are taken in by their own web of deceit.

The theme of housekeeping with 'no house to keep', a front with nothing behind it, runs through the film, with all its paradoxical implications (for Anne does in fact have to engage in housework, and the drudgery of daily routines). It becomes at one level a metaphor for Emmet's own revolution. Emmet, as portrayed in the film, is not the daring adventurer of nineteenth-century melodrama, but a reticent figure strangely removed from action, an idealist more at home in contemplation and in his laboratory than in the field of battle. (It is hardly a coincidence that we see him with Sarah Curran in 'the Philosophers' Walk' behind the Curran home, when word comes through of the explosion in the Thomas Street arms depot, which doomed the rebellion.) To Anne, this realm of ideas and principles, of planning and calculation, is

8.2

something of a mystery, a world apart. In the extraordinary trance-like scene in which she first discovers Emmet's study, invading as it were his secret lair, we see her silently negotiating through her senses this obscure array of military plans and abstractions – touching, almost caressing, scientific instruments, smelling gunpowder, and staring uncomprehendingly at pages of Emmet's handwriting.

Yet so far from being the groundwork of action, the basis of political change, there is a clear suggestion that Emmet's ability to think things out in his head with no regard to social circumstances, his desire to represent the people rather than letting them represent themselves, is the cause of his downfall – as it must be, by implication, with any nationalist movement divorced from material struggles. Emmet's political activity seems to operate largely at the level of *signs* and *representations*. To the amazement of the down-to-earth guerrilla leader Michael Dwyer, Emmet is prepared to launch the rebellion with little or no artillery or popular support; his experiments with rockets deriving not from any ballistic interest in their use as missiles, but rather as *signals*, as the means of a spectacular call to arms. To Jemmy Hope, the revolutionary with an indigenous base in the urban poor, this devotion to appearances and outward show is a constant source of frustration. Describing how a bonfire lit to celebrate Bastille day was enough to prompt some of the rebels inside an adjoining arms depot to start making speeches as if the revolution had arrived, Hope remarks: 'It is amazing how people are slaves to their own images of freedom.' Hope does not object to emblems as such, indeed he is fully aware of the power of utopian images when harnessed to genuine social upheavals. But ideals and representations can never be a substitute for material forces, and to allow a revolutionary movement to detach itself from its social base is to convert it into an instrument that could just as easily advance the interests of those it seeks to oppose. A revolutionary movement obsessed with symbols exists at one remove from reality, in Hope's eyes, and can never, as he puts it, amount to anything more than an abject form of 'coat-trailing'.[7]

This throwaway remark is particularly appropriate to Anne's situation because, for her, Emmet's concern with insignia and 'coat-trailing' becomes apparent in the scene where she finds his imposing green uniform spreadeagled across a chair, disembodied but seemingly possessing a life of its own. Anne stands before a mirror and holds up the jacket in front of her body – the nearest she comes to having access to the male symbolic order. At this point Emmet enters the room and interrupts her reverie, asking her what does she think of his outfit. When Anne replies that she doesn't care much for uniforms, Emmet reproaches her, eulogizing the dramatic effects of a military costume on a marching army. Anne immediately protests: 'They look like a green version of redcoats' uniforms. We are ourselves. We should rebel as ourselves.' Emmet responds with a flight of impassioned rhetoric: 'Anne, it will be like a green wave, like the land itself rising up . . .' – to which Anne can only reply, with an exasperated matter-of-factness: 'But the fighting will be in the streets. You will be seen a mile off. How will the men get away?'

It is significant that both in Emmet's case, and in the anecdote recounted by Hope, speech-making and high flown oratory are the ultimate expression of the male mastery of symbolic forms. When Anne is finally pitted against her interrogator, Major Sirr, bedecked in his splendid red uniform, his study littered with fossils and relics in a manner reminiscent of Emmet's laboratory, it becomes clear to her that, as a woman, she is estranged from a discourse of power to which men, regardless of political affiliation, have privileged access. The fact that Major Sirr uses the Irish language to communicate with the informer Halpin is the final proof that language is inherently bound up with the source of her oppression. As the film develops, it is possible in fact to trace a process in which language becomes increasingly disembodied, detached from any material or tangible medium. When we first encounter Emmet, it is solely through his voice, while he remains invisible, temporarily off-camera. During Anne's first night in Butterfield Lane, the conversation of Emmet and his conspirators wafts through the floorboards of her bedroom, faint and indistinct by the time it reaches her ears. Towards the end of the film, when Anne is in her cell, she again hears the voices of her fellow insurgents through prison walls, except now they belong to the informers, Fleming and Quigley. The voice of the revolution has become finally adrift from its physical moorings.

It is hardly surprising that, faced with this attenuation of language and its identification with both male and imperial domination, Anne should have recourse to silence, to the mute condition of her own body, as a site of resistance.[8] But at this point the question surely arises: is this retreat into silence,

and the unmediated realm of inner, bodily experience, not precisely a rein-
forcement of the traditional stereotype which decrees that woman exists
'outside' reason and language, representing 'nature' and 'biology' as against the
male domain of 'culture' and 'society'? More specifically in an Irish context,
does it not lend support to the opposition between language and silence,
action and passivity, which, in Marina Warner's view, lies at the basis of the
submissive models of women central to both Catholicism and mainstream
nationalism in post-Famine Ireland?

Certainly in *Anne Devlin* there are clear indications that Anne falls increasingly
back on her inner resources, on the density and resilience of her own body, in
order to withstand the encroachments of Major Sirr and Dr. Trevor, the prison
physician. As the film moves gradually from daylight and exteriors to the
claustrophobic interiors of her cell, Anne is forced to make sense of her surroundings, and indeed of space and time, the basic co-ordinates of all knowledge,
through the medium of her body. We see her pacing up and down the cell in
what is almost an attempt to cancel the constraints of space, and later, when it
appears she has lost all track of time, she says in voice-over, a kind of inner
speech, that it was only the monthly flow of her periods which represented her
last tenuous hold on the passing of time.

As if to drive home the finality of this relapse into the body, into a pre-social,
biological sense of female identity, Anne's recourse to silence culminates in her
adoption of the mother-role, exemplified by the motionless scene near the end in
which we see her as the pietà, her dead brother cradled in her lap in the prison
cell. Yet there is a profound underlying irony here, for while the image at one
level is the ultimate affirmation of the natural, of woman's biological, procreative
'destiny', at another visual level it works in the opposite direction. The 'natural'
role of mother is offset by the deliberately posed and 'artificial' character of the
image; so far from depicting woman as nature, it points to woman as *representation*, the coded, tableau-like composition constituting what is virtually a direct,
iconographic quotation from the history of art. Woman at her most natural is
reclaimed as a sign, a part of a corporeal signifying system (albeit one greatly at
odds with the abstract, symbolic character of verbal language). Thus, in the scene
which follows the pietà image, the simulated or counterfeit nature of Anne's
status as mother is borne out when her menstrual periods cease, as if displaying
the symptoms (or rather the signs) of an imaginary pregnancy. Anne enters into a
form of confinement from which there appears to be no issue or delivery.

Anne's role as servant and housekeeper is, as we have seen, no different – she
acts the part, seeing it as a fictive performance rather than as the natural calling of
women. In fact, it would seem that according as Anne assumes a domestic or
maternal guise, she moves farther away from any kind of familial ties. In the
opening sequences, Anne is defined entirely in terms of her family, but as the film
progresses, there is a gradual disengagement not only from her family, but also
from any kind of dependence on men. Though the suffering she has brought
upon her family is a source of intense anguish, she will not let it override her

political convictions: 'What kind of loyalty is it,' Major Sirr asks, 'that makes you work against them?' [i.e. her family]. As a last resort, Major Sirr tries to interest her in the reward money by pointing to the merits of an attractive dowry. His proposal, however, falls on deaf ears. 'And who would I be marrying, with all the men killed or in prison?' Anne replies later in a mocking tone to the suggestion of Mrs. Dunn, the jailer's wife, that if she had abandoned politics, she might be happily married with a number of children.

Anne's silence is similar to her domestic or maternal persona. It is not a submissive silence, standing outside signification and, by extension, language, power and representation. This should be clear from the very fact that, throughout the film, Anne is pre-eminently a messenger, a vehicle or *medium* of communication between Emmet and his various contacts: Michael Dwyer, the organizers in the various arms depots or, indeed, Sarah Curran. Yet Anne is a medium with a difference, a medium which is not a means to an end. When Emmet commits a message to writing, or takes his male comrades into his confidence, it is in danger of being intercepted, and the information is easily extracted – or extorted – from its source. This is what is rendered impossible in the case of Anne; it is as if the message is secreted so deeply in her person that it is inscribed on her flesh, bound up with the privacy of her body. It is her body which the redcoats scar and disfigure through bayoneting and half-hanging when they are first seeking information about Emmet's whereabouts, as if somehow the act of physical violation could release the required information. This is not to say, however, that the body gives rise to a more 'authentic' or reliable form of knowledge than verbal discourse. Aware that she is being watched during her last meeting with Emmet in the yard at Kilmainham, Anne dissembles the act of removing a stone from her shoe in order to exchange a few, final surreptitious words with a man she is not supposed to know. Her movements say one thing, while her words say something else: the body can lie just as effectively as language.

This idea of the body as somatic sign recurs at key moments in the film. In one particularly charged scene at the beginning, Anne's sister Julia is shown framed against the landscape, untying her long hair before brushing it out with deliberate, almost sensual strokes. But this is no cosmetic exercise; it is a sign which activates the appearance of Michael Dwyer and, as it happens, Emmet in the film, an indication that the coast is clear for them to emerge from their hiding places in the Wicklow countryside.[9] The body here does not transmit a signal: it is a signal. In the scene which immediately follows, Dwyer has to intervene abruptly to stop one of his men caressing, however absent-mindedly, Julia's hair. For Dr. Trevor, on the other hand, there are no such prohibitions. In what turns out to be Anne's last contact with another person in the film, we see him manhandling her hair in the course of informing her, with perverse satisfaction, that she is to be moved indefinitely to Dublin Castle, while the other state prisoners are to be released. If, on this occasion, Anne does not finally break, it is because her body has lost or, rather, has been extended beyond its biological functions such as hunger and menstruation. When someone says to her at one point: 'Don't let them break you,' she retorts: 'Break what? They don't know what it is. There is nothing to break.'

Implicit in these scenes is a suggestion that when words fail, other forms of communication take over. 'There are many ways of giving information,' Anne reminds Emmet when he renews his misplaced confidence in the double-dealing Quigley. Within the structure of the film, this theme is developed in terms of an opposition between word and image or, more precisely, between narrative and spectacle. It is precisely at those points, where the burden of meaning is transferred from language and action to other, silent modes of expression, that the narrative slows down, reverting to the painterly, tableau-like compositions discussed above. At these moments, the visual excess of the images and the heightened music, not only arrest the flow of events, but also stretch realism and verisimilitude to their limits.[10] Conventionally, the superiority of images to words resides in their transparency, their power to resemble the world and give unmediated access to reality, much as bodily sensations are supposed to give us direct access to our inner experiences. But just as the body is traversed by language in the film, so also are images refigured as signs, as coded representations referring not so much to reality as to other pictures, whether it be the composed stillness of Dutch interiors or the light effects of a painter such as de la Tour. These considerations are crystallized in one of the opening shots in which we see Anne and a group of women rising up in statuesque fashion on the cart in which they are travelling, in order to place their bodies between the redcoats and the United Irishman they have just exhumed [Fig. 8.3]. The female body here offers

8.3

resistance to vision, just as the obvious contrivance of the image points to the refractory, allusive nature of any visual medium which seeks to address itself to female experience.[11]

Anne Devlin is a powerful rejoinder to the view that because women do not (or do not wish to) participate in male forms of action and discourse, they are thereby disenfranchised from power and are removed to the margins of passivity and silence. This is indeed as the stereotype would have it, and where the figure of the silent, suffering mother leaves its imprint on Irish history. But there is no need to revert to a feminine mystique of the body (and related concepts of nature and organicism) to reaffirm the presence of women in a world dominated by men. Anne Devlin is not a feminist inversion of the psychotic IRA leader played by James Cagney in *Shake Hands With the Devil* (1959) who appears to be at war with England, but is really at war with women. Though the film hints provocatively at various affinities between Emmet and Major Sirr, Anne's enemy is not men as such, but Major Sirr and the paternalistic colonial regime which he represents. Conversely, though it is clear that the almost clandestine solidarity between women accounts for much of Anne's strength throughout her ordeal, this solidarity does not extend across the colonial or even the class divide. Anne, it would seem, has more in common with James Hope than with Sarah Curran. She is prepared to commit herself to a struggle in which she shares some common interests with men, except her participation is on her own terms, terms which are often at cross-purposes with the remote, instrumental uses of reason which characterize male conceptions of power. This is evoked visually in the last meeting between Anne and Emmet in the yard at Kilmainham. Emmet is playing a game on his own against the prison wall, and pleads with Anne to break her silence in the mistaken belief that she is holding out for him. 'It was not for you we did it,' Anne replies resolutely, while crossing and recrossing the yard at a right angle to Emmet's private game.

Anne Devlin points to a political project in which the silent bearers of history, whether they be women or the labouring poor, cease to be instruments of social designs worked out by others (for example, Emmet's 'investors', as Hope sarcastically calls them), but actively intervene in bringing about their own emancipation. In a similar manner, the mute eloquence of the body points to a use of language in which the medium is no mere instrument or 'carrier' of information, but is so visceral and dense as to be inseparable from the multiple meanings it conveys. In the traditional female stereotype, silence and resignation are seen as part of a natural order which ensures that women do not so much act themselves but are acted upon. By contrast, Anne's silence is not a given, it is an achievement: it is the silence that comes from holding something back rather than from having nothing to say. By the same token, her suffering and endurance have nothing to do with acquiescence or passivity but are a mode of resistance, an act of intransigence which places a formidable barrier in the path of those who seek to exploit and dominate others.

9. 'LIES THAT TELL THE TRUTH':
Maeve, History and Irish Cinema

From its beginnings in the early decades of the present century, Irish cinema has been dominated by a number of pervasive and interconnected themes: the idealization of the landscape, the persistence of the past, the lure of violence and its ominous association with female sexuality, and the primacy of family and community. In one of the first films shot in Ireland, Sidney Olcott's *Rory O'More* (1911), these elements are already visible, albeit in an attenuated, rudimentary form. Set in the period of the 1798 rebellion, this historical melodrama deals with the escape of the daring rebel Rory O'More from British custody. In a characteristic sequence, Rory is warned of his impending arrest by his faithful girlfriend Kathleen, and takes to the hills – which conveniently happen to be in the vicinity of Killarney! This provides the pretext for a series of picturesque set-pieces in which Rory and Kathleen are framed dramatically against the wild, rugged landscape, with key changes of scenery being preceded by appropriate titles in case we miss the whole point of the exercise: 'The Gap of Dunloe', 'The Lakes of Killarney' and so on. Through the agency of an informer (the archetypal source of corruption in the community), Rory is eventually arrested and sentenced to death. However, family and female devotion triumph once more over adversity, as Rory's mother and Kathleen, in league with the priest, arrange for a last-minute rescue from the gallows.

Few subsequent films on Ireland parade the motifs and devices deployed in their own construction with such a lack of irony, and in such a transparent manner. Yet in different ways, representative films such as *Man of Aran* (1934), *The Quiet Man* (1952), *The Gentle Gunman* (1952), *The Rising of the Moon* (1957) and *Ryan's Daughter* (1970), return to these considerations of landscape, the past, violence and sexuality, varying from one another in emphasis and approach rather than in any fundamental change of subject matter. This body of imagery has informed the representation of Ireland to such an extent that any new departure in cinema which addresses itself to one of these themes, even in a sustained critical manner, runs the risk of being appropriated back into the very tradition which it is opposing. In this respect, Pat Murphy's film *Maeve* (1981) represents an important achievement, for it deals not just with one or two of these areas in an isolated fashion, but in fact confronts the whole romantic tradition head-on.

Maeve deals with the return from exile of a young feminist, Maeve Sweeney, to her family and friends in Belfast. Maeve's exile is both physical and political, in that she feels alienated not only from the threatening British military presence on the streets, but also from the ideological climate of her own community which revolves around a traditional, male-dominated republicanism. The film charts Maeve's attempts to come to terms with her own biography, and traces the different ways in which her identity as a young woman in Ireland is crossed by forces of time and place, and by social constraints of culture, gender and politics. The film, therefore, is not just conducting a debate with the way in which the northern 'troubles' have been represented on television and documentary, but is in fact engaging with a wider set of questions centring on the foundational images of Ireland, and their role in the development of cultural nationalism. That it tackles this complex array of issues successfully, moreover, is due to the manner in which it explores a crucial formal problem which, in a sense, overrides all the others. This has to do with the nature of artistic representation and signification, in particular as it bears on the relationship in Irish history between narrative, fiction and reality.[1]

Landscape, narrative and memory

One of the central concerns in *Maeve* is the way in which representations or narrative forms in Irish culture do not simply describe but are often bound up with the realities they purport to represent. It is in this sense that the rediscovery of the past, according to Standish O'Grady, one of the main architects of the Literary Revival, should consist in 'a reduction to its artistic elements of the whole of that heroic history taken together'.[2] In the reconstruction of Irish history undertaken by O'Grady and his associates, the past was transformed into a stirring narrative of heroes and battles, of 'gods and fighting men' inspired by the warrior virtues of chivalry, purity and violence. The mere presence of a woman posed a threat to this ascetic, male universe, so when in the most famous of all the historical sagas, the *Táin Bó Cuailgne*, Ulster is invaded by Maeve, the warrior queen of Connacht, we find O'Grady's narrative powers stretched to their very limits. It is clear, moreover, that this was not simply a response to the dictates of the action, for in a revealing aside written many years later, he points to one pressing reason why the selection and abbreviation of events required by an orderly narrative was forced upon him. In popularizing the early texts, he informs us, he found some things which he 'simply could not write down and print and publish', such as the 'very loose morality' of Queen Maeve and her companions.[3] As Philip Marcus describes it:

> The treatment of Medb [i.e. Maeve] was perhaps most at variance with the source materials. O'Grady tried to make her seem more 'feminine', to endow her with some of the personality traits traditionally associated with the 'weaker sex', and at times the proud amazon of the sources seems more like the delicate fainting heroines of the nineteenth-century novel.[4]

Sexuality, in other words, as represented by powerful female figures such as Maeve, had to be written out of Irish history, a task for which a heightened Victorian narrative impelled by action and violence was eminently suitable.[5] It is hardly surprising then that in the modern setting of Pat Murphy's film, the return of another Maeve to Ulster should bring about a direct confrontation

9.1

with this mythic version of the past. The only difference is that now the drama is taking place on the streets.

One of the main effects of imposing 'artistic elements' or a conventional narrative form on history is that the past tends to be structured in terms of a beginning, a middle and end, as if an inexorable logic were driving events towards their modern denouement. The past is recreated in the image of the present, in anticipation, as it were, of things to come.[6] In Pat Murphy's earlier short film, *Rituals of Memory* (1979), we are already given a suggestion of how 'artistic elements', in this case visual representations, can enter into and constitute memory. This involves the use of photographs as mementoes, as when in a family album we encounter photographs whose principal function is to record important occasions such as weddings, holy communion and other family get-togethers. Counterpointed in the film against casual snapshots of informal occasions, these photographs invariably appear posed and stilted, unwittingly rigging the very past they are attempting to preserve. In this way, representations – photographs, film, drama, fiction – can orchestrate any future readings of events: 'The past is a way of acting on the present' as it is put in one key exchange in *Maeve*.

In *Maeve*, landscape becomes one of the primary means of arresting the flow of events, becoming in effect a form of congealed memory. The apparent continuity between past and present is brought out in the film by a series of flashbacks inserted into the narrative without the usual demarcating devices of blurred focus or dissolves – as if to say, in Maeve's own words, that 'the more you focus on the past, the more reality it gains'. Many of these flashbacks involve scenes from Maeve's childhood, in which she travels through the countryside surrounding Belfast in her father's van, while he regales her with stories and folklore, stories he eventually comes to believe himself. The landscape is scarred with ruins and antiquities, the circular remains of ring forts in particular echoing this idea of a continuous, recurring past. It is interesting to note that it was precisely this prominent feature of the Irish landscape which was seized upon by O'Grady to confer permanence on the legacy of the heroic age. As he expresses it himself, there are two kinds of 'pre-historic narrative' at work in Irish history, one which is found in texts and writing, and the other which is embedded in 'the early Irish tales that cling around the mounds and cromlechs' of the Irish countryside. He writes that this latter

> sort of pre-historic narrative clings close to the soil, and to visible and tangible objects. It may be legend, but it is legend believed in as history, never consciously invented . . . and drawing its life from the soil like a natural growth.[7]

It is this romantic idea of stories in stones, of a naturalistic narrative denying its own construction and posing as an organic creation of history, which presides over the flashback sequences in *Maeve*. O'Grady himself expressed regret that he could not conceal his own presence in his stories, thus belying their origins as 'conscious inventions' of a dominant male subject.[8] In *Maeve*, by way of contrast, we are left in no doubt that the account of history we are receiving is inscribed with a male authorial voice. In the opening scene of the film, Martin Sweeney, Maeve's father, escapes from the oppressive reality of a bomb-scare outside the front window of their house, and retreats to the safety of the back kitchen. Entering what is conventionally designated as female space, he removes various obstacles such as washing and clothing, and proceeds to write a letter to Maeve which we hear in voice-over – at which point Maeve herself first appears on the screen. Throughout the film, Martin's intrusions and storytelling attempt to occupy woman's space, usurping and pre-empting alternative female versions of reality. In one scene, he interrupts an anecdote about a neighbour which Eileen, Maeve's mother, is recounting, and converts it into a self-indulgent narrative of his own. The extent to which this continual appropriation of history removes women to the periphery is suggested in one striking, later sequence in which Martin loses himself in an even more drawn-out narrative than usual, while the young Maeve hovers in the background, edging herself slowly along the circular walls of a ring-fort. As she reaches the centre of the frame, directly behind Martin, she alights from the stone wall of the fort thereby parting company with this dominant conception of history. Martin's authority has been displaced, a fact which is expressed cinematically in both of the storytelling sequences in question by the manner in which he is prevented from assuming the role of an invisible, omniscient narrator, and is forced instead to relate his story in the form of a direct address to camera. By drawing attention to the authorial presence of the camera, and reminding the audience that they are in fact looking at a visual construction of reality, one of the main conditions of classical, illusionistic narrative is undermined and with it any possibility, as O'Grady expresses it, that 'history culminates in art' in an invisible manner.[9]

The manner in which both landscape and narrative bear the imprint of a male controlling vision is taken up again at a visual level in a key sequence in which Maeve and Liam, her republican boyfriend, engage in an extended political argument on Cave Hill overlooking Belfast (renowned for its United Irishmen connections). The camera pans slowly in an arc giving a commanding view of the city and its environs, while Maeve's voice, off-camera, intones a series of word associations which address themselves directly to this underlying matrix of landscape, narrative and memory:

> a centre, a landmark . . . a space for things to happen, a technique, a way in, a way out, a celebration, a guide, a release, a lie, a truth, a lie that tells the truth, a projection, a memory . . .

In this scene, the camera, articulating Maeve's point of view, expropriates the space provided for the male spectator in the traditional linear perspective of western painting, thus eroding one of the central tenets of classical visual realism. Perspective was traditionally conceived as a window on the world, providing the spectator with a detached, privileged vantage point from which to exert a visual mastery over nature.[10] In *Maeve*, by contrast, the frequent looks and glances through windows which recur in the film invariably take the form of point of view shots, the use of subjective camera underlining the vulnerability of a viewing object that is no longer distanced from reality. This dismantling of the conventions of pictorial realism, moreover, is carried beyond the visual level and into the dramatic structure of the Cave Hill sequence. The introductory monologue and subsequent non-naturalistic dialogue between Maeve and Liam serve to disrupt further the semblance of reality, in effect suspending the flow of the dominant narrative to afford Maeve space for her own activity and aspirations. As Liam says to her with characteristic bluntness: 'What you're proposing is no story at all.'

This is indeed what *Maeve* is proposing, a history divested of myth and (self-) deception. As the action in the film progresses, many of the images which help to insulate people from reality are removed, forcing them to come to terms with a world, as Barthes would put it, without 'the alibi of art'. Television, in this context, acts as a metaphor for the way in which images and representations often function as protective measures against the encroachments of an intolerable reality. In the opening scenes of the film, alluded to above, television violence competes for attention with the real life threat of the bomb-scare outside the front window, allowing Martin to retreat to the back kitchen to compose the letter to Maeve which initiates the action of the film. The feelings of security generated by representations which place the spectator at one remove from reality are shattered, however, in a subsequent scene (a flashback to the past) in which Maeve's family, watching July 12th celebrations on television, are abruptly brought back to earth by a brick coming through the window of their front room. In a later episode, the use of television as a security monitor in a republican pub shows how representations no longer merely simulate but actively participate in the violence they portray, the image becoming an accomplice in, rather than a refuge from, the propaganda of the deed. In a scene towards the end, it is in fact television which exposes the fictive nature of the teenage Maeve's excuses for her absence from school, and implicates her in the street riots shown on the six o'clock news. In a similar manner, it is suggested, Martin's stories and fictions no longer serve to prevent his immersion in reality, a point illustrated to stark effect in one strange, almost surreal, sequence in which he is forced by a squad of British troops to unload a consignment of televisions from the back of his van onto the street, their screens silent, blank and ineffectual [Fig. 9.2].

9.2

The memory of the dead

One of the most striking features of *Maeve* is the manner in which problems connected with art and politics, feminism and history, are explored not simply at the level of 'content' but are also reworked in terms of formal strategies, the structure of the film itself constituting a commentary on the events it portrays. In this sense, Maeve's ambivalent relationship to her family and community, the need to feel a part of and yet disengaged from the action, is articulated formally by her relationship to the narrative in the film. Though the leading character in the story, Maeve is nevertheless decentred throughout, making nothing happen, existing at the edges of the frame and indeed of people's lives. There is no question of Maeve adopting the kind of affirmative role normally accorded to the hero in a classical narrative, for this is based precisely on the values of masculinity, violence and sublimated sexuality from which she is seeking to distance herself.[11] Yet it is by no means clear that this detachment from the action amounts to a failure of commitment on Maeve's part, a total renunciation of her past, her family and her community. Though disengagement is, on the face of it, the very opposite of involvement, one of the central themes running through the film is the belief that certain ideals, wishes and aspirations may often be realized, paradoxically, in conditions that appear most opposed to their fulfilment. When Maeve and Liam meet for the first time in his flat, they both remark on the absurdity of his neighbours downstairs who, as part of a spiritualist group, engage in regular seances in order to further the cause of peace in Ireland. That night in his room, in the afterglow of making love for the first time, Maeve reflects on how the sordid nature of their environment did not take at all from the experience, despite her previous expectations of the kind of escapist, romantic surroundings associated with such intimacy. She says to Liam: 'Sometimes I think it is just as useful to do something totally contradictory' – as if to say that the very squalor of the room ironically made it perfect for the occasion.

The profound anti-romantic sentiments implicit in this remark have an important bearing on the role of the seance, being held underneath Liam's flat, in the overall context of the film. It suggests that for all its naivety, it may have more to do with traditional views of the violence in Northern Ireland than might appear on the surface. And in fact it has, for what is a seance but a memory of the dead, an invocation of the past, a crystallization of precisely the kind of history from which Maeve is trying to extricate herself. It answers, moreover, to the exact terms of O'Grady's conception of a mystical history relayed through 'visible and tangible objects', in that the past, in this instance, needs to be conducted through a body or a medium – in this case the physical presence of the medium organizing the meeting. Hence, it is all the more ironic that when the session reaches its climax, the strange sounds heard from above by the participants in the seance should emanate not from the memory of the dead, but rather from the language of the flesh upstairs where Maeve and Liam are making love. Desire and sexuality, in other words, both having their focal point in the women's movement, become key elements in the struggle to release history from the cycle of myth and violence in which it has been traditionally encased. As Maeve herself puts it in her final protracted argument with Liam, set significantly in a graveyard in the middle of Belfast: 'When you're denied power, the only form of struggle is through your body.'

Maeve's position here does not amount to a facile substitution of the personal for the political, but represents rather an attempt to question the whole basis of this distinction between the private and the public which lies at the heart of bourgeois social relations. One of the classical methods of delineating gender roles in the mainstream Hollywood narrative has been the construction of a private space – centring on the home, the mother, the family and personal relations – as a respite from the public domain of intrigue, machismo and violence. In *Maeve*, no such hiding places exist. Indeed, in a ghettoized society in which housing itself is one of the main areas of social contention, it would be surprising if the home were portrayed as a sanctuary from the conflict on the streets. In an early scene in the film, the adolescent Maeve lashes out at a group of schoolboys on discovering that they had attacked her younger sister, Roisin, with stones. The action then cuts to the Sweeney's kitchen where Maeve's mother is attending to Roisin's wounds, chiding her for not staying in the safety of their own back garden. This remark is no sooner uttered than it is undermined by the appearance at the back of the house of the mother of one of the boys, intent on having it out with Maeve. This depiction of the kitchen and the garden as extensions of the struggle, rather than as secluded havens from the outside world, is applied in turn to the other rooms of the house – the front room (in the scene where a brick comes in through the front window) and the upstairs bedrooms (as in the case of Roisin's anecdote about the British soldier who forces his way into her bed during a party, proposing to rape her or her female companion). The implication in Roisin's story is that even women's bodies are subjected to a constant threat of invasion, a suggestion that is made explicit in a subsequent scene (this time set on the streets) where Maeve and Roisin are humiliated in public by being ordered to jump up and down while soldiers leer at their breasts.

It is against this background that we should view Maeve's statement that women's bodies become sites of struggle in a conflict dominated, as she puts it herself, by 'purity and death', complementary forces in the annihilation of desire and the flesh. This adds a new dimension to the scene in which Maeve and Liam make love in his flat, for it also constitutes the only occasion on which they succeed in cutting themselves off from the troubles, and finding their own space. However, far from corresponding to the traditional romantic interlude promulgated by Hollywood, everything in the scene works in the opposite direction: the room, in Maeve's words, is 'full of other people's smells and dirt' and they are forced to sleep on the bare floorboards in the darkness, having used the mattress as a barricade to shut themselves in. Yet the experience, as we have seen, is not debased but is in fact enhanced by the absence of the conventional romantic trappings associated with such occasions: 'That's the thing, don't you see,' Maeve explains to Liam, 'Your fantasy gets acted out in the shape that fits itself around your surroundings. Like there's wine, and there's firelight, and those are the basic romantic needs. If someone were to write about this, the descriptions would fit the magazines . . .'

By the same token, the process of divesting the past, at a more general level, of the romantic aura with which it has been surrounded by mythic nationalism is bound up with the task of reinstating women, and the sexual discourse represented by feminism, on the agenda of Irish history and politics. This argument is worked into the structure of the film by the manner in which the gradual fragmentation of a narrative idiom centred on the male voice is offset by a converse movement whereby women renew contact, establishing a new sense of identity and solidarity with each other. This is brought out in the bedroom scene following the Cave Hill sequence in which a verbal disagreement between Maeve and Roisin on the need for an organized women's movement is undercut by the kind of intimacy that comes from a relaxed, unselfconscious awareness of each other's nudity. As the film progresses, Maeve's reticence, and her reluctance to assume the role of the assertive, self-contained individual required by conventional narrative forms, becomes a source of strength rather than of weakness on her part. Her isolation in the hospital, for instance, allows her to cross the sectarian divide by bringing her into contact with the old Protestant woman who sings plaintively 'Abide With Me'. Towards the end of the film, she returns to a republican drinking club, such as provided the occasion for her row with Liam and her initial decision to leave earlier in the film. This time, however, she is in the company of Roisin and her friends, and what was originally a source of alienation and departure is now a pretext for a night on the town, forging new bonds of friendship and community.

Many of these concerns – landscape and memory, history and narrative, male discourse and female solidarity – converge in the penultimate scene set in the Giant's Causeway, one of the most important scenic sites in Ireland. The total disintegration of the male controlling voice is evident in the figure of the ranting orator, hurtling the rhetoric of the Ulster covenant at the sea while Maeve, Roisin and Eileen find refuge behind the rocks, sharing jokes and confidences and experiencing a new collective identity as they abandon themselves to a bottle of

9.3

whiskey. In the final scene, Martin is shown alone in the darkness, talking to himself about the arrest and interrogation by the RUC, a victim of his own self-deception: 'I used to think that these things would never happen to me, even when they did. 'Cos you see, that's the only way to go on . . .' It is he, and not Maeve, who is the outsider in the end.

The ambivalent resolution, whereby Maeve's aloofness and detachment constitute both 'a way in, [and] a way out' of her past and her environment, suggests that the film is undertaking a debate not only outside the republican movement but also within it. As against Liam's view that republicanism should not jettison the mythic dimensions in its history but should annex them for a new set of object-ives, Maeve argues that these myths cannot simply be controlled at will but must be totally re-figured if people are to escape their influence. This is an important rejoinder to an uncritical acceptance of the view that strategic realignments in the republican movement, such as a 'left turn' and a greater concentration on material issues, will automatically dispel the overpowering legacy of romantic nationalism. These 'masterful images', in Yeats' phrase, have to be attacked on their own terms as cultural and aesthetic forms, all the more so when they are woven, as we see in the film, into the very fabric of everyday life. For this reason, local forms of resistance centring on culture and on women's issues do not become (in Liam's words) simply 'one more faction to contend with', but are in fact intrinsic to any attempt to free republicanism from its image of a mystical communion with the past, and by so doing to prevent it falling back on fictions

9.4

when faced with the possibility of mass mobilization (as in the case of the images of religious martyrology which surfaced in the H-Block campaign) or even a radical transformation of society. The kind of local strategies elaborated in *Maeve* may appear marginal to what is conventionally understood as politics. Yet one of the central arguments running through the film, as we have seen, is that certain ideals and aspirations, particularly those labouring under a burden of myth and romanticism, may often be realized in conditions that appear most opposed to their fulfilment. In the final analysis, *Maeve* is itself an example of an ideal served by its opposite, an imaginative construct which brings us closer to reality, in its own words, 'a lie that tells the truth'.

10.1 James Coleman, 'guaiRE' (1985)

10. NARRATIVES OF NO RETURN:
James Coleman's guaiRE

'In using what I considered traditional symbols,' W. B. Yeats observed ruefully toward the end of his life, 'I forgot that in Ireland they are not symbols but realities.'[1] Culture in these circumstances cannot be reduced to an aesthetic pursuit at one remove from reality; it is a material force in its own right, as its role in turn-of-the-century Irish nationalism attests. Indeed, the later Yeats was tormented by the thought that some of his plays might have contributed to the violence of the Irish War of Independence (1916–22). He may have had in mind not just his incendiary *Cathleen ni Houlihan*, of 1902, but his less-known *The King's Threshold*, staged a year later, which introduced hunger-striking into Irish politics as a form of symbolic resistance.[2]

Drawing on Irish legend, *The King's Threshold* describes a struggle between Guaire, a seventh-century king of Connacht renowned for his generous banquets, and Seanchan, his chief bard. Guaire accuses the poet of an excess of words that is inimical to orderly statecraft, the practical obligation to attend to material needs and get things done. Seanchan responds with a hunger strike, which he sees as a way of releasing the imagination: 'For when the heavy body has grown weak,/ There's nothing that can tether the wild mind.'[3] In early versions of the play the king yields, but in 1922, probably as a result of the death on hunger strike of Terence McSwiney, the nationalist lord mayor of Cork, Yeats gave the play a new, tragic conclusion. What is interesting here is the notion of narrative as an event informed by its historical moment: the 'original' version of 1902 was no longer possible given the events of the War of Independence. The question is not just one of revision but of a story structured by the circumstances of its telling.

James Coleman too has dealt with the Guaire legend, in *guaiRE: An Allegory* (1985), a complex reenactment of the myth using video, gesture, text, and music. And though his work is usually discussed in terms of a European and American tradition of conceptual art, *guaiRE* reveals it as deeply informed by its Irish context and situation. The Guaire of Irish legend would not have approved of exposing the legacy of the past to the vicissitudes of narration. In popular tradition, he was fighting with Seanchan because the poet could remember only fragments of the *Táin Bó Cuailgne*, a key repository of Irish mythology. Guaire asked Seanchan's son to restore the original, as if the power of the state depended on preserving the continuity between past and present. It was precisely such narratives of return that Coleman countered in *guaiRE*.

Narrative in this staged allegory did not just take the form of a story: it *took place*, the place in question being Dun Guaire Castle in County Galway, suppos-edly Guaire's stronghold. The initial act of restoration that Coleman contested by working here was the Irish heritage industry's version of history: the 'authentic' banquets laid on for tourists at castles like Dun Guaire, to give the illusion of communion with the medieval past.⁴ Indeed, on the way into the 'throne room' in which *guaiRE* was performed, the audience was shown the backstage of such illusions – a painter at work on the set, costumes being prepared.

From the performance's opening words, it was clear that Coleman's Guaire too is obsessed with continuity – with lineage and pedigree, the foundations of his legitimacy as king. A prophecy has foretold that he will be overthrown by the son of his rival Ceallach, whom he has disposed of to assert his claim to the throne: 'My will be done . . . a formula to dissect . . . thwart the course of destiny . . . the prophecy . . . Yet it can be employed to extend life . . . Nobody can rob me of my formulae . . . Buried deep inside.' 'Will' here signifies not just volition but inheritance, which is in turn secured by the 'formula', an elixir of life (or death), but also the source of repetition and continuity in oral culture.⁵

In the legend, when Guaire has Ceallach murdered, the body is stuffed in a hollow tree.⁶ In Coleman's work, however, an obstetrician rather than a coroner appears on the scene. It is as if Ceallach had been returned to the womb – as if Guaire had sought to remove his rival from affairs of state by inserting him into a maternal narrative. For Coleman, though, this insertion becomes a form of empowerment. The maternal gestures toward an alternative public sphere that jams the machinery of patrilineal power.

Though the voices of *guaiRE*'s 'characters' are mainly male, they are articulated through a masked female actress (Olwen Fouere), the only on-stage presence. At one point in the text her body is explicitly linked to Ceallach's tree. Does it follow from this that the female body is merely a hollow vehicle for a male line of transmission? Is it devoid of its own narratives? Marina Warner points out that the allegorical use of the female form to embody abstract ideas such as 'Justice' and 'Liberty' does not mean that these virtues are actually extended to women. Indeed, it often implies the opposite: the materiality of women's bodies is emptied out to carry what are essentially masculine ideas. Hence the reduction of woman's body to a shell in icons such as the Statue of Liberty: 'The statue's hollowness, which we occupy literally when we make the ascent to Liberty's empty head, is a prerequisite of symbols with infinite powers of endurance and adaptability. She is given meaning by us, and it can change, according to what we see or want.'⁷

Yet an allegory that insists on the corporeality of the sign would seem to obstruct such instrumental uses of the female form. In *guaiRE*, the maternal body is such a figure. As the performance opens, the actress's body comes alive, tentatively discovering itself from the inside. Her left leg twitches, but she grabs her right leg by mistake. She pinches her nipple and is startled by the pain. Her 'throne' is a plaster head, on which is projected a face; it is as if she were giving birth. It may be, of course, that the mother remains a 'relay' or extension of patriarchy, on the assumption that behind every maternal body lies a great man. This is no doubt as the king would like it to be. But *guaiRE* throws such notions into question; it is less allegory than a reflexive commentary on allegory's workings.

For Freud, every family romance contains the underlying anxiety that where-as 'paternity is always uncertain, maternity is most certain'.[8] James Joyce, writing within the colonial frame of turn-of-the-century Ireland, spells out the political implications of this when he has Stephen Dedalus exclaim in *Ulysses* that 'paternity may be a legal fiction', and is only as secure as the power of state and law to back it up.[9] (Hence Guaire's 'my will be done'.) The anomaly colonial Ireland posed to an equation of nation and fatherland was that Irish men lacked the control of the public sphere that paternal authority required. As Elizabeth Butler-Cullingford writes of the representation of Ireland in eighteenth-century '*Aisling*' poetry, a genre in which the male poet would personify Ireland as a woman, 'She is still a sexual object, for the poet lovingly describes her physical charms, and occasionally she is shown as ravished by the invader. Colonization, however, has destroyed native masculinity along with political independence, and no true Irishman remains to mate with her.'[10]

Hence the colonial construction of the Irish body politic as female, with its corollary that without 'manly' British rule, government was impossible in Ireland. (In 1898, Sir George Baden Powell contrasted the patriarchal benefits of Ireland's union with Britain to the 'emasculated' self-government that would result from Home Rule, the latter resembling the dependency of a 'southern señora on her father confessor'.[11]) It may be, then, that these female personifications of the nation in some sense do mask patriarchal power on the part of the *colonial* adminis-tration, but it is not clear that this instrumental use of allegorical forms extends to the colonized culture itself. As Anne Owens Weekes writes, Gaelic Ireland's dis-tance from power meant that the *entire* population, both male and female, shared the condition of women in the metropolitan centre: 'Colonization, then, makes female both country and people. . . . "Excluded from landed wealth, from political life, from the 'official' church . . . the Irish erected a counter-culture, not so much rebellious as evasive", also a strategy, like women's, decreed by their similar repression, and one whose end was survival.'[12] In these circumstances, the recourse to female imagery in poetry and popular protest turns the colonial stereo-type against itself, positing an alternative 'feminized' public sphere (imagined as the nation) against the official patriarchal order of the state.

In *guaiRE*, this refiguration of female allegory finds expression through *location*, the ruins of Dunguaire Castle. (For Walter Benjamin, the ruin is the most evocative of allegorical emblem, its fragments testifying to an unrestorable origin.) At one point the king's anxiety requires that he 'sponges his perspira-tion', an action accompanied by the line 'Sponging over a will'. The reference is to Lady Christabel Russell, who lived for a time at Dun Guaire Castle. Becoming pregnant soon after her marriage, Russell was sued for divorce by her husband in 1924 on the grounds that, since their marriage was uncon-summated, she must have committed adultery. Yet examination by two gynaecologists showed that she was a virgin. It followed that her son was the rightful heir, even if paternity could not be established. (Coleman's sponge remark – a sponge which she shared with her husband was found in Russell's bath – adverts to one lurid explanation of how she became pregnant.[13]) It was as though maternity had ceased to be a vehicle for the male line, the female body usurping the 'meaning' it was patriarchally intended to carry.

In one of Coleman's recent works, *Charon* (1989), a series of fourteen photographic vignettes, a baby gazes intently at the camera, and hence, as Lynne Cooke suggests, at 'the photographer who seems to be both father of the child and allegorical father of the image'.[14] In *guaiRE*, the temporal lapse which characterizes allegory, the delay between the sign and what it signifies, displaces the sovereignty of the eye. In the set (designed by Dan Graham), a curved two-way mirror acts as a video screen behind the 'throne', providing the audience with a panning shot of the room from the point of view of the king. (For Michel Foucault, analysing the birth of 'classical representation' in Velazquez's *Las Meninas*, the individual subject/spectator is constituted by an identification with the king.[15]) At the end of the performance, this pan dissolves into an image of the throne/head on which the performer sits, with its lifelike face. The masked performer turns her back on the audience, and reveals her face – which turns out to be the face projected on the plaster head – but her reflection in the real time of the mirror is mediated by a time-delay video, which superimposes on the mirror/screen a flashback of her removing the mask. It is as if the mirror possesses memory. 'The mirror stage' on which the performance literally takes place is not a medium of representation so much as a pretext for the uncanny, a reminder, in the phrase Jo Anna Isaak adapts from Joyce, of 'the ineluctable temporality of the visible'.[16]

It is a conventional critique of allegorical idealizations of the female that they privilege the relation of the image to other images rather than to women in the real world. This spiriting away of the physical body is addressed in Paul Muldoon's 'Aisling', a parody of the eighteenth-century Irish visionary poems: 'Was she Aurora, or the goddess Flora,/Artimedora, or Venus bright,/or Anorexia, who left/a lemon stain on my flannel sheet?/. . . In Belfast's Royal Victoria Hospital/a kidney machine/supports the latest hunger-striker/to have called off his fast, a saline/drip into his bag of brine.'[17] Here the *aisling* figure is linked to the harlot ('the lemon stain') and the hunger-striker, the anorexic bodies of all three sharing the rarefaction of the flesh.

This image of decomposition assumes a different valency, however, if we recall Benjamin's reclamation of the prostitute's sensuality through the image of the ruin.[18] The fragmentation of the ruin is an allegory of *desire* as well as of death, its incompletion finding expression in a ceaseless quest that acknowledges rather than reverses the passage of time. In *guaiRE*'s enigmatic maternal narratives, the denial of the body that is implicit in virginity is recuperated through the desire of the harlot. So, in the Russell case, the absence of an identifiable father was read as evidence not of parthenogenesis but of promiscuity, the likelihood of many fathers in her mansion. Outside the family structure, the maternal becomes a figure of erotic abandon.

During the preparation of *guaiRE*, such anxieties returned to haunt the Irish state in the forms of a divisive abortion referendum in 1983, and of the

Kerry babies controversy shortly after. Two babies were found dead in County Kerry, at locations fifty miles apart. A young woman, Joanne Hayes, confessed under police questioning to the killing of the first baby, then withdrew her confession, admitting to the killing only of her own, different, child. The state insisted that she had carried, and killed, *both* babies – an implausible accusation, for it was shown that the blood group of her own baby's father was incompatible with that of the other infant. The prosecution charge then rested on the suggestion that she had carried babies by two fathers at the same time – a legal fiction that even the power of the state could not uphold against a vulnerable single mother. Paternity had to be established at all costs, as if the inability to name the father called the legitimacy of the state itself into question.[19]

Clearly, allegory in *guaiRE* derives its impact not from a suppression of the real but from an anchorage in *events*, in narratives of time and place. Its engagement with questions of narrative, representation, and sexuality paradoxically depends on the contingency that, set in another time and place, it would be a different story. Erich Auerbach has noted the links between allegory and prophecy in scripture, both looking *through* signs for other meanings; for Auerbach, though, prophecy differed from allegory in its insistence on grounding its interpretations in 'literal truth' (for the early Church fathers 'refused to consider the Old Testament as mere allegory', insisting that 'it had real, literal meaning throughout'[20]). Coleman's *guaiRE* attempts a kind of prophecy in reverse, inserting allegory back into history by denying that the real is the sole preserve of the literal. This version of allegory opens rather than closes narratives, establishing a gap between the present and a past that awaits completion.

11. IDENTITY WITHOUT A CENTRE:
Allegory, History and Irish Nationalism

The state is concentric, man is eccentric.

James Joyce

In the memorable closing scene of James Joyce's story 'The Dead', the composure of the urbane and self-centred Gabriel Conroy is shattered when he
discovers that his wife, Gretta, still pines for a young man, Michael Furey,
whom she knew years earlier in the west of Ireland. The night before she left
for Dublin, the seriously ill Michael Furey had risen from his bed to see her,
and died a week later from a chill caught standing in the cold winter rain. As
snow begins to fall outside their hotel window, Gabriel's thoughts drift towards
the west of Ireland in a trance-like reverie:

> The time had come for him to set out on his journey westwards. Yes, the news-
> papers were right: snow was general all over Ireland. It was falling on every part
> of the dark central plain, on the treeless hills, falling softly upon the Bog of Allen
> and, further westwards, softly falling on the dark mutinous Shannon waves. It
> was falling, too, upon every part of the lonely churchyard on the hill where
> Michael Furey lay buried. It lay thickly drifted on the crooked crosses and
> headstones, on the spears of the little gate, on the barren thorns.[1]

It is striking that for all its evocations of the sacred (the crosses, spears and
thorns), Gabriel's mental journey westwards is recreated in the profane image of
the newspaper. According to Benedict Anderson, newspapers, and print culture
in general, introduce a secular 'transverse, cross-time', which allows people to
establish links with parts of their country they have never directly experienced,
thus laying the basis for the 'imagined community' of nationalism.[2] Gabriel's
hollow, transverse relationship to the west of Ireland contrasts starkly with that of
his wife, Gretta, whose memories of Michael Furey are precipitated by the chance
hearing of an old Irish ballad which he used to sing, 'The Lass of Aughrim', as she
is preparing to leave the dinner party on the feast of the Epiphany which forms
the centrepiece of the story.

For Joyce, it is this remnant of oral culture, rather than the 'empty, homogeneous time' of the newspaper, which is characteristic of the most resilient
strains in Irish nationalism – or any subaltern culture, I would contend, which
attempts to speak in the aphasic condition of colonialism. Gabriel writes for a

134

newspaper and identifies with the latest European ideas, but this has little to do with the social milieu in which his wife, Gretta, grew up. Earlier in the story, he is upbraided by the nationalist Miss Ivors for refusing to travel to the west of Ireland and encounter native Gaelic culture at first hand, and – a related misdemeanour in her eyes – for writing in the Dublin *Daily Express*, which she considers an imperialist organ, and an adversary of the national revival.[3] Anderson is correct in stating that the emptying out of time in print culture is constitutive of certain kinds of nationalism, but this applies mainly to forms of nationalism driven by state formation of the advanced Western kind, characterized by centralization, unification and, one might add, colonial expansion. In contradistinction to this, as E. J. Hobsbawm points out, are those versions of nationalism intent on fragmentation and disaggregation, motivated by separation rather than unification.[4] Such good words as Hobsbawm can muster up for nationalism are reserved for the former kind, and he can scarcely conceal his contempt for those 'fissiparous' tendencies in nationalism which mobilize outside or against the centralized state, even for purposes of decolonization. Unlike the viable 'ethnically and linguistically homogeneous entities which came to be seen as the standard forms of "nation-state" in the west', these aberrant strands in nationalism are 'politically fluctuating and unstable'. According to Hobsbawm, the nation must evolve under the aegis of the state: otherwise it is like a mollusc extracted from its shell, emerging in a 'distinctly wobbly state'.[5]

It could be argued, however, that most of the justified criticism of nationalism as masking over internal divisions, inventing tradition, or retreating into xenophobia and racialism, are properly directed at the classical European model rather than its more idiosyncratic peripheral variants. Literacy, and in particular print culture, is often presented as rescuing a 'pre-political' populace from the torpor and dogmatism of oral tradition. Yet while an alliance of print culture and Protestantism played a crucial role in laying the conditions for the Enlightenment and liberal democracy in Europe, it is worth recalling that it also consolidated logocentrism at the level of *popular* religious practice, establishing the immanence of the living word, the Voice of God, in the transparent text of the Bible. As Terry Eagleton puts it:

> Of course, for the puritan tradition, script has a privileged status. But that is no more than to say that the enigmatic materiality of the biblical text must be dispersed and deciphered by the power of grace, so that the living speech of its Author may be freed from its earthly encasement.[6]

In the twentieth century, this suspicion of hermeneutics was linked to modernism itself, as part of an attempt to innoculate Western culture against the multivalence of tradition. For Susan Sontag:

> *Transparence* is the highest, most liberating value in art – and in art criticism – today. . . . Once upon a time (say, for Dante), it must have been a revolutionary and creative move to design works of art so that they might be experienced at

several levels. Now it is not. It reinforces the principle of redundancy that is the principal affliction of modern life.[7]

In this sense, the modernist project of the Enlightenment and advanced print cultures stands as much in need of deconstruction as many of the traditional societies it purports to bring into the contemporary world. It is true that many non-Western or 'pre-modern' cultures have shown a proclivity for dogmatism and fundamentalism, but it is far from clear that this is a result of their opposition to Western values. The insistence on the univocal and literal meaning of sacred texts among present-day fundamentalist movements would seem to owe as much to Lockean-type conceptions of language, and scientific notions of clarity, as to the obscurantism of traditional or so-called backward societies. As Rosemary Radford Reuther contends, summarizing recent research in this area, fundamentalist movements arise not only as a response to Western culture but may actively draw inspiration from it, 'by selective adaptions to modern organizational and technological methods and scientific thought'. She continues:

> Fundamentalism is not simply a historical conservatism. It is often militantly hostile to much of past tradition, which is seen as having become corrupted. Many fundamentalist movements see themselves as purging this corrupted tradition, but also as retrieving . . . some absolute truth beyond historical relativity and change. Thus most fundamentalisms claim some inerrancy of Scripture, or infallibility of teachers, or both.[8]

Thus in the context of Irish Catholicism, for example, it was the modernizers, the centralizing forces, in the church who pressed the claims for papal infallibility at the Vatican Council in 1870, a paradox of progress that did not escape the attention of James Joyce. In his story 'Grace', one of the characters exults over the fact that of the two senior churchmen who held out against this high-handed arrogation of authority, one was the nationalist Archbishop MacHale of Tuam from the west of Ireland, who presided over a wayward popular religion that was inimical to the very idea of certainty.[9] One of the main tasks of the 'Devotional Revolution' which swept the Catholic church in post-Famine Ireland was to exorcise the baneful influence of traditional cultural practices (such as wakes, 'keening', 'patterns' at holy wells, and other 'pagan' rituals) from religious devotions, thus bringing Irish Catholicism into line with *Roman* Catholic orthodoxy.[10] This augmentation of Catholic power was part of a wider transformation which also sought to dislodge nationalism from popular insurgency, integrating peasant culture into the institutions of state power – defined, in this period, in terms of an imperial administration, at least where constitutional nationalists were concerned. The writer Seán O'Faoláin was closer to the mark than even he perhaps realized when he observed that before the Whig-inspired accommodation with state power under the leadership of Daniel O'Connell, the Irish people had 'no *absolute* sense of *themselves* as a nation (first italics mine).[11]

Allegory and agrarian insurgency

Jacques Derrida's contention that 'logocentrism is a uniquely European phenom-enon'[12] may be usefully extended to European conceptions of nationalism, in that the premium placed on coherence and abstraction, and the clarity of political consciousness, comes to resemble the unmediated self-presence of the individual subject. It is this sense of unity and national integration which Western imperial-ism prided itself on exporting to what were referred to as the 'discordant races' of its empires. On 1 January 1877, the day Queen Victoria was proclaimed Empress of India, the (London) *Times* paid homage to the civilizing mission of English imperialism as it confronted the otherness of Asia, a continent vitiated by con-tingency and instability:

> It can hardly be to share the rapid vicissitudes of Asia, and to prove that policy is the creature of accident, that we have entered that new sphere. It is rather that we may introduce into it the deeper sentiments and grander ideas that have made Europe hitherto the leading quarter of the world. India, in itself, never had the prospect or even the thought of a political unity. Like Africa, the region was peopled with numberless races, who had their quarrels, but who were apparently capable of no grander objects than could be attained within their own territories, which were sufficient for the population. . . . Politically, they represent altogether one great fact, which is the single-all-sufficient justification of this day's ceremony. They represent the proved impossibility of India uniting herself by her own internal development, or by any Asiatic agency. A self-made Indian union is as much an impossibility as a self-made African union.[13]

– or, one might add, a self-made Irish union. According to Sir George Baden-Powell, writing during the Home Rule controversy at the turn of the century, 'Ireland does not contain the necessary elements of a separate nationality – for among the inhabitants there is no unity or individuality of blood, religion, laws, occupations, sentiments, history, or even tradition'.[14] There is little trace here of the primordial unity and plenitude which Western phonocentrism is apt to visit upon pre-literate societies: a 'self-made' identity is decidedly the prerogative of the colonizer.

In recent years, versions of this thesis, filtered through the work of modern historians such as Anderson, Hobsbawm and Ernest Gellner, have surfaced in Irish cultural debates as part of a revisionist challenge to the exaggerated ancestry bestowed on the Irish nation by romantic historians of the old school. Such mythic accounts of Ireland as 'the oldest nation in Europe' can be seen as part of an attempt to smuggle into Irish culture the continuity and permanence of English tradition as venerated by Edmund Burke, but while notions of stability and security come readily to colonial powers, they hardly make sense in societies uprooted by the expansionist designs of the West.[15] 'The rapport of self-identity', as Derrida puts it, is 'always a rapport of violence with the other'.[16] This helps to place in perspective the argument of the Irish historian Tom Dunne that not alone does Irish nationalism lack an ancient pedigree, it cannot be said to have emerged as a significant force until it identified with the nation state as conceived by Anglocentric, or mainstream European, political discourse. Though he makes no explicit connection between nationalism and print culture, the main target of Dunne's and other related critiques is the vernacular culture of the so-called 'hidden Ireland' of the eighteenth century, a communal culture largely oral in nature, except for those poets, scribes and scholars who had regular access to written sources.[17]

According to Dunne, native Irish culture in the early modern period failed to develop a coherent nationalist ideology because it lacked the centralizing mechanisms of the absolute monarchies that provided the infrastructure of the first nation states:

> A national monarchy did not emerge in Ireland to form the nucleus of a cen-
> tralized state, as happened in other countries. Outside pressure failed to bring
> political unity also, and instead newcomers were absorbed into the system of
> competing lordships.[18]

It is hardly surprising that 'outside pressures' did not succeed in producing a clone of the centralized state, for it was precisely such a concentration of power in the centre that native culture was resisting. The stratagem of 'divide and rule' is one of the bogies of the imagined community of nationalism, but in certain cases it was the amorphousness of native cultures, the mollusc-like qualities excoriated by Hobsbawm, which offered the most effective long-term defence against conquest. While it took almost four centuries to subdue the sprawling Indian peoples of North America, historians have suggested that it was the excessive centralization of the far more powerful Aztec and Inca civilizations which brought about their rapid downfall – once the emperors Montezuma and Atahualpa fell into Spanish hands, as Richard Peet describes it, their empires became 'bodies without heads'.[19]

This principle did not go unnoticed by nationalist propagandists in Ireland, and even as late as the cultural revival at the turn of the century, it was used by some leftist commentators as a pretext for forging links between traditional Gaelic culture and the syndicalist version of Marxism promulgated by James Connolly, with its declared aversion to centralized power and the state. According to Aodh de Blacam, an English-born critic who came to Irish nationalism with the zeal of a convert, 'it was the many-headedness, as of the hydra, of the Irish constitution that perplexed the enemy, who knew not where to strike'. It is true, he adds, that pre-invasion Gaelic culture 'was weak in central authority', and the lack of 'a strong military monarchy' ensured that 'when the most unscrupulous and most militaristic nation of Europe sent ravaging armies into Ireland, there was a tragic want of ruthlessness in the opposition that was offered'.

> And yet [he continues] this want of centralization proved, in a sense, the nation's
> salvation. Had the Irish State [sic] hung upon central institutions, the destruction
> thereof would have meant the nation's destruction. Thus one great battle might
> have ended Irish independence.[20]

What Dunne sees, then, as a weakness in native culture, and the factor which inhibited the development of national consciousness, could be interpreted as its strength. This point is more or less conceded when he argues that the introduction of a state apparatus into Irish society with its attendant cultural and ideological agencies (such as institutionalized religious authority) saw to it that the quest for a unified identity worked *against* Irish independence: 'Political unity and the transformation in attitudes and identity which accompanied it were imposed by English conquest in a manner which involved the destruction of the Gaelic system and political culture rather than its "modernization".' Yet, having demonstrated that political unity of this kind was a stalking horse for colonization, he nevertheless proceeds to concur with the orthodox nationalist view that its absence was the cause of the destruction of the old Gaelic order:

> Gaelic Ireland did have important unifying features – common social and economic systems, law-codes, literature and religion. . . . Yet, while all of this points to a collective sense of Gaelic identity, it was a sense which conspicuously lacked a political dimension, even on the very basic level of a commitment to unity against foreign aggression. Looking at the European context, this was hardly surprising. The development of 'national consciousness' (to call it that) was one of the products of political unity under expansionist monarchies. This was the case, for example, in sixteenth-century England and such 'national consciousness' formed an important part of the dynamics of Elizabethan imperialism in Ireland, just as its absence in Gaelic Ireland contributed to the failure of resistance to this imperialism.[21]

What this attempt to measure an emergent Irish nationalism against British or European standards fails to recognize is that the bondsman is in no position to emulate the lord, for he is already implicated in his master's identity. This is the fatal weakness in Marx's famous dictum, frequently quoted in defence of Marxist appropriations of modernization theory, 'The country that is most developed industrially only shows, to the less developed, the image of its own future.'[22] If this is interpreted to mean that, say, Ireland or Scotland should have looked to England, the workshop of the world, as a prototype of their own future development, it conveniently overlooks, as Colin Leys points out, that the confidence and self-assurance of the English nation state derived partly from the fact that its sovereignty extended to 'not just Manchester and the Midlands, but also the Scottish "deer forest" (that is, vast regions of the "development of underdevelopment") and the oppressed and stagnant home colony of Roman Catholic Ireland'.[23] If Ireland looked to the image of England, in other words, it would end up seeing its own distorted reflection – as if in the 'cracked looking glass of a servant' with which Joyce liked to compare his work.

One of the basic assumptions in arguments designed to rule out any semblance of nationalism before the development of the nation state is that members of pre-modern cultures are totally immersed in their own localities, and are not capable (as the London *Times* would have it) of elevating their minds to grander notions. This hypostatization of the local is simply the unified subject of the nation state viewed through the reverse end of a telescope. As critics of Clifford Geertz's ethnographic work have argued, the very attempt to seal off the local from the wider social networks in which it is inserted is the conceptual equivalent of proclaiming a district: it is to place it in political quarantine.[24] For all Geertz's careful elucidations of the local intricacies of the Balinese cockfight, he fails to tease out the wider implications of his own observation that the Balinese project on to the shape of their island the image of a cock taunting its more powerful neighbour, Java. This is not to say that the particular and the general are fused: however, it does suggest, as William Roseberry avers, 'that the cockfight is intimately related (though not reducible) to political processes of state formation and colonialism'.[25]

This is how we should understand the sense of time and place in the symbolic practices of Irish culture and politics in the formative stages of nationalism, whether they take the form of poetry, popular ballads or agrarian insurgency. In the case of rural disorder and agrarian unrest in the pre-Famine period (1760–1845), the trend in revisionist Irish social history has been to dismiss it as an essentially local phenomenon, lacking political consciousness, and certainly operating without a wider sense of the colonial subjugation of Ireland. But while such agrarian violence was indeed 'sporadic, local, unpredictable, continual, anonymous', it also, as Tom Garvin has pointed out, 'showed distinct signs of politicization and articulation over long distances, although no really effective central authority emerged'. There is evidence to suggest that both Ribbonism (as its post-1800 manifestation is usually called) and Defenderism (the highly politicized Catholic agrarian movement of the 1790–1800 period) possessed a structure of delegate meetings, and that quite elaborate, underground inter-county structures existed, as well as extensive contacts with Irish groups overseas.[26] So pervasive and clandestine were these networks that Garvin discerns in them the infrastructure of the later Fenian organization, or Irish Republican Brotherhood, which was responsible for the Easter Rising of 1916, and which established the Irish Republican Army, or IRA, in 1919.

Agrarian protest in the early nineteenth century had demonstrably acquired a complex political consciousness, in many ways more influential and certainly more subversive than the 'official' constitutional nationalist campaigns of Daniel O'Connell, or even the more revolutionary Young Ireland movement of the 1840s, both of which helped to bring Irish nationalism into the mainstream European discourse of the nation state. What is interesting for our present purposes, however, is the shadowy precursor of Ribbonism and Defenderism, the constellation of agrarian protest and secret societies known as the Whiteboy movement, which first came to public notice in the mid-eighteenth century. While clearly local and class-based in their immediate manifestations, the forms of material struggle in which Whiteboys were engaged had a wider remit than purely economic interests: they were also concerned, as Michael Beames puts it, 'with the establishment and maintenance of alternative codes and values, and in defending those codes against attack from whatever source'. Agrarian violence not only borrowed its practices from the kind of peasant rituals associated with wakes and weddings, but outbreaks of Whiteboy activity also intensified around the time of important seasonal festivals such as Mayday, Halloween (Samhain), and the aftermath of Christmas (St. Stephen's Day, New Year's Eve).[27]

The most conspicuous evidence of the cross-over with other forms of peasant custom such as Mummers and Strawboys was the symbolic dress of male insurgents, and in particular the systematic adoption of female clothing: bonnets, veils, gowns and petticoats were pressed into service in this transgressive costume drama. This was a notable feature of rural uprisings in other peasant societies but, as Natalie Zemon Davis points out, 'in Ireland . . . we have the most extensive example of disturbances led by men disguised as women'.[28] The assumption of a female persona was taken to the point where some of the Whiteboy organizations ('Whiteboy' itself signifies the wearing of a white smock) masqueraded under female soubriquets: the Lady Clare boys, Lady Rock, Terry Alt's Mother and, in the nineteenth century, the Molly Maguires from the west of Ireland who later resurfaced as a militant organization in the coalfields of Pennsylvania in the 1870s.

The threat posed by the anonymity and inscrutability of these societies was such that the authorities felt compelled to lift the veil, as it were, and impute some kind of organizing consciousness behind the scenes to their otherwise incomprehensible behaviour. It was as if the very fact that certain activities were imbricated in a narrative without a determinate leader or organizing consciousness was sufficient to constitute them as 'violent'. Given the basic assumption, moreover, that a subaltern culture was incapable of achieving unity or even intelligibility on its own terms, the organizing principle was invariably ascribed to some external agent, or form of manipulation from above. The landing of the French adventurer, Thurot, in the north of Ireland in 1760 sent shock waves into the colonial administration, and the alleged appearance of the Pretender, disguised as a woman, in the south of Ireland the following year was believed to be the immediate cause of the rise of the Whiteboys in 1761, confirming to the authorities' satisfaction their own worst fears of an imminent Jacobite invasion.

Although the Whiteboys did indeed march to the tune of 'The Lad with the White Cockade' and carried the white lily (both emblems of the Stuart dynasty deposed by the Williamite settlement), there is no reason to believe that they subscribed to the fully elaborated theories of paternalism and patriarchy which informed Jacobite ideology among English Tories.[29] In fact, they owed their allegiance to a series of enigmatic female figures who hovered between the other world and everyday life in the imagination of the peasantry: 'Shevane (Joanna) Meskill' or 'Sieve Oultagh'. According to James Donnelly, these incendiary images found their way into peasant consciousness through cultural forms such as the ballad and prophetic poetry:

> Precisely how this usage originated is unknown, but it almost certainly derived its currency from the popular tradition in song and poetry of personifying Ireland as a

woman and its people as her children . . . it would be wrong to interpret 'Queen
Sieve' as a symbol of Ireland in a consciously nationalistic sense, but the common
people were undoubtedly accustomed to this manner of representing the plight of
the Irish poor as a collectivity.[30]

Although these personifications may not meet the specifications of nationalism in an abstract or an 'absolute sense' (to cite O'Faoláin's terms above), they
nonetheless provided a powerful symbolic means of lifting a set of grievances
above local horizons. Natalie Zemon Davis points out with regard to peasant
consciousness in France in the early modern period that:

In the 1540s, the Rouen festive society could count on spectators and readers
knowing the facts of local political life, but references to national or European
events were usually general and even allegorical.

– the important point being, in Ireland at any rate, that it was not always possible
to clearly distinguish what was factual and what was allegorical.[31] Hence, the
dying declaration of five Whiteboys hanged in Waterford in 1762 that, by the
mysterious Queen Sieve, 'we meant a distressed harmless old woman, blind of
one eye, who still lives at the foot of a mountain in the neighbourhood'. Allegory
here is not just a personification of an abstraction: it is part of the language of
personal acquaintance. This intimate and yet otherworldly relationship with a
female personification places it on a continuum with the allegorical figures of
'Dark Rosaleen', and 'Cathleen Ní Houlihan' in the visionary poetry and ballads
of the period, who promised apocalyptic deliverance from the Williamite
confiscations in Ireland.[32]

The instability of these images, and the absence of an unmediated concept of
nationalism, proved an embarrassment to later cultural nationalists intent on
establishing the kind of 'self-present' identity required for state-formation. One of
the ways of explaining away the recourse to figuration was to construe it as a
strategic device, deliberately coding information and sentiments that were already
known in a literal sense, but which could not be uttered directly because of the
fear of being charged with sedition.[33] This explanation is on a par with functional
accounts of Whiteboy dress which reduce it simply to disguise, a way of deceiv-
ing others. The French commentator Augustin Thierry was more to the point
when he observed that those who had recourse to such symbolic practices also
succeeded in placing a barrier between *themselves* and a reality that was too
painful for clear and distinct ideas:

The Irish love to make their country into a loving and beloved real being, they
love to speak to it without pronouncing its name . . . it seems as if, under the
veil of these agreeable illusions, they wished to disguise to their minds the
reality of the dangers to which the patriot exposes himself.[34]

It is not simply, therefore, that allegory comes after the event, a mask that can
be removed at will: it is part of consciousness itself under certain conditions of

colonial rule. 'The very extravagance of allegory employed on these occasions', wrote Edward Hayes, 'is an unmistakable index to the intensity of the persecution which produced it in the first place'.[35] This disjunction between expression and experience, between the outward sign and its recondite meaning, reinforced the colonial prejudice that the Irish were inveterate liars, constantly reacting against the despotism of fact. In an article written in 1833 comparing Ribbonism in Ireland to the Thuggee in India, the Rev. Samuel O'Sullivan complained that even legal language, which drew on the coercive power of the state to stabilize meaning, was not immune to subversion from within:

> What is Ribbonism . . . but a species of political Thuggee, in which the conspirators are of one religion, and bind themselves by an oath of blood to the extermination of all in whom opposition to their evil designs might be apprehended . . . if the Thugs are their superiors in the article of safe and expeditious murder, they are immeasurably beyond the Thugs in the article of skilful perjury, by which they make the very forms of law contribute to defeat the ends of justice.[36]

The peasantry may have been subject to the law but they did not owe their allegiance to it: their lives were regulated by an alternative public sphere which was not allowed material expression but which was nonetheless capable of negating what overlaid it. The mollusc in this case could not be contained within its outer shell. As with law, so with linguistic shifts in a colonized culture. According to Edward Hayes, although 'we are English in expression', it is still the case that 'we can be thoroughly Irish in thought': 'The fathers of the early church struck down paganism with weapons borrowed from its own armoury . . . and so, also, has Ireland conquered in her captivity, by her successful cultivation of the English tongue'.[37] This, no doubt, is an over-optimistic reading of what was, after all, the virtual destruction of the old Gaelic order, but Hayes is correct in maintaining that it possessed what might be referred to as 'negative capability' (to misappropriate Keats' phrase), acting as a vestigial, destabilizing force in the interstices of colonial discourse. As Stephen Dedalus reflects when the Dean of Studies eulogizes the English language in a well-known passage in *A Portrait of the Artist as a Young Man*:

> The language in which we are speaking is his before it is mine. How different are the words *home*, *Christ*, *ale*, *master*, on his lips and on mine! I cannot speak or write these words without unrest of spirit. His language, so familiar and so foreign, will always be for me an acquired speech. I have not made or accepted its words. My voice holds them at bay. My soul frets in the shadow of his language.

The secret scripture of 'The Dead'

In the Christmas-dinner scene in the same novel, Joyce depicts a bitter row between members of the Dedalus household over the Catholic church's role in bringing about the fall of Parnell. The acrimony which has soured the festive atmosphere takes a turn for the worse when Mr. Dedalus points to a portrait of his grandfather on the wall, and boasts to his friend John Casey that his grandfather, for one, never let a priest sit at his table:

> – Do you see that old chap up there, John? he said. He was a good Irishman when there was no money in the job. He was condemned to death as a white-boy. But he had a saying about our clerical friends, that he would never let one of them put his two feet under his mahogany.[38]

This piece of ancestry is borrowed from the history of Joyce's own family for, as Richard Ellmann informs us, the novelist's great-grandfather, also called James Joyce, was condemned to death in Cork for Whiteboy activities, but was pardoned before execution.[39] On a later visit to Cork in the *Portrait*, the young Stephen meets an old man who actually knew his great-grandfather: 'old John Stephen Dedalus, and a fierce old fireeater he was. Now, then! There's a memory for you!'[40] The avatar of the Whiteboys found a kindred spirit in Stephen Dedalus for whom the past prefigured the present: 'through the ghost of the unquiet father', he states in his commentary on *Hamlet* in *Ulysses*, 'the image of the unliving son looks forth'.[41]

It is these restless shades, and the culture of the west of Ireland imbued with the memory of the dead, which come to haunt Gabriel Conroy in the closing scenes of the story 'The Dead'. When the thoughts of Gabriel's wife, Gretta, turn westward, opening up an irreparable gulf between them, it is because of her hearing 'The Lass of Aughrim', the ballad once sung by her dead lover. In the allegorical mode of both poetry and popular insurgency which followed the Williamite confiscations in the eighteenth century, the refusal to name, for all its eloquence, is akin to the silence induced by the traumatic experience of loss.[42] Gretta's muteness, her 'veiled and sad voice', can be seen in this context. Though transfixed by the ballad, its name has escaped her memory:

> 'Mr. D'Arcy,' she said, 'what is the name of that song you were singing?'
> 'It's called *The Lass of Aughrim*,' said Mr. D'Arcy, 'but I couldn't remember it properly. Why? Do you know it?'
> '*The Lass of Aughrim*,' she repeated. 'I couldn't think of the name.'[43]

Aughrim, a small village near her home town Galway in the west of Ireland, was the site in 1691 of the final battle in the Williamite wars which resulted in the destruction of the old Gaelic order. Though Gabriel consciously turns his back on this shattered culture, a second, inner voice infiltrates his thought and speech, threading allusions to King William and his colonial legacy in an almost liminal manner through the text. The ballad itself has political resonances in view of the tendency to allegorize Ireland as a female, for it relates the story of a young peasant woman who is seduced, and then abandoned, by a noble lord, an emblematic encounter, in Richard Ellmann's words, of 'the peasant mother and the civilized seducer'.[44] On each occasion, as Gabriel nervously contemplates his after-dinner speech, his thoughts turn to the snow-capped Wellington monument in the nearby Phoenix Park, and the adjoining 'white field of Fifteen Acres' where military reviews were staged as a form of colonial spectacle. After he finishes his speech – in which he assures his listeners that he 'will not linger on the past' or 'let any gloomy moralizing' intrude on the festive atmosphere – he is drawn to relate an amusing anecdote about his grandfather Patrick Morkan, and his horse Johnny who spent his life 'walking round and round in order to drive the mill' where he was working. One day Morkan decided to drive up to the Phoenix Park with his horse to see a military review:

> 'And everything went on beautifully until Johnny came in sight of King Billy's statue: and whether he fell in love with the horse King Billy sits on or whether he thought he was back again in the mill, anyhow he began to walk round the statue . . . Round and round he went . . .' (209)

Revenants of the Williamite past make their presence felt once more when members of the dinner party cross O'Connell Bridge in a cab on their journey home. One of the party remarks: 'They say you never cross O'Connell Bridge without seeing a white horse' (the white steed being a traditional emblem of King William's charger). Gabriel replies that all he can see is a white man pointing to the snow-covered statue of Daniel O'Connell.[45]

Public monuments are expressions of official memory, and bear witness to the power of the state to legitimate its triumphant version of the past, and assert its authority over its citizens. By their imposing presence, and their control of public space, they stand in stark contrast to the memories of the vanquished which attach themselves to fugitive and endangered cultural forms such as the street ballad. Yet it may be that monuments do not embody memory but efface it, absolving the citizen of the burden of remembering by relocating it in a static form: 'The less memory is experienced from the inside', writes Pierre Nora, 'the more it exists only through its exterior scaffolding and outward signs'.[46] Gabriel Conroy negotiates his life through such outward signs, in the hope that they will provide direct access to what they represent. He calls love by its name, and is unsettled when, somehow, the use of the correct word does not call up the experience: 'Why is it that words like these seem to me so dull and cold? Is it because there is no word tender enough to be your name?' (215). Like Patrick Morkan's horse, he is so inured to habit that the outer shell loses its own materiality, becoming a substitute for the thing itself.

It is striking that Gretta does not answer directly when Gabriel asks her (twice) if she loved Michael Furey, but looks instead to a half-remembered street ballad to come to terms with an unfathomable loss. Unlike monuments, ballads were excluded from the public sphere, and hence carried on a fugitive existence in the margins between the personal and the political, charging a personal event or memory with the impact of a political catastrophe – and vice versa. As Donal O'Sullivan points out, this was often no more than the result of an accident, a patriotic song taking a familiar tune – usually that of a love song – and retaining the name of the girl in the love song, if only to indicate the original air. 'There is nothing romantic in all this', he assures us, since 'the choice of names is quite fortuitous'.[47]

In fact, as Gabriel admits, such a contingent relation can lead to a romantic intensity which he can barely comprehend: 'So she had that romance in her life: a man had died for her sake. It hardly pained him now to think how poor a part he, her husband, had played in her life' (223). For Gretta, it is not the transparency of the sign but the veiling of the voice, the dislocation between inner and outer, which enables her to break her silence. As in Joyce's notion of an 'epiphany', the difference and incongruity of the surface manifestation, the maintenance of boundaries, is essential, for if it is fused with the experience, it would preclude its straining after some more elusive or ineffable meaning:

> Ever mindful of limitations, [the true artistic sensibility] chooses rather to bend upon these present things and so to work upon them and fashion them that the quick intelligence may go beyond them to their meaning which is still unuttered.[48]

In a short article surveying the political situation in Ireland in 1907, James Joyce wrote that Irish nationalism is characterized by 'a double struggle' – the anti-imperial struggle, on the one hand, and, on the other hand, an internal struggle, 'perhaps no less bitter', between constitutional nationalism and a dissident, insurrectionary tradition beginning with the Whiteboys and passing through to the Fenian (IRB) movement.[49] Within the narrative framework of 'The Dead', and indeed in terms of popular cultural forms, this internal struggle is articulated through the competing strategies of the newspaper, and the popular ballad, in addressing questions of history and identity. This does not mean that modern media forms are confronted by a primordial oral tradition, at one with itself in an imaginary wholeness before the fall brought about by letters and universal reason. As David Lloyd has argued, not least of the reasons the popular ballad attracted the opprobrium of state-builders intent on an unproblematic 'unity of culture' was its ephemeral, fragmented status, its refusal to act as a source of originary plenitude for the higher self of the nation.[50]

In the construction of 'the national', therefore, complexity and cultural critique are not the sole preserve of the newspaper and print culture, or the type of abstract consciousness required by state formation in advanced Western countries. By the mid-nineteenth century, it was apparent to William Thackeray that the 'rationality' which print culture was expected to cultivate was already skewed in Ireland by oral tradition and popular religious practices which he dismissed as 'lies and superstition':

> Leave such figments to magazine writers and ballad-makers; but, corbleu! it makes one indignant to think that people in the United Kingdom, where a press is at work and good sense is abroad . . . should countenance such savage superstitions and silly, grovelling heathenisms.

By superstition here, Thackeray means the redundancy of speech, the 'loud nothings, windy emphatic tropes and metaphors' that abound in a recalcitrant culture traversed, but not yet fully regulated, by the book: 'If I were Defender of the Faith', he declares, 'I would issue an order to all priests and deacons to take to the book again . . . mistrusting that dangerous facility given by active jaws and a hot imagination'.[51] It is important to bear in mind, moreover, that such indeterminacy as speech possesses in this context is historically bounded, for even though a level of undecidability is a feature of all language, some cultures are in a better position than others to stabilize the allegorical impulse in a given speech community. As James Clifford puts it:

> Whereas the free play of readings may in theory be infinite, there are, at any his-
> torical moment, a limited range of canonical and emergent allegories available to
> the competent reader (the reader whose interpretation will be deemed plausible
> by a specific community). . . . Reading is indeterminate only to the extent
> that history itself is open-ended.[52]

It may well be that under certain conditions of relative historical continuity or legal-rational administration, such as those which obtained in the exemplary European nation states invoked by Hobsbawm, language and identity acquired the kind of fixity that monuments confer upon memory. But this option is not open to all national cultures, particularly those subject to centuries of colonial rule, which have known otherness from the inside. Mikhail Bakhtin writes that 'it is quite possible to imagine and postulate a unified truth that requires a plurality of consciousnesses, one that cannot in principle be fitted into the bounds of a single consciousness, one that is, so to speak, by its very nature *full of event potential* and is born at a point of contact among various consciousnesses'.[53] The Hegelian standards of clarity and abstraction prescribed for political consciousness in the metropolitan centre do not exhaust all possibilities of national identity. The owl of Minerva may only fly at dusk, but Dedalus was able to wing his way through the Celtic twilight, albeit by flying close to the ground.

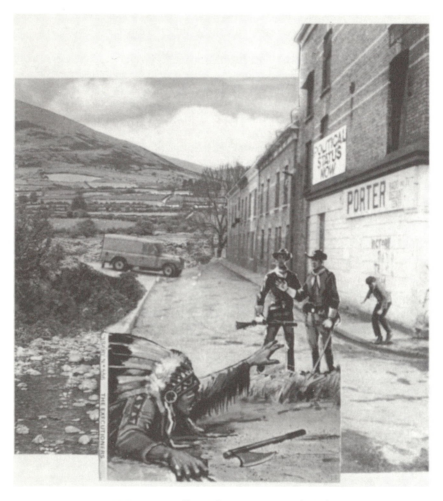

12.1   Seán Hillen, 'The Executioners' (1996)

12. RACE AGAINST TIME:
Racial Discourse and Irish History

He was a young Irishman . . . he had the silent enduring beauty of a carved
ivory negro mask, with his rather full eyes, and the strong queerly-arched brows,
the immobile, compressed mouth; that momentary but revealed immobility, an
immobility, a timelessness which the Buddha aims at, and which negroes express
sometimes without ever aiming at it; something old, old, and acquiescent in the
race! Aeons of acquiescence in race destiny, instead of our individual resistance.
And thus a swimming through, like rats in a dark river.

D. H. Lawrence, *Lady Chatterley's Lover*

During the twilight of colonialism, a children's toy circulated in the 'Big
Houses' of the Irish Ascendancy which purported to give the 'British Empire
at a Glance'.[1] It took the form of a map of the world, mounted on a wheel
complete with small apertures which revealed all that was worth knowing
about the most distant corners of the Empire. One of the apertures gave a
breakdown of each colony in terms of its 'white' and 'native' population, as if
both categories were mutually exclusive. When it came to Ireland, the wheel
ground to a halt for here was a colony whose subject population was both
'native' and 'white' at the same time. This was one corner of the Empire,
apparently, that could not be taken in at a glance.

In his analysis of colonial discourse, Homi Bhabha has written that 'colonial
power produces the colonized as a fixed reality which is at once an "other" and
yet entirely knowable and visible': hence 'in order to conceive of the colonial
subject as the effect of power that is productive – disciplinary and "pleasurable"
– one has to see the surveillance of colonial power as functioning in relation to
the regime of the scopic drive'.[2] The apparent ease with which colonial discourse establishes its legitimacy derives from the paradox that it locates
discrimination in a primal act of *visual* recognition – notwithstanding the fact
that the visual, in this Lacanian sense of the Imaginary, obviated the very basis
of difference in the first place. For this reason, it is clear that a native population
which happened to be white was an affront to the very idea of the 'white man's
burden', and threw into disarray some of the constitutive categories of colonial
discourse. The 'otherness' and alien character of Irish experience was all the
more disconcerting precisely because it did not lend itself to visible racial divisions, as is evident from Charles Kingsley's anxious ruminations on a visit to
Sligo, Ireland, in 1860:

149

> I am haunted by the human chimpanzees I saw along that hundred miles of hor-
> rible country. I don't believe they are our fault. I believe . . . that they are happier,
> better, more comfortably fed and lodged under our rule than they ever were. But to
> see white chimpanzees is dreadful; if they were black, one would not feel it so
> much, but their skins, except where tanned by exposure, are as white as ours.[3]

Carlyle expressed similar impatience with the resistance of the Irish to neat classifications: 'Black-lead them and put them over with the niggers' was his perfunctory solution to the Irish question.[4]

This lack of fixed boundaries, of clear racial markers, has led some commentators to conclude that there was no rational basis for the 'ancient quarrel' between Ireland and England, and that the separatist movement was fuelled simply by the wilful obscurantism of Irish nationalism. In a trenchant discussion calling for a reappraisal of Irish colonial stereotypes, Sheridan Gilley argues that 'since an objective criterion of race like skin colour is lacking to define Saxon dislike of the Celts, there is a difficulty of definition in deciding at what point vague talk about Celtic character amounts to "racial prejudice"'.[5] So far from evincing the kind of repulsion and hatred characteristic of racism, Gilley contends that English attitudes towards the Irish were distinguished by a spirit of toleration and a willingness to accommodate Irish difference. As *The Times* put it in an editorial after the Clerkenwell prison bombing in 1867:

> This is not a quarrel of race with race, nation with nation, or people with people,
> but between isolation, exclusion, inhospitality, and egotism, on the Irish side, and
> liberality, hospitality and neighbourliness on ours. . . . The Irish portion of this
> mixed community [in England] is quite as large as any that could call itself pure
> Saxon.[6]

Oblivious to the irony in the phrase 'Killing Home Rule with Kindness', Gilley proceeds to point out that apologists for imperial rule such as Matthew Arnold advocated a commingling of the Saxon and the Celt, and called for an infusion of Celtic blood into the enervated body politic of post-Benthamite England. This apparent magnanimity is hardly consistent with the fears about intermarriage and miscegenation which stalked the deep south in America, and as such it is an important corrective to a simplistic equation of the plight of the native Irish with that of the black population in the southern states of the USA, or in other British colonies. But while Gilley is right to emphasize that the analogy with the oppression of black people cannot be fully sustained, it does not follow that this was the only model of racism available to colonial regimes.[7] Far more important for understanding the distinctive character of Irish stereotypes was the analogy with the native Americans, or American Indians, an analogy, moreover, which had a foundation in the shared historical experience of being at the receiving end of the first systematic wave of colonial expansion. Research by historians such as D. B. Quinn and Nicholas Canny has suggested that it was Ireland – 'that famous island in the Virginian sea', as Fynes Morison called it – which helped to turn the attention of the Elizabethan settlers towards America, and many of the earliest colonizers of the New World such as Humphrey Gilbert and Walter Raleigh alternated between Ireland and Virginia or Newfoundland.[8] In this initial phase, there was far less confidence about the absorptive powers of English civilization, and Lord Mountjoy, for example, warned of the dangers of succumbing to the primitive native culture in Ireland (the fate of the previous settlers which he designates the English-Irish):

> Because the Irish and English-Irish were obstinate in Popish superstition, great care was thought fit to be taken that these new colonies should consist of such men as were most unlike to fall to the barbarous customs of the Irish, or the Popish superstition of Irish and English-Irish, so as no less cautions were to be observed for uniting them and keeping them from mixing with each other than if these new colonies were to be led to inhabit among the barbarous Indians.[9]

This type of comparison between the subject populations of both colonies established a network of affinities that was to recur in descriptions of both the Irish and the Indians. Referring to the 'booleys' or wigwams built from the bark of walnut trees and mats, Thomas Morton remarked in 1632 that 'the natives of New England are accustomed to build their houses much like the wild Irish' and this perception of a common primitive culture also extended to dress and sleeping habits. When Shane O'Neill presented himself at the court of Queen Elizabeth in 1562, decked out in a vivid saffron cloak, the historian Camden wrote that he was looked upon with as much wonderment as if he had come from 'China and America'. William Strachey frequently couched descriptions of the Indians in Irish terms, remarking of their sleeping habits that 'some lie stark naked on the ground from six to twenty in a house, as do the Irish', and observing of their fashions that 'the married women wear their hair all of a length, shaven, as the Irish, by a dish'.[10] What is important for the purposes of understanding the implicit primitivist assumptions underlying these apparently casual observations on the state of the Irish peasantry is that comparisons with the American Indians persisted well beyond the initial period of conquest. Visiting Ireland on the eve of the Famine in 1839, Gustave de Beaumont, who had travelled widely in both the old and the new world, wrote ominously that the state of the Irish peasant was so wretched that he did not even have the redeeming qualities of the noble savage:

> I have seen the Indian in his forests and the negro in his irons, and I believed, in pitying their plight, that I saw the lowest ebb of human misery; but I did not then know the degree of poverty to be found in Ireland. Like the Indian, the Irishman is poor and naked; but he lives in the midst of a society which enjoys luxury, honours and wealth. . . . The Indian retains a certain independence which has its attraction and a dignity of its own. Poverty-stricken and hungry he may be, but he is free in his desert places; and the feeling that he enjoys this

liberty blunts the edge of his sufferings. But the Irishman undergoes the same
deprivations without enjoying the same liberty, he is subjected to regulations: he
dies of hunger. He is governed by laws; a sad condition, which combines the
vices of civilization with those of primitive life. Today the Irishman enjoys neither
the freedom of the savage nor the bread of servitude.[11]

There is even evidence that the comparison of the native Irish to American
Indians as a justification of conquest has survived down to the present day in
loyalist popular memory in Northern Ireland. As Anthony Buckley reports in
his ethnographic study of Ulster Protestants:

I have heard many individuals separately state, viz. 'nobody expects that
America should be given back to the Indians' (or Australia to the Aborgines). In
part, this familiar statement is a plea to let bygones be bygones: 'it all happened
a long time ago'. In part, however, it also contains an imperialist rhetoric that
Protestants in Ireland, like white people in America, Australia, and elsewhere in
the British Empire, have been the bringers of Christianity and civilization.[12]

De Beaumont's sympathetic observations show that the apparently carefree
lifestyle of the Indian was not without its appeal to the white sensibility: yet there
is little doubt that the American Indians were also the victims of some of the
gravest acts of genocide ever perpetrated by white supremacist policies, policies,
moreover, which owed a considerable amount of their impetus to the initial Irish
pattern of conquest.[13] In a recent comparison of the image of the Indian and the
black in American history, Michael Rogin has pointed out that Indians were not
viewed with the kind of virulent hatred which whites reserved for blacks, but
were often treated with bemused fascination and the type of paternalist affection
which adults display towards children. Like the Irish, and in marked contrast to
blacks, fears of miscegenation and interracial contact did *not* figure prominently
in the white demonology of the Indian. In fact, all the mitigating or 'positive'
features which, in Sheridan Gilley's view, extenuate the British from charges of
racism with regard to Irish people, were evident in American attitudes towards
the Indians, including the crucial expectation that they commingle with the
whites and, in Andrew Jackson's words, 'become merged in the mass of our
population'. The alternative to assimilation, however, was the stark prospect of
annihilation: like Shakespearean drama, this particular racist scenario ended in
either marriage or tragedy. As the US House Committee on Indian Affairs forecast
in 1818: 'In the present state of our country one of two things seem to be necessary, either that those sons of the forest should be moralized or exterminated.'[14]

The extermination of the Indian way of life, if not the Indians themselves, was
facilitated by the convenient belief that they were children of nature, 'sons of
the forest', and thus were bereft of even the most meagre forms of civilization:

The Indian is hewn out of rock. . . . [wrote Francis Parkman] He will not
learn the arts of civilization, and he and the forest must perish together. The

stern, unchanging features of his mind excite our admiration from their very immutability; and we look with deep interest on the fate of this irreclaimable son of the wilderness, the child who will not be weaned from the breast of his rugged mother.[15]

The Indian remained at a primitive oral stage, and had not made the transition to the symbolic order of civilization. Ironically, this was the attribute of Indian society, translated into an opposition between speech or oral tradition on the one hand, and the acquisition of writing on the other, which led to its rehabilitation by Rousseau, and indeed by a tradition of romantic primitivism in anthropology extending down to Claude Lévi-Strauss at the present day. Oral culture, in this sense, is seen as a source of plenitude and stability, of a prelapsarian innocence or communion with nature before the fall brought about by the invention of letters. The primacy of speech, the voice of experience, attests to the authenticity of a culture, presenting, as Derrida puts it, 'the image of a community immediately present to itself, without difference, a community of speech where all the members are within earshot' of one another.[16]

The problem with this form of romantic primitivism, as it presented itself to native Irish historians in the eighteenth century, was that such a state of primordial innocence offered an open invitation to conquest. The plenitude of an original, oral state of nature, as Derrida argues, is paradoxically constituted by what it lacks, in this case the absence of 'civilization': 'the unity of nature or the identity of origin is shaped and undermined by a strange difference which constitutes it by breaching it'.[17] If apologists for colonialism in the new world insisted on portraying America as 'virgin' territory, as if its native inhabitants were simply hewn out of the rock formations which dominated the landscape, then it was decidedly in the interests of native Irish historians to deny that Ireland was ever in a state of nature, and that it was culturally inscribed from the dawn of antiquity. The difficulty with this position was that the testimony on which it was based depended to a large extent on an oral heritage, and thus had to contend with a prejudice *against* popular memory, derived ultimately from the Protestant valorization of the written word at the expense of custom and tradition. The *locus classicus* for this attack on oral culture was John Locke's argument that whereas an original text ('the attested copy of a record') bears witness to truth, in tradition '*each remove weakens the force of the proof*; and the more hands the tradition has successively passed through, the less evidence and strength does it receive from them'.[18] In this schema, the *written* text enjoys the status of an originating presence, and is the standard against which the inferior claims to truth of speech and tradition may be judged.

Hence the relative ease with which those who opposed the enlisting of cultural nationalism in the cause of Catholic emancipation at the end of the eighteenth century could reject native pretensions to an ancient Irish civilization. According to David Hume, tradition lacked the clear-cut simplicity of scripture in that it was 'complex, contradictory and, on many occasions, doubtful'. 'Popish legends' not only led to a fragmentation of truth – 'though every one, almost, believed a part of these stories, yet no one could believe or know the whole' – but also lacked foundations, the grounds of knowledge: 'all must have acknowledged [of tradition], that no one part stood on a better foundation than the rest'.[19] Hume lost little time in extending this critique to Irish culture, arguing that tradition and popular memory were indistinguishable from credulity and superstition:

> As the rudeness and ignorance of the Irish were extreme. . . The ancient superstitions, the practices and observations of their fathers, mingled and polluted with many wild opinions, still maintained an unshaken empire over them, and the example alone of the English was sufficient to render the reformation odious to the prejudices of the discontented Irish . . . The subduing and civilizing of that country seemed to become every day more difficult and impracticable.[20]

Faced with this dismissal of what they considered their intellectual birthright, it is not surprising that Irish historians, whether of native or old English stock, took considerable pains (and an even more considerable degree of poetic licence) to argue that the ancient Irish acquired literacy and kept written records in the pre-historic era. As early as 1633, in what is perhaps the pioneering work in Irish historiography, and the last great Irish book to be circulated in manuscript form, Geoffrey Keating wrote that both the accuracy and the extent of the ancient 'chronicles of the Kingdom' was such that it procured for the Irish 'a superior esteem to the antiquities of any other nation, except the Jewish, throughout the world'.[21] By the eighteenth century, this had been transformed into an argument that the Irish, by virtue of their alleged Phoenician ancestry, had actually invented letters, and introduced the alphabet to classical Greece. In 1753, in the first systematic history of Ireland in the modern mode, Charles O'Conor could assert 'that our nation and language are coeval':

> the annals of the nation were, from a very early age, committed to writing. Blind tradition, or ulterior invention, could never, in ages of simplicity, and so distant from each other, concur in so many marks of authenticity.

This was part of a general counter-offensive by a new wave of Irish historians which posited the existence of an *original* Irish civilization, rivalling Greece and Rome in its cultural attainments. If subsequent generations – indeed epochs – have receded from the plenitude of this founding moment, then there is at least the consolation, as O'Conor puts it in characteristically Lockean terms, 'that our copy of the earliest times, is pretty just to the original'.[22]

The difficulty with this argument was that it had to account for an extensive amount of mimetic shortfall to compensate for the gap between the glories of the past and the destitute condition of the mass of the Irish population in the eighteenth century. Native historians had to face Edmund Spenser's taunt, quoted with evident satisfaction by Thomas Campbell as part of an assault against native historians in 1789: 'if such "old scholars", why so unlearned still?'[23] Why, in other words, was there so little to show of the achievement of remote antiquity? The obvious answer was the destruction wrought by conquest; but to acknowledge the disruptive effect of successive invasions was to concede the discontinuous, fragmented nature of Irish history – the charge levelled at tradition by critics such as Hume. It was precisely for this reason that conservative minded nationalists sought to impose a coherent narrative form on the amorphous mass of Irish history, discerning a totalizing design in what A. M. Sullivan was later to refer to as 'the Story of Ireland'. As Charles Gavan Duffy expressed it in the 1840s: 'The history of Ireland abounded in noble lessons, and had the unity and purpose of an epic poem'.[24]

This provided a cue for *race* to enter the proceedings on the nationalist side, securing the image of an embattled people surviving intact and maintaining unity in the face of two thousand years of upheaval, invasion and oppression. The concept of race also helped to explain the persistence of continuity in the midst of change and, even more to the point, the racial notion of an original native purity allowed nationalists to cite the effects of conquest to explain away some of the less desirable aspects of Irish life, attributing them to the slave's propensity to mimic his master's vices. As Douglas Hyde expressed it in his lecture on 'The Necessity for De-Anglicizing Ireland', one of the founding texts of the Literary Revival:

> The Irish race is at present in a most anomalous position, imitating England and yet apparently hating it. How can it produce anything good in literature, art, or institutions as long as it is actuated by motives so contradictory? Besides, I believe it is our Gaelic past which, though the Irish race does not recognize it just at present, is really at the bottom of the Irish heart, and prevents us becoming citizens of the Empire.[25]

In the hands of less astute propagandists, race became a scouring agent, removing from the Irish people all the impurities acquired through contamination by the 'Saxon foe'. In an unabashed tirade entitled *The Celt Above the Saxon*, published at the turn of the century, Fr. C. J. Herlihy sought to restore Ireland's reputation as an island of saints, scholars and sobriety:

> How many Englishmen ever reflect that England is responsible for [the] intemperance of the Irish? Our Celtic ancestors were a very temperate people before the English landed on their shores. In the time of St. Patrick drunkenness was unknown amongst them. In all his writings the great apostle does not even refer once to Irish intemperance. It was only after they lost their independence that this vice broke out among the Irish; and when we take into consideration all they suffered from English tyranny during the last seven hundred years, can we be astonished that they turned to drink?[26]

For Gilley this would exemplify the ambivalence and essentially contested nature of Irish colonial stereotypes, for here is clearly a case of attributing an

English provenance to a trait of national character that was, unfortunately, home grown: 'behind the English conception of the Irish', concludes Gilley, 'lies the Irish idea of the Irishman', as if colonial rule had no role at all to play in fabricating the self-images of the Irish.[27] What Gilley conveniently overlooks, however, is that the process is a two-way (albeit unequal) transaction, and that many of the concepts requisitioned by nationalist propagandists in defence of Irish culture are, in fact, an extension of colonialism, rather than a repudiation of it. The racial concept of an Irish national character is a case in point: the mimicry of English life castigated by Douglas Hyde may have extended down to the concept of 'the Irish race' which he posited to counteract alien influences. The 'Celt', and by implication the Celtic revival, owed as much to eighteenth-century primitivism and the benevolent colonialism of Matthew Arnold as it did to the inner recesses of the hidden Ireland, and the facility with which Gilley construes the Arnoldian stereotype as benign – in fact, as not a stereotype at all – explains how it could be taken to heart by Irish revivalists. The racial mode is, moreover, the version of Irish nationalism which has passed into general academic circulation in recent years through the revisionist writings of Conor Cruise O'Brien and F. S. L. Lyons (among others) – largely, one suspects, because it redefines even resistance within a racist colonial frame and thus neutralizes the very idea of anti-colonial discourse.[28]

Yet not all the concepts of Irishness which emerged under the aegis of cultural nationalism were dependent on racial modes of identity. Indeed, it is worth noting that while moderate, anti-republican politicians such as Arthur Griffith voiced some of the most bigoted expressions of nationalism (to the point of condoning black slavery, for instance), others associated with militant republicanism rejected racial concepts out of hand on account of their exclusivity, and their simplistic approach to historical change.[29] In his posthumous work *Literature in Ireland* (published after his execution as one of the leaders of the 1916 Rising), the poet and critic Thomas MacDonagh took issue with the Arnoldian idea of 'the Celtic Note' on the grounds that it carried with it unacceptable racial undertones:

> I have little sympathy with the criticism that marks off subtle qualities in literature as altogether racial, that refuses to admit natural exceptions in such a naturally exceptional thing as high literature, attributing only the central body to the national genius, the marginal portions to this alien strain or that.[30]

MacDonagh's thinking on this point was greatly influenced by the outstanding translator and scholar, Dr. George Sigerson (to whom, in fact, he dedicated his book). In a series of works beginning as early as 1868, Sigerson sought to remove the racial epithet 'Celtic' entirely from the cultural canon, arguing that Irishness incorporated the residue of several cultural or 'racial' strains, as befitted a country exposed to successive waves of invasion and internal strife over the centuries.[31] This carried with it the implication that history did not run in a straight line from the Milesians to the Celtic revival, but was closer to an alluvial deposit, secreting an unstable, porous version of Irish identity. As David Hume rightly observed, the lack of secure foundations prevented the most dynamic strands in Irish nationalism from succumbing to 'fixed dogmas and principles'.[32]

The construction of a continuous, unaltered tradition, stretching back to remote antiquity, can be seen, in fact, as precisely a colonial imposition, an attempt to emulate in an Irish context the Burkean model of the English constitution based on an organic theory of community and the inherited wisdom of the ages. The past can be eulogized when it is truly dead and gone and when even revolution leads to social stability, but these comforting sentiments were not so easily transferrable to a country such as Ireland in which history was still a matter of unfinished business. As a commentator in *The Nation* newspaper put it, writing at the height of the Famine in 1847, England's reassuring image of a common, unified past — a society in which 'history knits together all ranks and sects' — is strangely at odds with the uneven, fractured course of Irish history:

> There are bright spots in our history; but of how few is the story common! and the contemplation of it, *as a whole*, does not tend to harmony, unless the conviction of past error produces wisdom for the future. We have no institution or idea that has been produced by all. We must look to the present or future for the foundations of concord and nationality.[33]

There was nothing organic about Irish history, despite the best attempts of the editors of *The Nation* to make it 'racy of the soil'.

Hence in the case of the Ossian controversy that raged in the latter half of the eighteenth century, it was precisely Macpherson's claim to faithfully reproduce the originals, to be in perfect communion with the past, which aroused the suspicions of his most perceptive Irish critics. Notwithstanding his emphasis elsewhere that 'many volumes of well-authenticated records have escaped the ravages of time and of foreign spoils', the antiquarian Joseph Cooper Walker's comments on Oisin (as he was called in Ireland) show that he had no illusion about the preservative power of either antiquarian texts or traditions:

> Only a few fragments of his works, and those much mutilated and ill-authenticated, have come down to us. Indeed, had his productions reached us in a state of original perfection, our best Irish scholars would have found much difficulty in translating them; for there are many passages, in Irish poems of the fifth and sixth centuries, which seem at present, and *probably ever will remain*, inexplicable. Yet, we are told, that the poems of Oisin are recited and sung, at this day, by ignorant Scottish hinds, though the characters of the language, in which they were composed, are as unintelligible to the modern Scots, as the hieroglyphics of the Egyptians.[34]

The impossibility of gaining direct access to the past is not because it is sealed off, as in a time capsule, but because it is part of an unresolved historical process which engulfs the present. It is lived history that prevents the kind of omniscient narration envisaged by Locke which sees texts as transparent windows on the past. The romantic nostalgia for Ossian, and its vogue in the metropolitan centre, was not unrelated to the fact that after the Battle of Culloden, and the elimination of the Jacobite threat, it was relatively safe to rake over the embers of the Scottish past.[35] But such an option was not available in Ireland: the past was not simply part of recorded history but *remembered* history, an open-ended narrative which was not safely interred in texts (as Hume would have it) but continued to haunt contemporary political struggles. As Donal McCartney has written with reference to the constant invocation of key historical events such as the 1641 rebellion and the 1691 Treaty of Limerick, in the campaign that led to Catholic emancipation in 1829:

> With our eyes on the 1829 act, we may say that a single topic from Irish history kept constantly before an organized people and forced upon the intentions of parliament, had tremendous influence in altering the law of the United Kingdom. The treaty argument [of Limerick, 1691], which passed out of the written page and penetrated the walls of parliament, was more than the mere spearhead of the emancipation struggle. For, like 1641, the interpretations of 1691 never passed into history, inasmuch as they never passed out of politics.[36]

Texts, in other words, were not simply *about* history: they were part of history, fragments of a past that still awaited completion.

In his essay on '*Ulysses* in History', Fredric Jameson cites Roland Barthes in support of his observation that under the impact of modernity, the gap between meaning and existence, the representation and the real, has widened:

> The pure and simple 'presentation' of the 'real', the naked account of 'what is' (or what has been), thus proves to resist meaning; such resistance reconfirms the great mythic opposition between the vécu [that is, the experiential or what the existentialists called 'lived experience'] and the intelligible . . . as though, by some de jure exclusion, what lives is structurally incapable of carrying a meaning – and vice versa.[37]

Reality has become dislocated from structures of signification, and takes the form of the random impression, the passing moment or the descent into the contingency of the detail. Yet, as David Frisby writes, if

> modernity as a distinctive mode of experiencing (social) reality involves seeing society and the social relations within it as (temporally) transitory and (spatially) fleeting then this implies, conversely, that traditional, *permanent* structures are now absent from human experiences.[38]

As to the source of these 'traditional, permanent structures', Nietzsche, for one, had no doubt where it lay: in history, or more accurately in historicism, precisely that view of the past which looks to tradition to confer a permanent structure on experience.[39] If we turn to Ireland, however, it will be seen that it is history itself which is irrevocably scarred with the traces of contingency. The fall from grace brought about by writing, the violent wrenching of tradition by the advent of the text, was present in Irish history from the very outset. In the novels of Walter Scott, or even in the Ossianic poems, the invocation of the past often had a therapeutic effect, the distance in time affording a common ground and a sense of stability which ensured that history was kept firmly in its place. This is the complacent historicism to which Nietzsche objected so strenuously. But in Ireland the recourse to history was the problem. As a writer in the appropriately entitled *The Voice of the Nation* expressed it in 1844:

> In other countries the past is the neutral ground of the scholar and the antiquary; with us it is the battlefield.[40]

As a result of this Irish culture did not have to await modernity to undergo the effects of fragmentation – the cult of the fragment was itself the stuff from which history was made. The sense of disintegration and 'unconditional presentness' (Simmel) which exerted such a fascination for writers from Baudelaire to Benjamin was pre-eminently spatial, the result of a new topology of social relations in the metropolis. In Ireland, however, it was bound up with *temporality*, as the endless preoccupation with ruins and remnants of ancient manuscripts in cultural nationalism made all too evident. In mainstream romanticism (if such a generalization may be permitted), ruins represented the triumph of natural forces over human endeavour, and if at one level this was a process of destruction and decay, at another level it was redeemed as a higher totalizing moment, in the form of a trans-historical communion with nature. For George Simmel, the nature-encrusted ruin was of a piece with the organicist conception of history which came so easily to countries in control of their own destinies:

> The charm of a ruin resides in the fact that it presents a work of man while giving the impression of being a work of nature. . . . The upward thrust, the erection of the building, was the result of human will, while its present appearance results from the mechanical force of nature, whose power of decay draws things downwards. . . . Nature has used man's work of art as the material for its own creation, just as art had previously taken nature as its raw material.[41]

In Ireland, by contrast, as David Lloyd has shown, ruins were the result not of a clash between nature and culture, but between several opposing cultures, the debris of a history of invasions. In a state of seditious reverie, the United Irishman William Drennan meditated on the round tower of Glendalough, Co. Wicklow, which he saw as 'raising its head above the surrounding fragments, as if moralizing on the ruins of the country, and the wreck of legislative independence.'[42] Or as the narrator of James Clarence Mangan's lament on the ruins of the Abbey at Timoleague has it:

– Tempest and Time – the drifting sands –
The lightning and the rains – the seas that sweep around
These hills in winter-nights, have awfully crowned
The work of impious hands! . . .

Where wert thou, Justice, in that hour?
Where was thy smiting sword? What had those good men done,
That thou shouldst tamely see them trampled on
By brutal England's Power?[43]

The conviction that it was history in its refractory Irish variant which led to the shedding of experience formed the basis of one of the most powerful contemporary critiques of James Joyce, that formulated in Wyndham Lewis' *Time and Western Man*. Lewis was impatient enough with the accumulation of detail in naturalistic fiction as language sought to catch up with the proliferation of sense-data unleashed by modernity. But in Joyce, even this took a turn for the worse, for in his obsession with place and the relations between objects, his writing dispenses with the graphic clarity that is necessary to fix the contours of, and impart solidity to, the objects in our environment:

The local colour, or locally coloured material, that was scraped together into a big variegated heap to make *Ulysses*, is – doctrinally even more than in fact – the material of the Past. . . . As a careful, even meticulous craftsman, with a long training of doctrinaire naturalism, the detail – the time detail as much as anything else – assumes an exaggerated importance for him. . . . The painful preoccupation with the *exact* place of things in a room, for instance, could be mildly matched in his writing. The *things themselves* by which he is surrounded lose, for the hysterical subject, their importance, or even meaning. Their *position* absorbs all the attention of his mind.[44]

If Joyce's language dissolved the objective world into subjective experience, then that at least would offer the consolation of stabilizing the subject, of consolidating the ego of the narrator, the author and, indeed, the reader. But this is not what happens: the torrent of Joyce's prose carries all before it, leaving no room for a transcendental essence on either side: at the level of brute reality, or the numinous realm of the sovereign self. 'No one who looks *at* it,' Lewis writes, 'will ever want to look *behind* it', and he continues, with reference to the persistence of history in related, aberrant forms of modernism:

You lose not only the clearness of outline, the static beauty, of the things you commonly apprehend; you lose also the clearness of outline of your own individuality which apprehends them . . . 'you' become the series of your temporal repetitions; you are no longer a centralized self, but a spun-out, strung along series . . . you are a *history*: there must be no Present for you. You are an historical object, since your mental or time-life has been as it were objectified. The valuable advantages of being a 'subject' will perhaps scarcely be understood by the race of *historical objects* that may be expected to ensue.[45]

Joyce's use of language – in *Ulysses* at any rate – bears an inescapable resemblance to the fractured course of oral tradition which drew the fire of Lockean inspired critics of native Irish history in the eighteenth century. It is akin to the language of rumour, as analysed by Gayatri Chakravorty Spivak, that is to say, to a form of spoken utterance which carries back into its innermost structure the effects of spacing and rupturing which, according to Derrida, characterize written texts.[46] Rumour or tradition, in this sense, is not available to the detached reader or spectator but only to the active – one is tempted to say the *committed* – participant in social communication. Yet if it presupposes a face-to-face setting, it cannot be taken at face value for, unlike the phonocentric voice, it does not carry with it its own authenticity. As Spivak writes:

> Rumour evokes comradeship because it belongs to every 'reader' or 'transmitter'. No one is its origin or source. Thus rumour is not error but primordially (originarily) errant, always in circulation with no assignable source. This illegitimacy makes it accessible to insurgency.[47]

The amorphousness which Barthes attributes to existence, to the surplus or excess of the real which constantly eludes signification, is here the hallmark of language itself, and it is this above all which threatens the imperious eye of Wyndham Lewis: 'whatever I, for my part, say, can be traced back to an organ; but in my case it is *the eye*. It is in the service of the thing of vision that my ideas are mobilized.'[48] The problem with Joyce, however, was that 'He thought in words*, not images', and this forfeited any chance of stabilizing the flux of events by discerning the organic totality of experience:[49]

> Where a multitude of little details or some obvious idiosyncracy are concerned, he may be said to be observant; but the secret of an *entire* organism escapes him.[50]

As Fredric Jameson has stated, 'the visual, the spatially visible, the image is . . . the final form of the commodity itself, the ultimate terminus of reification', and yet, as he goes on to note, one of the minor but astonishing triumphs of Joyce's prose is that he succeeds in inserting even a sandwichboard man – the ultimate in both visual and human reification – back into a network of social and historical relations: 'Everything seemingly material and solid in Dublin itself can presumably be dissolved back into the underlying reality of human relations and human praxis.'[51]

Jameson's and Lewis' insistence on the unremitting temporality of Joyce's writing contrasts starkly with Franco Moretti's attempt to annex Joyce for the metropolitan centre, and to disenfranchise him of both his Irishness and his profound engagement with history:

> *Ulysses* is indeed static, and in its world nothing – absolutely nothing – is great. But this is not due to any technical or ideal shortcoming on Joyce's part, but rather to his subjection to English society: for Joyce, it is certainly the only society imaginable . . . (whatever has emerged from the studies that interpreted Joyce on the basis of Ireland?)[52]

Whatever about Moretti, Wyndham Lewis, for one, had no illusions about
Joyce's Irishness, and it is difficult not to suspect that underneath the elaborate
tracery of his critique of Joyce lay a colonial frustration with a form of cultural
difference which offered intense resistance to what Homi Bhabha, following
Freud, terms the scopic drive – or what an Irish dramatist has called 'the artillery of the eye'. In an extraordinary appendix to his study of Shakespeare, *The
Lion and the Fox*, Lewis launched a sustained assault on those critics such as
Renan, Lord Morley and Matthew Arnold who claimed that Shakespeare owed
his genius to the Celtic strain in his personality. This was too much to take.
Lewis heaped abuse on the exponents of this heresy and sought, in the process, to demolish the very foundations of the Celtic claim to be a separate
race. Interestingly, these foundations, in his estimation, could only be based
on *visual* characteristics, and their absence, for Lewis, was sufficient proof
there was no difference at all between the Irish and the English. In a remarkable passage, he writes of his response to the funeral of Terence McSwiney, the
republican lord mayor of Cork, whose death by hunger strike in 1920 proved
a turning point in the Irish War of Independence:

> During the martyrdom of the Lord Mayor of Cork I had several opportunities of
> seeing considerable numbers of irish people [Lewis refused to capitalize adjectives
> referring to nationality] demonstrating among the London crowds. I was never able
> to distinguish which were irish and which were english, however. They looked to
> me exactly the same. With the best will in the world to discriminate the orderly
> groups of demonstrators from the orderly groups of spectators, and to satisfy the
> romantic proprieties on such an occasion, my eyes refused to effect the necessary
> separation, that the principle of 'celtism' demanded, into chalk and cheese. I should
> have supposed that they were a lot of romantic english-people pretending to be
> irish people, and demonstrating with the assistance of a few priests and pipers, if it
> had not been that they all looked extremely depressed, and english-people when
> they are giving romance the rein are always very elated.[53]

There is a certain macabre irony in Lewis' persistence in adhering to an
'epidermal schema' (to cite Franz Fanon's phrase), to visible bodily differences,
in a context in which the dematerialization of the body through hunger
striking is itself a means of affording political resistance. Lewis's dogged refusal
to register the traumatic reverberations of McSwiney's funeral at anything
other than a visual level is, in effect, an attempt to reduce it to *spectacle*. As
such, it is consistent with his desire to remove all traces of history from the
colonial experience, for it was precisely spectacle, in its collective modern
variant, which sought to step outside history, transforming it into a set of
horizontal, spatial relations.[54] As if to pre-empt this erasure of history, the
nationalist response to McSwiney's funeral inserted history back into spectacle,
seeing it as a means, in Benjamin's terms, of blasting open the centuries-old
continuum of British rule in Ireland. As the anonymous writer of a contemporary pamphlet on the hunger strike wrote:

A prominent man, occupying an eminent position, holding the chief office in one of the most important cities in his country, offers himself as a *spectacle* to the world that it may behold in him a *living document* of the secular injustice of England. . . . The crisis has come . . . with a swiftness that is without parallel in our time. Old solutions are discarded. The new wine is bursting in old bottles. . . . There may be other factors in the accomplishment of this astounding conversion, brought about as it has been in a space of time that is, compared to the slow march of events in history, phenomenally short. These other factors it will be for the historians to rehearse when the whole drama is unfolded.[55]

Lewis may have been indifferent to the impact of McSwiney's funeral, but it devastated Irish public opinion to such an extent that even James Joyce was forced to break his silence on the War of Independence, penning a scurrilous broadside against the English authorities. The difference between Irishness and Englishness escaped Lewis' notice, but it was all too plain to those Irish people who identified with the colonial administration in their own country. After all, it was the Unionist Provost of Trinity College, Dublin, J. P. Mahaffy, who remarked:

James Joyce is a living argument in favour of my contention that it was a mistake to establish a separate university for the aborigines of this island – for the corner-boys who spit in the Liffey.[56]

13.1   Seán Hillen, 'The Oracle at O'Connell St. Bridge' (1996)

13. MONTAGE, MODERNISM AND THE CITY

Cinema is recreated in the image of the city, its emergence as a cultural form coinciding with the growth of the modern metropolis. Writing as early as 1898 in the columns of the Dublin *Daily Express*, John Eglinton saw in the new medium a portent of modernity, an icon of a technological age. Enjoining W. B. Yeats and other 'dreamers who walk with their heads in a cloud of vision' to apply their creative faculties to 'the mechanical triumphs of modern life', Eglinton wrote:

> The epics of the present age are the steam-engine and the dynamo, its lyrics the kinematograph, phonograph, etc., and these bear with them the hearts of men as the *Iliad* and *Odyssey* of former times uplifted the youth of antiquity . . .[1]

This message was apparently lost on Yeats for whom even the neon lights of O'Connell Street were signs of Armageddon, but one wonders if the possibility of an Odyssey in an age of mass production, utilizing cinematic techniques, impressed itself on the young James Joyce.

Joyce's striking use of cinematic devices such as montage is often taken as one of the most innovative aspects of *Ulysses*, the incessant collision of images simulating the disorientation and fragmentation of life in the metropolitan centre. In the eyes of many otherwise perceptive critics, this is where Joyce parts company with his Irishness: indeed the more avant-garde the idiom, the less it has to do with what is perceived as the backward state of Irish culture. According to the Italian critic Franco Moretti:

> If Joyce were an Irish writer, comprehensible and containable without any loose threads within Irish culture, he would no longer be Joyce; if the city of *Ulysses* were the real Dublin of the turn of the century, it would not be the literary image *par excellence* of the modern metropolis.

Moretti concludes on the strength of this that '*Ulysses* fully belongs to a critical turning point of international bourgeois culture – a status it would not have achieved in . . . Ireland's peripheral and backward form of capitalism (which was, moreover, dependent on the destiny of British capitalism . . .)'.[2]

Moretti's dismissal of Joyce's Irish background is based on the assumption that, as a pre-modern society, Ireland was a cultural backwater which had yet to undergo the dislocations of modernity, and hence was hardly in a position to influence the most distinctive, estranging features of Joyce's writing. There is no doubt that in advanced western countries, traditional or pre-modern culture came to be associated with stagnation and conservatism (or, in its more nostalgic variant, stability and tranquillity) and, as such, provided a useful foil for the radical incursions of modernity. Moretti appears to have something like this in mind when he speaks of Irish culture, with the proviso that the enervating hold of the past also includes the city, preventing Dublin from attaining the status of a truly urban metropolis.

Yet while tradition may appear orderly and stable from the relatively secure vantage point of the imperial centre (the privileged terrain, after all, of the leading western powers), this comforting image of the past does not lend itself to cultures on the other side of the imperial divide – countries such as Ireland skewered not only by a 'peripheral and backward form of capitalism', but by centuries of colonial depredation. During the Tricentennial celebrations of the 'Glorious Revolution' in 1988, Margaret Thatcher declared that even the revolutionary settlement of 1688, which placed William of Orange on the throne, had failed to disturb the essential composure of the British constitution. What she conveniently overlooked was that the devastation wreaked by the Williamite wars was displaced onto Irish soil, with disastrous consequences which are still with us today. History may be recollected in tranquillity by colonial powers, but this luxury hardly extends to their subject colonies. Hence the kind of 'health warnings' which were frequently attached to general histories of Ireland designed for Victorian readers brought up on the linear narratives of the Whig interpretation of history:

> The history of Ireland is marked by peculiarities which do not affect that of any other country. It comprises the remotest extremes of the social state; and sets at nought the ordinary laws of social transition and progress, during the long intervals between them. Operated on by a succession of *external* shocks, the internal advances, which form some part of all other history, have been wanting; and her broken and interrupted career, presents a dream-like succession of capricious and seemingly unconnected changes, without order or progress.[3]

This could be a description of *Ulysses*, picking up on its refusal of narrative progression, its preoccupation with the contingency of 'seemingly unconnected' details, and, of course, the cascading sequences of 'dream-like' images re-enacting the stream of consciousness. What is even more important from the point of view of cinematic techniques is the emphasis on Irish history as 'a succession of external shocks', for it was precisely in this way that Eisenstein first developed his theory of montage as the systematic use of conflict within, and between, cinematic images. The 'montage of attraction', he wrote, utilizes

> every aggressive moment in it, i.e. every element of it that brings to light in the spectator those senses or that psychology that influence his experience – every element that can be verified and mathematically calculated to produce certain emotional shocks in a proper order within the totality.[4]

The persistent recourse to 'shock tactics' in modernism, whether in the form of the semiotic sabotage of Dada ('not so much a movement, more a virus'),

Eisenstein's montage or Joyce's assault on the novel, was endorsed by Walter Benjamin on the grounds that it jolted people out of the accumulated habits of tradition, the inertia of the old order. But what if the 'old order' was already shattered, and convulsed by social upheavals to the point of being in a state of anarchy (at least according to the 'civilizing' norms of culture laid down by colonial critics such as Matthew Arnold)? In a culture traumatized by a profound sense of catastrophe, such as Ireland experienced as late as the Great Famine, is there really any need to await the importation of modernism to blast open the continuum of history?[5]

It is interesting, moreover, that in the summary of Irish history quoted above, 'the ordinary laws of social transition and progress', and 'the long intervals' between social upheavals, are suspended, with the result that the course of history constantly veers from one extreme to another. This depiction of Ireland as a country of extreme situations is one of the most pervasive set-pieces in descriptions of the Irish 'national character', whether in Tom Moore's lachrymose fusion of 'the tear and the smile', or in the more menacing figure of the 'Celtic Jekyll and Hyde', who, as described by L. P. Curtis, 'oscillated between two extremes of behaviour and mood; he was liable to rush from mirth to despair, tenderness to violence, and loyalty to treachery'.[6] Irish narrative structures, in both drama and fiction, tended to follow suit. In the barn-storming melodramas of Dion Boucicault, for example, the abrupt transitions from levity to tragedy, high-jinks to high-seriousness, forced Boucicault to revolutionize the use of stage machinery to facilitate sudden shifts in the action. These audacious forays into stage-design pushed theatre to its limits, leading film historians such as A. Nicholas Vardac and John L. Fell to discern in Boucicault's stagecraft the rudiments of film syntax: dissolves, fades, tracking shots and, of course, editing, particularly the use of rapid 'cutting' during, and between, scenes.[7]

For Eisenstein, Charles Dickens was the true precursor of cinema, but when he goes on to demonstrate the principles of montage construction in Dickens' work, it is in terms similar to Boucicault's stage techniques. Dickens' extended digression on the nature of melodrama in chapter xvii of *Oliver Twist* is taken by Eisenstein as a reflexive commentary on the novelist's own work:

> It is the custom of the stage, in all good murderous melodramas, to present the tragic and the comic scenes, as in regular alteration, as the layers of red and white on a side of streaky well-cured bacon. The hero sinks upon his straw-bed, weighed down by fetters and misfortunes; and, in the next scene, his faithful but unconscious squire regales the audience with a comic song . . . such changes appear absurd; but they are not so unnatural as they would seem at first sight. The transitions in real life from well-spread boards to death-beds, and from mourning-weeds to holiday garments, are not a whit less startling.[8]

Eisenstein is insistent, however, that this 'head spinning tempo of changing impressions' in Dickens' work comes not from his living in '"cozy" old England', wallowing in a rural past, but rather from his being 'a city artist', in fact, 'the first to bring factories, machines, and railways into literature'. It is noteworthy, by contrast, that rural Ireland – a countryside in which even the landscape is riven by political conflict – activates the same principle of montage in Boucicault's 'sensational' melodramas such as *The Colleen Bawn*, *The Shaughraun* or (Joyce's own favourite) *Arrah-na-Pogue*. It is as if the disintegration of experience visited by the city and modern life on Dickens' work was brought about by the antinomies of colonial rule in Ireland. Even before the modern era, the centre did not hold in this 'uneven and backward' culture.

If we return then to the terms of Moretti's critique of Joyce's Irishness, quoted at the outset, it can be seen that it was precisely those aspects of Irish development described as 'uneven and backward' which exerted a dynamic, formative influence on Joyce. This is not to diminish the importance of Joyce's vital contacts with the European modernist movement, but rather to say that they were enhanced and given greater intensity by his response to the cultural ferment in Ireland at the turn of the century. Unlike other urban intellectuals in both Ireland and England, Joyce had no romantic illusions about the restorative powers of the countryside and did not look to a pre-lapsarian past for an unbroken, pristine Irish identity:

> Our civilization is a vast fabric, in which the most diverse elements are mingled, in which nordic aggressiveness and Roman law, the new bourgeois conventions and the remnant of a Syriac religion are reconciled. In such a fabric, it is useless to look for a thread that may have remained pure and virgin without having undergone the influence of a neighbouring thread.[9]

This is the language of montage, the structuring of identity as the juxtaposition and commingling of opposites. Given John Eglinton's express desire, moreover, to bring cinematic techniques to bear on the Literary Revival, it is ironic that in the National Library (or 'Scylla and Charybdis') episode in *Ulysses*, Eglinton himself is identified as one of the main obstacles preventing the realization of such a project. When Eglinton, in the original 1898 controversy on 'What Should be the Subjects of a National Drama?', advised Yeats to turn to the culture of the 'kinematograph' and the phonograph, it was at the expense of ancient Irish epics which, in his view, should be safely interred, like history itself, in the past. In his fictional encounter with Stephen Dedalus in the library, Eglinton agrees that Shakespeare introduced elements of Celtic legend into *King Lear* to good effect, but denies that such intercalations of the past are permissible in modern texts:

> That was Will's way, John Eglinton defended. We should not now combine a Norse saga with an excerpt from a novel by George Meredith. *Que voulez-vous?* Moore would say. He puts Bohemia on the seacoast and makes Ulysses quote Aristotle.[10]

Stephen is not convinced by this reasoning, which is hardly surprising, seeing that he is part of a historical montage in which Ulysses speaks through the mouths of Dubliners.

In recent years, a version of Eglinton's argument has gained credence in Irish cultural debates, taking the form of a steady chorus of complaints against the disabling influence of the past, and of nationalist history in particular, on contemporary culture. Literature and cinema, according to this view, should address themselves to the realities of modernization and urban life, rather than the complacencies of traditional culture. Not least of the difficulties with this argument is that the pastoral image of the countryside singled out for criticism – that of an organic community with an enclosed, continuous past – is itself an urban construct, having little or no connection with the actualities of life in what was far from an idyllic, agrarian order. Modernity, on this reading, can do little more than deny the past (when it is suitably refashioned to suit its own dictates). Joyce's vision was more complex and unsettling than this. When Stephen Dedalus spoke of the 'nightmare of history', it was out of a conviction that the past was a destabilizing rather than a conservative force. History was a source of both attraction and repulsion – 'the montage of attractions' that is *Ulysses*.

"Begob, Eamon, there's great changes around here!"

(AUGUST, 1948)

14.1

14. UNAPPROVED ROADS:
Ireland and Post-Colonial Identity

> There might be more to be learned through a careful tracing, along paths not already guarded by the intellectual patrols of neo-imperialism, of the border lines where comparative experiences of imperial victimization and resistance meet and separate. These paths and borders, of course, are not to be found on any Cartesian plane, nor will they stay in the same place as we change our relation to them.

Jonathan Boyarin, *Storm from Paradise*

In 1948, the Irish humorous journal *Dublin Opinion* published a cartoon depicting the removal of the statue of Queen Victoria from in front of Leinster House, the Irish seat of parliament. 'Begob, Eamon', the dejected Queen commiserates with de Valera who had just lost office in a general election, 'there's great changes around here!' [Fig. 14.1]. This was indeed true, for the removal of the statue was a prologue to the official declaration of an Irish Republic in 1949, an act which formally severed the imperial connection that reached its apotheosis during her reign in the nineteenth century.

Yet the queen, for all her legendary absence of humour, may have had the last laugh. Early in 1995, a public controversy ensued when University College, Cork, as part of its 150th anniversary celebrations, decided to exhume a statue of Queen Victoria which had been buried in the grounds of the college since the 1930s, and put it on public display. This, it was argued, was doing no more than setting the historical record straight, a public acknowledgement of the fact that the university (originally called Queen's College, Cork) was founded under a Victorian administration.

But this is not the way history, or rather memory, operates in a culture with a colonial past; for 1845 was not only the year in which the Queen's Colleges were established, it also marked the beginning of a more painful reminder of Victorian rule, the Great Famine (1845–8).[1] At the opening of the exhibition in which the statue was included, a protester was arrested for interrupting the proceedings with shouts of 'What about the Famine?' Though dismissed by some as a nationalist crank, the protester was also seeking to register a profound loss of memory, a traumatic episode in Irish history that was no less effectively buried by officialdom, both before and after independence, than Queen Victoria's moving statues.[2]

How is it possible to accommodate these disparate legacies of the Victorian era within the narratives of Irish identity? According to one influential strand in contemporary cultural theory, the answer lies in post-colonial strategies of cultural mixing, that is, embracing notions of 'hybridity' and 'syncretism' rather than

171

obsolete ideas of nation, history or indigenous culture. This, after all, is what is meant by the designation 'post'-colonialism, and all its works and pomps, is deemed to be over and done with (if, indeed, it ever existed in the first place), and the time has come to draw a line over the past. In his highly schematic but instructive overview of the four stages of culture formation mapped out by post-colonial theory, Thomas McEvilley identifies, first, the idyllic pre-colonial period, the subject of much subsequent nationalist nostalgia; second, the ordeal of conquest, of alienation, oppression and internal colonization; third, the nationalist reversal 'which not only denigrates the identity of the colonizer, but also redirects . . . attention to the recovery and reconstitution of [a] once scorned and perhaps abandoned identity',[3] and fourth, the stage ushered in by the generation born after the departure of the colonizing forces, which is less concerned with opposition to the colonial legacy – a situation which arose in India and Africa 'about 25 years after the withdrawal of colonialist armies and governments'. It is this latter phase which lends itself to the free play of hybridity and cultural mixing – and also to the distancing project of the diaspora in which immigrants from ex-colonies renegotiate their ancestral ties in terms of the global demands of their new host culture.

But while the past may be a distant country, it is not so different for those cultures engaged in a centuries-old struggle against western colonization. The belief that the restoration of Queen Victoria's statue was an inoffensive gesture in the context of an historical arc spanning 1845–1995 could only make sense if the Great Famine in Ireland was a thing of the past, a phase of history that could now be safely consigned to the communal Prozac of the heritage industry. But can the wounds inflicted by a social catastrophe be so easily cauterized? Would anyone seriously suggest that the traumatic lessons of the Holocaust shouldn't be as pertinent in a hundred years time as they are today? Or – to take an example that touches directly on colonialism and the displacement of the diaspora – that novels such as Toni Morrison's *Beloved* are valuable merely for their re-creation of the ordeal of slavery as it was endured 150 years ago but have little to do with the *lived experience* of the African-American population in the contemporary United States?

What we are dealing with here are different registers of memory, one that is contained and legitimized within the confines of the monument and the museum, and the other having to do with the endangered traces of collective memory, as transmitted by popular culture, folklore, ballads, and so on. In this respect, the contestation of museum space in Philip Napier's exhibit, *Ballad* [Fig. 14.2], at the 'Beyond the Pale' exhibition in the Irish Museum of Modern Art (1994–5) is remarkable.[4] It features an accordion mounted on a wall whose intake and expelling of air allows it to double up as an artificial lung attached to the barely decipherable image of the republican hunger-striker, Bobby Sands. The blown-up photogravure effect of the image is achieved through small nails, a reminder of the aura of martyrdom which surrounded Sands' death on hunger strike in 1981. The wheezing moans of the accordion extend beyond the individual body, however,

14.2 Napier, 'Ballad no. 1' (1992–4)

14.3 'The Ballad Singer', from *Illustrated London News* (29 October 1881)

evoking some of the more discordant strains in Irish vernacular culture. Not only do the eerie sounds waft through museum space like the wail of the mythical *banshee* in Irish folklore[5] but the instrument itself signifies traditional music, more particularly the street singer and the popular ballads that were repeatedly targeted by the authorities as cultural expressions of insurgency [Fig. 14.3]. By linking the famished body with mourning and collective memory, the off-key image becomes, in effect, a living monument for the Famine and the dark shadow which it cast on the lung of the Irish body politic.

The mythic resonances of the *banshee* and vernacular culture are also evident in the figurations of hair and long female tresses central to Alice Maher's recent work. Although the *banshee* is more often heard than seen, sightings of the phantom figure portray her as an old woman, combing her long white hair as she laments. In Alice Maher's *Familiar* [Fig. 14.4] series, undulating braids of hair are given an additional historical twist by being recreated through the medium of flax – a material, according to the artist, that is 'interwoven with a thousand meanings and histories'.[6] One of the meanings is the association with women's work and the relative financial independence which cottage industry afforded for women in pre-Famine Ireland. Another historical connection, however, derives from the destruction of the once thriving Irish wool trade by British colonial policy, and its replacement by a linen industry, based mainly in northern Ireland. The 'hybridity' of these exhibits is clear from their indeterminate boundaries: between organic and fabricated materials, nature and culture, native and newcomer.

Of course, there are proponents of hybridity who refuse to consider Ireland as a suitable case for post-colonial treatment at all. Though the authors of one 'comprehensive study' find the term 'post-colonial' expansive enough to include not only the literatures of India, Africa, and the Caribbean but also Canada, Australia, and even the United States, no place is found for Irish literature. The reason for this becomes apparent later on, when Irish, Welsh, and Scottish literatures are discussed 'in relation to the English "mainstream"':

> While it is possible to argue that these societies were the first victims of English expansion, their subsequent complicity in the British imperial enterprise makes it difficult for colonized peoples outside Britain to accept their identity as post-colonial.[7]

This remarkable statement (which does not appear to include Ireland as one of those countries 'outside Britain') only makes sense if one identifies the Irish historically with the settler colony in Ireland, the ruling Anglo-Irish interest, thus erasing in the process the entire indigenous population – a view closer, in fact, to 'Commonwealth' than post-colonial literature.[8] This indiscriminate application of the term 'post-colonial' is indeed a recurrent feature of *The Empire Writes Back*, with the result that Patrick White and Margaret Atwood are considered post-colonial in the same way as Derek Walcott or Chinua Achebe.[9] This is not to say, of course, that some Catholic or indigenous Irish did not buy into hegemonic forms

14.4   Alice Maher, 'Familiar 1' (1994)

of racism in the United States and Australia when they themselves managed to throw off the shackles of slavery or subjugation. But it is important to recognize this for what it is, a process of identifying with the existing supremacist ideologies, derived mainly from the same legacy of British colonialism from which they were trying to escape. In Charles Gavan Duffy's words, commenting on the upward mobility of some of the Irish Catholic diaspora in Australia:

> To strangers at a distance who read of Barrys, MacMahons and Fitzgeralds in high places, it seemed the paradise of the Celts – but they were Celts whose forefathers had broken with the traditions and creed of the island [i.e. Ireland].[10]

This is an important corrective to the essentialist myth that racist attitudes were already present in Irish emigrants – by virtue of their 'whiteness', their backwardness, or 'national character' – before they emigrated to Britain, the United States or Australia.[11] What the immigrant Irish brought with them from the homeland were not the habits of authority fostered by the colonizer but, in fact, a bitter legacy of servitude and ignominy akin to that experienced by native and African Americans. Indeed, from the colonial perspective, the racial labels 'white/non-white' did not follow strict epidermal schemas of visibility or skin colour so that, in an important sense, the Irish historically were classified as 'non-white', and treated accordingly. The widespread equation of the 'mere Irish' with the native Americans in the seventeenth century served as a pretext for wholesale confiscations and plantations, and more ominous expressions of genocidal intent as in Edmund Spenser's advice to Queen Elizabeth that 'until Ireland can be famished, it cannot be subdued'.[12] The transportation of the Irish to the New World featured prominently in the 'white slave trade' in the seventeenth century, and throughout the eighteenth and early nineteenth centuries the Penal code which systematically excluded Catholics from citizenship and political life rendered them, in Edmund Burke's phrase, foreigners in their native land. There was no need to go abroad to experience the 'multiple identities' of the diaspora valorized in post-colonial theory: the uncanny experience of being a stranger to oneself was already a feature of life back home.

As David Roediger remarks of the ambivalence of Irish attitudes to racism in America, 'shared oppression need not generate solidarity but neither must it necessarily breed contempt of one oppressed group for another'.[13] The need to define themselves as white presented itself as an urgent imperative to the degraded Irish who arrived in the United States after the Famine, if they were not to be reduced to servitude once more. This was the political climate in which Ralph Waldo Emerson could write:

> I think it cannot be maintained by any candid person that the African race have ever occupied or do promise ever to occupy any very high place in the human family. The Irish cannot; the American Indian cannot; the Chinese cannot. Before the energy of the Caucasian race all the other races have quailed and done obeisance.[14]

It was in these circumstances that many Irish sought to identify with the manifest destiny of whiteness, finding in the anti-abolitionist Democratic party a vehicle for their social and political aspirations. This, in effect, meant an uneasy accommodation with what Reginald Horsman describes as 'American racial Anglo-Saxonism' and, as Roediger comments, 'under other circumstances, Irish American Catholics might not have accepted so keenly the "association of nationality with blood – but not ethnicity", which racially conflated them with the otherwise hated English'. But, he continues:

> within the constrained choices and high risks of antebellum American politics such a choice was quite logical. The ways in which the Irish competed for work and adjusted to industrial morality in America made it all but certain that they would adopt and extend the politics of white unity offered by the Democratic party.[15]

The point of drawing attention to the unhealthy intersection of Irish Catholicism with supremacist Anglo-Saxon ideals of whiteness in the United States is to underline the risks inherent in uncritical adulations of 'hybridity' as an empowering strategy for diasporic or post-colonial identity – particularly when it involves accommodation with the values of powerful expansionist cultures already built on racism. As Ella Shohat and Robert Stam put it, undue haste in deconstructing essentialist notions of identity 'should not obscure the problematic agency of "post-colonial hybridity"'.

14.5   Willie Doherty, 'Evergreen Memories' (1989)

A celebration of syncreticism and hybridity per se, if not articulated with questions of historical hegemonies, risks sanctifying the fait accompli of colonial violence. For oppressed people, even artistic syncreticism is not a game but a sublimated form of historical pain, which is why Jimi Hendrix played the 'Star Spangled Banner' in a dissonant mode, and why even a politically conservative performer like Ray Charles renders 'America the Beautiful' as a moan and a cry. As a descriptive catch-all term, 'hybridity' fails to discriminate between diverse modalities of hybridity: colonial imposition, obligatory assimilation, political co-option, cultural mimicry and so forth.[16]

It is in this context that one should consider Willie Doherty's photographic triptychs *Fading Dreams* (1989) and *Evergreen Memories* (1989). In *Fading Dreams* we see redolent details of imposing Georgian architecture dating from the period in the eighteenth century when the majority Catholic population was kept in bondage, and then the obsequious 'hybridity' of reclaiming this heritage for a nationalist present by placing a brass harp on a panelled door. The green letters overlaid on the images, however, suggest that nostalgia – the 'fading dreams' and 'hospitable' welcome – for imperial splendour is not restricted to the relics of the old order but is possibly shared by the new 'nationalist' dispensation, notwithstanding its official condemnations (it is not clear, for this reason, to whom 'Depraved' and 'Unknown Depths' refers). As against this, *Evergreen Memories* [Fig. 14.5] shows another neo-classical building which has been more violently reclaimed by nationalist memory, the General Post Office in the centre of Dublin, scene of the 1916 rebellion which declared an Irish republic. On the one hand, this founding site of the state is an object of awe and reverence ('*Evergreen memories*' of '*Resolute*' revolutionaries); but the site is also one of disavowal and rejection (it is not clear whether the overlaid 'Psychopath' and 'Cursed Existence' emanate from the imperial building itself, or from its new custodians, the post-colonial state intent on forgetting its violent origins).[17]

In a similar vein, John Kindness's satirical panels for the DART (Dublin Area Rapid Transit) trains show the colonial mimicry of the consumerist Irish state as evidenced by the green bottle on the dinner table containing DE sauce (as in *D áil É ireann* [i.e. the Government of Ireland], and perhaps Eamon *de Valera*?). This craven hybridity is an imaginary rip-off of the original HP sauce bottle (as in Houses of Parliament) which adorns so many British dinner tables. The kind of homely ideology lodged in domestic details is again apparent in Kindness's recent *Belfast Frescoes* which depict, in comic-book fashion, scenes from an upbringing in Protestant Belfast. The affectionate memory of the father's cigarette moving around the room in the dark before breakfast is counterpointed by the imagery on the teapot and cup of the ill-fated Titanic,

Early in the morning in our house there was a cigarette that moved around in the dark. it was my father getting ready to go to work.

14.6 John Kindness, 'Belfast Fresco Series' (1994)

the pride of the loyalist shipyards, which was sunk by an iceberg on its maiden voyage in 1912. (In a later picture, a teapot displays the rose and thistle, emblems of the union between England and Scotland which initially constituted modern Britishness.) The link between the innocent detail of the cigarette and the imperial icon of the ocean liner is forged by the sustained visual pun in the border of the image in which the smoke of the cigarette is gradually transformed into the fog and mist which concealed the iceberg on the ship's fatal journey. The tigers, elephants and kangaroos in the borders of subsequent images also harbour imperial fantasies, as when the young boys are shown embarking on safari hunts in their neighbourhood in Belfast. In a later sequence, the closed culture of loyalism is characterized by an image of a unionist election poster blocking out labour and nationalist posters, and the young narrator and his friend being contemptuously labelled as 'Fenian-lovers', not because they are nationalists but merely because, as working-class children, they are not overtly unionist and supported labour.

If Ireland does not quite conform to the post-colonial condition, it is not for the reasons outlined by some critics – namely, that because it is 'white' and situated in Europe, therefore it cannot have been subject to colonization.[18] Anne McClintock is nearer the mark when she advises that:

> the term 'post-colonialism' is, in many cases, prematurely celebratory: Ireland may, at a pinch, be 'post-colonial', but for the inhabitants of British-occupied Northern Ireland, not to mention the Palestinian inhabitants of the Israeli Occupied Territories and the West Bank, there may be nothing 'post' about colonialism at all.[19]

'Post', in this context, signifies a form of historical closure, but it is precisely the *absence* of a sense of an ending which has characterized the national narratives of Irish history. This has less to do with the 'unfinished business' of a united Ireland than with the realization that there is no possibility of undoing history, of removing all the accretions of conquest – the English language, the inscriptions of the Protestant Ascendancy on the landscape and material culture, and so on. For this reason, there is no prospect of restoring a pristine, pre-colonial identity: the lack of historical closure, therefore, is bound up with a similar incompleteness in the culture itself, so that instead of being based on narrow ideals of racial purity and exclusivism, identity is open-ended and heterogeneous. But the important point in all of this is that the retention of the residues of conquest does not necessarily mean subscribing to the values which originally governed them: as Donald Horne has argued, even the sheer survival of cultural artefacts from one era to another may transform their meaning, so that the same building (or, perhaps, even the same statue) 're-located' in a new political era becomes, in a sense, a radically different structure.[20]

From this it follows that openness towards other cultures does not entail accepting them solely on their own terms, all the more so when a minority or subaltern culture is attempting to come out from under the shadow of a major colonial power. As Friedrich Engels remonstrated with those English comrades in the First International who objected to the formation of Irish national branches in England on the grounds that this was betraying the 'universal' ideals of internationalism, this proposal was seeking:

> not internationalism, but simply prating submission [on the part of the Irish]. If the promoters of the motion were so brimful of the truly international spirit, let them prove it by removing the seat of the British Federal Council to Dublin and submit to a Council of Irishmen.[21]

What Engels is pointing to here is the hidden *asymmetry* of many calls for internationalism – or its post-colonial counterpart, hybridity – emanating from the heartlands of colonialism. The need to address the other, and the route of the diaspora, is invariably presented as a passage from the margins to the metropolitan centre, but the reverse journey is rarely greeted with much enthusiasm. In fact, those who go in the opposite direction are invariably derided as 'going native', as slumming it when they should really be getting on with the business of persuading the natives to adopt their master's voice.[22] Yet it is only when hybridity becomes truly reciprocal rather than hierarchical that the encounter with the culture of the colonizer ceases to be detrimental to one's development.

Another way of negotiating identity through an exchange with the other is to make provision, not just for 'vertical' mobility from the periphery to the centre, but for 'lateral' journeys along the margins which short-circuit the colonial divide. This is the rationale for the present welcome cultural exchange between Irish and Mexican culture in the 'Distant Relations' exhibition of the Irish Museum of Modern Art. Hybridity need not always take the high road: where there are borders to be crossed, unapproved roads might prove more beneficial in the long run than those patrolled by global powers. So far from rejecting universal values, moreover, this may be the most productive way, as Engels recognized, of taking the Enlightenment to the limit.

NOTES AND REFERENCES

1 Introduction: Culture, History and Irish Identity

1   For a range of different perspectives on these issues, see Therese Cahery et al., *Is Ireland a Third World Country?* (Belfast: Beyond the Pale Publications, 1992).

2   According to Marshall McLuhan, the first broadcast in 'radio' history took place when volunteers during the Rising commandeered a transmitter to send news of the proclamation of the Republic across the airwaves, in the hope that a transatlantic ship would convey the information to sympathizers in the United States. See *Understanding Media* (London: Routledge & Kegan Paul, 1967) p. 304.

3   Martin Woollacott, 'Living in the Age of Terror', *The Guardian*, 22 April 1995. An extended discussion of the politics of televangelism can be found in Timothy Luke, *Screens of Power: Ideology, Domination and Resistance in Informational Society* (Urbana: University of Illinois Press, 1989), ch. 3. Similar strictures hold in relation to Islamic fundamentalism, which, so far from rejecting the west, is often in unacknowledged collusion with it. As Malise Ruthven summarizes fundamentalism's indebtedness to certain strands of modernization in the course of reviewing Azia Al-Azmeh's *Islams and Modernities* (Verso, 1993): 'In common with most other scholars, he emphasizes the highly selective way in which modern fundamentalists retrieve those elements from a real or mythical past they find convenient, or even invent them altogether. In his own area of speciality (the Arab world) he is alert to the infiltration of intellectual influences from the ostensibly rejected "West", notably social Darwinism and revolutionary ideals of total political action deriving from Rousseau and the Jacobins.' ('Veils of Distortion', *The Guardian*, 18 January 1994).

4   It is, of course, true that all expressions of a unified and harmonious past are mythic to the extent that they mask over the conflicts and divisions which impel historical change. But there is still a world of a difference between the discontinuities evident in the legacy of the 'free born Englishman' for example, and the devastation wreaked on cultures that have faced extermination, such as the native Americans, or, for that matter, the old Gaelic order in Ireland.

5   C. Litton Falkiner, 'Youghal', in *Essays Relating to Ireland: Biographical, Historical and Topographical* (London: Longmans, 1909), p. 165. Falkiner goes on to complain about Armagh, Ireland's oldest city: 'Nowhere is the contrast more marked between the remote antiquity of Irish historical origins and the long silences which intervene between recorded episodes to destroy all natural continuity and intelligible sequence' (p. 180).

6   Alice Stopford Green, 'The Way of History', in *The Old Irish World*, (Dublin: Gill, 1912) p. 16.

7   Brendan Bradshaw, 'Nationalism and Historical Scholarship in Modern Ireland, *Irish Historical Studies*, vol. xxvi, no. 104 (November 1989), p. 338. Bradshaw

adds about his use of the term 'holocaust': 'The reference to the mid-nineteenth century famine is intended to refer to the scale of a disaster which was, it is clear, humanly avoidable; it is not intended to carry connotations of genocide.' For extended discussions of the revisionist debate in contemporary Irish historiography, to which Bradshaw's article has made a major contribution, see my section on 'Challenging the Canon: Revisionism and Cultural Criticism', in Seamus Deane, ed., *The Field Day Anthology of Irish Writing* (Derry/London: Field Day Publications/ Faber and Faber, 1991), vol. iii, and Ciaran Brady, ed., *Interpreting Irish History: The Debate on Historical Revisionism* (Dublin: Irish Academic Press, 1994).

8   Henry Giles, 'Spirit of Irish History,' *Lecture and Essays on Irish and Other Subjects* (New York: D. & J. Sadlier & Co., 1869), pp. 14, 29, 70.

9   Paul Gilroy, *The Black Atlantic: Modernity and Double Consciousness* (London: Verso, 1993), p. 221. Gilroy is elaborating on Toni Morrison's work here, particularly Morrison's statement that 'black women had to deal with post-modern problems in the nineteenth century and earlier. These things had to be addressed by black people a long time ago: certain kinds of dissolution, the loss of and the need to reconstruct certain kinds of stability. . . . These strategies for survival made the truly modern person. They're a response to predatory western phenomena' ('Living Memory: Meeting Toni Morrison', in Paul Gilroy, *Small Acts* [London: Serpent's Tail, 1993], p. 178).

10   James Joyce, *Ulysses* (New York: Modern Library, 1946), p. 25. For a number of recent discussions which address these issues, particularly in relation to Joyce, see Eamonn Hughes. 'It seems history is to blame: Ulysses and cultural history', *Ideas and Production*, no. vi, 1987; Emer Nolan, *James Joyce and Nationalism* (London: Routledge, 1995); Terry Eagleton, *Heathcliff and the Great Hunger, Studies in Irish Culture* (London: Verso, 1995), especially chs. 5, 6 and 7; and Declan Kiberd, *Inventing Ireland: The Literature of the Modern Nation* (London: Jonathan Cape, 1995).

11   See Eric Hobsbawm and Terence Ranger, *The Invention of Traditions* (Cambridge: Cambridge University Press, 1984). This is decidedly not to concur with a nativist mythos which sees all evil as coming from the outside – the point is simply that it does not all come from the inside either, any more than 'the inside' has a monopoly on perfection. It is precisely such clear-cut boundaries between outside and inside that are contested in colonized societies, and to different degrees in all subaltern cultures.

12   Barbara Johnson, 'Woman and Allegory', in *The Wake of Deconstruction* (Oxford: Blackwell, 1994), p. 61.

13   Hans Kohn, *Nationalism: Its Meaning and History* (New York: D. Van Nostrand, 1965), pp. 29–30, cited in Alok Yadov, 'Nationalism and Contemporaneity: Political Economy of a Discourse', *Cultural Critique*, no. 26, Winter 1993–4, pp. 218–19. Yadov's fine discussion does much to clear the ground for new concepts of nationalism that acknowledge 'the heterogeneity of social groups, [the] need to foster alternative, decentralized public institutional sites and more participatory forms of political activity beyond the centralized state structure' (p. 207).

14   'In a statement yesterday, Mr. Molyneaux said that residents in the solidly middle-class constituency had "suffered least from the terrorist savagery and can afford to forget people in the frontier counties"' (*The Irish Times*, 17 June 1995). For the

historical affinities between Ulster loyalism and the frontier ideology in the United States, see below, p. 12–14, 151–2.

15 According to Fredrick Jackson Turner's influential formulation, borrowed from official census definitions in the United States, the frontier was a place occupied by fewer than two people per mile (Patricia Nelson Limerick, 'The Adventures of the Frontier in the Twentieth Century', in James R. Grossman, ed., *The Frontier in American Culture* [Berkeley: University of California Press, 1994], p. 67). For a discussion of the distinction between borders and frontiers, see Anthony Giddens, *The Nation State and Violence* (London: Polity Press, 1985).

16 For an authoritative discussion of Geoffrey Keating's enormously influential manuscript history of Ireland (which was translated by, amongst others, John O'Mahony, the Fenian leader, in 1867) and other early expressions of Irish nationalism, see Joep Leerssen's *Mere Irish & Fíor Ghael: Studies in the Idea of Irish Nationality, its Development and Literary Expression prior to the Nineteenth Century* (Amsterdam/ Philadelphia: John Benjamins Publishing Company, 1986, new edition forthcoming in this series from Cork University Press).

17 For an incisive discussion of the Arnoldian project as it related to Ireland, see Marjorie Howes, *Yeats's Nations: Gender, Class and Irishness* (Cambridge: Cambridge University Press, forthcoming), ch. 1.

18 As a recent summary describes this anti-culturalist position: 'Because of their epiphenomenal nature, cultural patterns are seen as being derived from the particular historical constellations of economic and political structures. Since matters of culture are interpreted as having no significant impact – either alone or even in interaction with the economy or political system – on the emergence and transformations of social formations in the historical process, the study of culture is as epiphenomenal as its object itself.' (Ewa Morawska and Willfried Spohn, '"Cultural Pluralism" in Historical Sociology: Recent Theoretical Directions', in Diane Crane, ed., *The Sociology of Culture: Emerging Theoretical Perspectives* [London: Blackwell, 1994], p. 50).

19 Raymond Williams, *Politics and Letters: Interviews with the New Left Review* (London: New Left Books, 1979), pp. 352–3.

20 Quoted in Tzvetan Todorov, *Mikhail Bakhtin: The Dialogical Principle* (Manchester: Manchester University Press, 1984), p. 85. See also E. P. Thompson's influential formulation that class consciousness is no more than the cultural dimension of economic and political struggle, 'the way in which these experiences [of production relations] are handled in cultural terms: embodied in traditions, value-systems, ideas, and institutional forms' (*The Making of the English Working Class* [Harmondsworth: Penguin, 1975], p. 10).

21 Anthony D. Smith, *National Identity* (London: Penguin, 1992), p. vii.

22 One notable exception to this trend in Irish cultural history is W. J. McCormack's intensive study of the pamphlet war in the 1780s which led to the emergence of the Protestant 'Ascendency' as a distinctive political force, and which attends closely to the precise nature of the publications involved. See W. J. McCormack, *The Dublin Paper War of 1786–88: A Bibliography and Critical Inquiry* (Dublin: Academic Press, 1993).

23 Samuel Clark, *Social Origins of the Irish Land War* (Princeton: Princeton University Press, 1979), p. 269.

24   This is not to say that the impression conveyed was entirely illusionistic, effacing its simulation of reality – in fact, the limited camera movements and long takes gave a staged impression not unlike that of early cinema. This contrived effect was augmented by the theatricality of many of the actors, due to their long apprenticeship in the 'fit-ups' which toured rural Ireland, as against the more illusionistic drama of conventional theatre.

25   For a critical reconsideration of the public/private distinction as it affects the family and the domestic sphere in Ireland, see Clair Wills, 'Rocking the Cradle? – Women and the Family in Twentieth-Century Ireland', *Bullán: An Irish Studies Journal*, vol. 1, no. 2, Autumn 1994.

26   It is for this reason that it is important to question the futile opposition of 'anthropological' to 'aesthetic' definitions of culture, as if great art somehow loses its value the more it comes into contact with the world it tries to represent. Of course, it is distanced from 'reality' by virtue of its generic conventions, stylistic devices, narrative structures, etc.; but it is precisely the imaginative space afforded by these symbolic forms which endows it with the capacity to provide frames of reference and alternative 'paradigms' for even the most familiar aspects of everyday experience.

27   Significantly, areas such as abortion and gay rights which were to prove so controversial in the 1980s and 1990s did not figure on the agenda of these early groundbreaking programmes, or, indeed, on television agendas to any great degree subsequently.

28   Richard Slotkin, *The Fatal Environment: The Myth of the Frontier in the Age of Industrializaton, 1800–1890* (New York: HarperPerennial, 1994), p. 16.

29   The contradictions inherent in the frontier ideology become most apparent in its deployment by the corporate sector to clear away impediments to endless accumulation and expansion, and yet its being mobilized by 'the small man', the petty bourgeois individual, to oppose big business and monopoly capital. The introduction of the railway, strained the western genre to its limits, even if, as Leo Marx has observed, the complex theme of 'the machine in the garden' was devised to reconcile the competing claims of eastern industrial progress and the agrarian, entrepreneurial vision. (See Leo Marx, *The Machine in the Garden: Technology and the Pastoral Ideal in America* [New York: Oxford University Press, 1976].)

30   As the Waco siege and the Oklahoma bombing have tragically shown, the 'right to bear arms' in American society is considered by some zealots to have a group or collective dimension, insofar as it extends to private armies (such as David Koresh's millenarian sect, or the self-styled 'Michigan Militia') and male confraternities (such as the Ku Klux Klan). But as Ann Swidler correctly points out, these movements 'rest on the cultural assumption that social groups . . . are constituted by the voluntary choices of individuals' – hence the often ludicrous initiation rituals required to lose one's individualism, and to join the group. The collective right itself is based on the supposed prior 'right' to keep weapons, even military assault rifles, in the privacy of one's own home. The collective is seen as invalid unless it is an extension of individualism. As Steve Derne argues, citing Swidler's research, 'American social movements which focus on group justice are often seen as illegitimate, and meet with public disapproval. Even in accomplishing collective acts, then, Americans may be constrained by the individualistic framework for understanding action that focuses on individual choices' (Steve Derne, 'Cultural Conceptions of Human Motivation and their Significance for Culture Theory' in Diane Crane, ed., op. cit., p. 283).

31 Cited in Slotkin, op. cit., pp. 475–6. This is not, of course, to deny that there were Irish-Americans who were far from being sympathetic to the Indians, and accommodated themselves to versions of the dominant frontier ideology (for a discussion of this, see below 'Ireland and Post-Colonial Identity'). The *Irish World*, however, catered for the newly arrived, lower-income Irish, and, under the editorship of Patrick Ford, was the main organ of Irish nationalist opinion in the United States.

32 *The Scotch-Irish and Ulster: The Scotch Irish and American History* (Belfast: Ulster-Scot Historical Society, 1965), pp. 4–5. As an unabashed American commentator describes these lineages of conquest: 'The great emigration [to America] of three hundred thousand or more people from Ireland before 1750 was from Ulster Province, which has a history which may well be called one of the romances of colonization. This ancient division of Erin has in it nine counties, in which are many hills and bogs and much worthless land, yet good colonists made it one of the fairest and richest portions of the earth. . . . They made of the wilderness a garden and of Ulster a hive of industry.' It was, the author reassures us, 'the best sort of colonists' who came to American shores: 'Most of these emigrants were not poor bog-trotters or potato-eaters who had lived in hovels, but were industrious, well-educated, thrifty, virtuous people of faith and character' (William Elliot Griffis, *The Romance of American Colonization: How the Foundation Stones of our History were Laid* (1898), reprint [New York: Research Reprints, 1970]).

33 See also, my extended discussion of the resistance to romantic conceptions of nature in Irish cinema and culture in Kevin Rockett, Luke Gibbons and John Hill, *Cinema and Ireland* (London: Routledge, 1988), pp. 203ff, and the shorter account in 'Romanticism in Ruins', *The Irish Review*, 2 (1987).

34 Roy Foster, 'The Lovely Magic of its Dawn: Reading Irish History as a Story', *The Times Literary Supplement*, December 16, 1994, pp. 4–5.

35 William O'Brien, 'The Irish National Idea', in *Irish Ideas* (London: Longmans, Green, and Co., 1893), p. 4.

36 Summarizing the narrative interpretations of history in the work of Hayden White, Louis Mink and Paul Ricouer, David Carr writes: 'Narrative structure, particularly the closing off of a sequence of events provided by the stories' beginning and end, is a structure derived from the telling of the story itself, not from the events it relates' (*Time, Narrative, and History* [Bloomington: Indiana Press, 1986], p. 10). Carr – to my mind correctly – challenges this view: narrative 'in its literary guise', he argues, 'arises out of and is prefigured in certain features of life, action and communication. Historical and fictional narratives . . . reveal themselves to be not distortions of, denials of, or escapes from reality, but extensions and configurations of its primary features' (p. 16).

37 See p. 6 above. For the use of the term proto-modernism to describe early examples of this fiction, see Katie Trumpener's valuable discussion, 'National Character, Nationalist Plots: National Tale and the Historical Novel in the Age of *Waverley*, 1806–1830', *English Literary History*, vol. 600, no. 3, Fall (1993), p. 690.

38 See Gary Owens, 'Nationalist Monuments in Ireland, *c.*1870–1914: Symbolism and Ritual' in Brian P. Kennedy and Raymond Gillespie, eds., *Ireland: Art into History* (Dublin: Town House, 1994), and Timothy O'Keefe, 'The 1898 Efforts to Celebrate the United Irishmen: The '98 Centennial', *Eire-Ireland*, vol. xxiii (1988).

39 F. S. L. Lyons, *The Burden of Our History*, The W. B. Rankin Memorial Lecture (Belfast: Queen's University, 1978), pp. 13–14.

40   Ibid., pp. 8, 12.
41   T. W. Moody, 'Irish History and mythology', *Hermathena*, no. cxxiv (Summer, 1978), p. 7. I have reprinted sections from both Lyons' and Moody's articles in my section 'Challenging the Canon: Revisionism and Cultural Criticism', in Deane, op. cit., vol iii.
42   Joel C. Weinsheimer, *Eighteenth-Century Hermeneutics: Philosophy of Interpretation in England from Locke to Burke* (New Haven: Yale University Press, 1993), p. 129.
43   Brendan Bradshaw, op. cit., p. 337.
44   Robert Darnton, 'Peasants Tell Tales: The Meaning of Mother Goose', *The Great Cat Massacre, and other Episodes in French Cultural History* (London: Penguin, 1984), p. 30.
45   As Dominic La Capra comments, 'Rarely do historians see significant texts as important events in their own right that pose complex problems in interpretation and have intricate relations to other and to various pertinent contexts. Nor are [they] inclined to raise the more "rhetorical" question of how texts do what they do – how, for example, they may situate or frame what they represent or inscribe (social discourses, paradigms, generic conventions, stereotypes, and so forth). The multiple roles of tropes, irony, parody, and other rhetorical devices of composition and arrangement generate resistances to the construal of texts in terms of their "representations" or narrowly documentary functions, and they disclose how texts may have critical or even potentially transformative relations to phenomena "represented" in them.' ('Rhetoric and History', in *History and Criticism* [Ithaca: Cornell University Press, 1985], p. 38).
46   It is important to emphasize that these areas of experience do not lend themselves to certainty, or even to the more prosaic types of veracity claimed by 'literal truth', in order to counter nativist postures which construe various 'national narratives' as self-validating, or beyond question. As Slotkin points out in relation to the western, even the most powerful 'national narratives' are subject to the transformations of both genre and history. It is the attempt to invest certain narratives with the authority of omniscient narration, denying the possibility of other voices or other ways of framing experience, that leads to cultural supremacy and related forms of fundamentalism.
47   'In the north of Ireland, the Molly Maguires, a very powerful organization, went in groups to local wakes, looking for an occasion to fight. The Mollies would take part in certain games with the sole intention of beating some man who had refused, for some reason, to join their ranks.' Seán Ó Suilleabháin, *Irish Wake Amusements* (Cork: Mercier Press, 1967), p. 71.
48   W. R. Wilde, *Irish Popular Superstitions* (1852), (Shannon: Irish University Press, 1972), p. 81.
49   See, respectively, Kevin Kenny, 'The Molly Maguires in Popular Culture', *Journal of American Ethnic History*, vol. xiv, no. 4, Summer 1995, and Slotkin, op. cit., pp. 349, 442, 463, 468.
50   As Fredric Jameson argues, 'generic affiliations, and the systematic deviation from them, provide clues which lead us back to the concrete historical situation of the individual text itself, and allow us to read its structure as ideology, as a socially symbolic act, as a protopolitical response to a historical dilemma.' ('Magical Narratives: Romance as Genre', *New Literary History*, 7 [1975], p. 157, cited in Michael Denning, *Mechanic Accents: Dime Novels and Working Class Culture in America* [London: Verso, 1987], p. 224.)

51 Denning, op. cit., pp. 120–1.
52 Miroslav Hroch, 'From National Movement to Fully-Fledged Nation', *The New Left Review*, no. 198, March/April 1993, p. 4.
53 Edward Hayes, ed., *The Ballads of Ireland* (London: A. Fullerton & Co., 1857), vol. 1, p. xxi.
54 Hayes, ibid.
55 Hroch, op. cit., p. 15.
56 On this in an Irish context, see Clair Wills, *Improprieties: Politics and Sexuality in Northern Irish Poetry* (Oxford: Oxford University Press, 1993) and Carol Coulter, *The Hidden Tradition: Feminism, Women and Nationalism in Ireland* (Cork: Cork University Press, 1993). For related theoretical discussions, see Seyla Benhabib and Drucilla Cornell, eds., *Feminism as Critique: On the Politics of Gender* (Minneapolis: University of Minnesota Press, 1987).
57 See Craig Owens, 'The Allegorical Impulse: Towards a Theory of Postmodernism', in Brian Wallis, ed., *Art After Modernism: Rethinking Representation* (New York/ Boston: The New Museum of Modern Art/Godine, 1984). For a wide-ranging discussion of the relation between allegory and realism in the nineteenth-century Irish novel, see David Lloyd, 'Violence and the Constitution of the Novel', in *Anomalous States: Irish Writing and the Post-Colonial Moment* (Dublin: Lilliput Press, 1993).
58 James Clifford, 'On Ethnographic Allegory', in James Clifford and George E. Marcus, eds., *Writing Culture: The Poetics and Politics of Ethnography* (Berkeley: University of California Press, 1986), pp. 119–20.

2 Synge, Country and Western: The Myth of the West in Irish and American Culture

1   Robert Ballagh, 'The Irishness of Irish Art', (1980), unpublished lecture, p. 2. I am grateful to Robert Ballagh for permission to quote from this paper.
2   One other interesting possibility presents itself, that of the Australian outback. As depicted in much of Australian cinema, it represents an uneasy blend of the masculinity of the American west, and, through an ethos of 'mateship', the sublimated violence and communal identity of the Irish western world.
3   J. M. Synge, 'The Aran Islands', in *Collected Works*, ii (Prose), ed. by Alan Price (London: Oxford University Press, 1966), p. 103.
4   Synge, ibid., p. 96.
5   Paul Hoch, *White Hero Black Beast* (London: Pluto Press, 1979), p. 118.
6   Philip French, *Westerns* (London: Secker and Warburg, 1973), p. 48.
7   Peter Homans, 'Puritanism Revisited: An Analysis of the Contemporary Screen-Image Western', in J. Nachbar, ed., *Focus on the Western* (Englewood Cliffs, N. J.: Prentice Hall, 1974), p. 85.
8   Jim Kitses, 'The Western: Ideology and Archetype', in Nachbar, op. cit., p. 67.
9   Cited in David Brion Davis, 'Ten-Gallon Hero', in N. Cords and P. Gerster, eds., *Myth and the American Experience*, vol. 1 (Beverley Hills: Glencoe Press, 1973), p. 91.
10 Of course, this did not prevent managerial élites and big business conscripting the frontier topos and related motifs in their struggles against organized labour, demonizing the working class (and particularly the Irish) as primitives and savages. See above, p. 184, note 29.

11   Karl Marx, 'The Eighteenth Brumaire of Louis Bonaparte', in *Surveys from Exile: Political Writings*, vol. 2 (Harmondsworth: Penguin, 1973), p. 239.
12   Emmet Larkin. 'The Devotional Revolution in Ireland, 1850–75', *American Historical Review*, 77(1972).
13   Brian Friel, 'Plays Peasant and Unpeasant', *Times Literary Supplement*, 17 March 1972, p. 305; C. Arensberg and S. T. Kimball, *Family and Community in Ireland* (Cambridge, Mass.: Harvard University Press, 1948), p. 154; J. Lee, *The Modernization of Irish Society, 1848–1918* (Dublin: Gill & Macmillan, 1973), pp. 5, 11.
14   P. A. Sheehan, *The Beauty of Summer* (Cork: Mercier Press, 1973), pp. 46, 48–9. See also John Wilson Foster, 'Certain Set Apart: The Western Island in the Irish Renaissance', *Studies*, 66 (1977), pp. 263–7.
15   Erwin Panofsky, '*Et in Arcadia Ego*: Poussin and the Elegiac Tradition', in *Meaning and the Visual Arts* (New York: Doubleday Books, 1955), pp. 297–302.
16   Synge, 'Autobiography', op. cit., p. 11.
17   G. J. Watson, *Irish Identity and the Literary Revival* (London: Croom Helm, 1979), p. 40.
18   Synge, op. cit., 'Various Notes', p. 349, and 'Autobiography', p. 14.
19   Synge, 'The Aran Islands', op. cit., p. 66. Subsequent references in parenthesis in text.
20   J. M. Synge, *Collected Works*, iv (Plays), ed. by Anne Saddlemyer (London: Oxford University Press, 1968), p. 111. Subsequent references to the *Playboy* are in parentheses in text.
21   Annelise Truninger, *Paddy and the Paycock* (Berne: Francke Verlag, 1976), p. 103.
22   Alan Price, *Riders to the Sea and The Playboy of the Western World* (Oxford: Basil Blackwell, 1969), pp. 69, 80.
23   Jenni Calder, *There Must be a Lone Ranger* (London: Abacus, 1976), p. 158.
24   Sean McMahon, 'The Road to Glenmalure', *Éire-Ireland* 8 (1972), p. 147. See also Elizabeth Coxhead's comment on this point: Synge's heroines 'are creatures caged and raging, given no scope for their powers, condemned to love men who are poor things beside them and do not really care for them at all' (*Lady Gregory* [London: Macmillan, 1966], pp. 137–8).
25   James Kilroy, *The Playboy Riots* (Dublin: Dolmen Press, 1971), p. 66, and Ruth Dudley Edwards, *Patrick Pearse* (London: Faber and Faber, 1979), pp. 102–3. Significantly, Pearse had changed his mind by 1915, and challenged peremptory nationalist dismissals of the *Playboy*.
26   Synge, op. cit. (1966), n. 1, p. 283.
27   Hoch, op. cit., pp. 118–44.
28   Synge, ibid., p. 54, n. 1.
29   See S. J. Connolly, op. cit., 195–6; Seamus Breathnach, *The Irish Police* (Dublin: Anvil Books, 1974), pp. 34–5; P. O'Donnell, *The Irish Faction Fighters* (Dublin: Anvil Books, 1975); and Samuel Clark, *Social Origins of the Irish Land War* (Princeton: Princeton University Press, 1979), pp. 66–86.
30   Daniel Corkery, *Synge and Anglo-Irish Literature* (Cork: Mercier Press, 1966), pp. 187, 185.
31   George Cornewall Lewis, *On Local Disturbances in Ireland* (London: B. Fellowes, 1836), pp. 251–2.
32   W. R. Rodgers, 'Introduction', to Peig Sayers, *An Old Woman's Reflections* (Oxford: Oxford University Press, 1978), p. viii.

3 Back Projections: John Hinde and the New Nostalgia

1   Cited in Ed Buscombe, 'Sound and Colour', *Jump Cut*, no. 17, p. 25.
2   Cited in Naomi Schor, '*Cartes Postales*, Representing Paris 1900', *Critical Enquiry*, vol. 18, no. 2, Winter 1992, p. 211.
3   For a perceptive comparison of *The Wizard of Oz* with *E.T.*, see Inez Hedges, *Breaking the Frame: Film Language and the Experience of Limits* (Bloomington: University of Indiana Press, 1991), ch. 7.
4   Sigmund Freud, 'On Narcissism: An Introduction', in Philip Rieff, ed., *General Psychoanalytic Theory* (New York: Collier, 1976), p. 70.

4 From Kitchen Sink to Soap: Drama and the Serial Form on Irish Television

1   For the text of Eamonn Andrews' speech, see 'One of the Most Exciting Years of my Life', *RTV Guide*, 12 January 1962, p. 3.
2   *Irish Times*, 1 January 1962, p. 3.
3   David Thornley, 'Television and Politics', *Administration*, vol. 15, no. 3 (1967), p. 218. At the time of writing, the author had just joined the *Seven Days* programme whose turbulent history placed current affairs firmly on the map of Irish television.
4   'MRBI 21st Anniversary Poll', *Irish Times*, 27 June 1983, p. 6.
5   For some interesting observations on this point, see T. J. M. S., 'Success of the Indirect Approach', *Irish Catholic*, 18 April 1968, p. 1: 'One of the paradoxes of television is the fact that the most successful way to present quite serious ideas is often through the lightest of entertainment. . . . To put across very serious ideas on television, the obvious way would seem to be to present experts on the subject either in interviews, or involved in a debate or discussion. . . . But when the same serious views are neatly woven into a popular entertainment programme, like *Tolka Row*, the impact on the public covers a much wider range of viewers, and in many cases makes a much more definite impact.'
6   See George Brandt, ed., *British Television Drama* (Cambridge: Cambridge University Press, 1981), especially Martin Banham's article on Jeremy Sandford, pp. 194–217.
7   John Caughie, 'Progressive Television and Documentary Drama', *Screen*, vol. 21, no. 3 (1980), pp. 36–9.
8   W. Stephen Gilbert, 'The TV Play: Outside the Consensus', *Screen Education*, no. 35 (Summer, 1980), pp. 36–9.
9   Caughie, op. cit., p. 16. Among the film directors who made the transition from television to cinema were Arthur Penn, Robert Mulligan, John Frankenheimer, Sidney Lumet, and George Roy Hill. See Michael Kerbel, 'The Golden Age of TV Drama', in Horace Newcomb, Newcombe, ed., *Television: The Critical View* (New York: Oxford University Press, 1982).
10   See the remark by Sydney Newman, the Canadian producer who was perhaps the most significant figure in the development of British television drama in the late 1950s and 1960s: 'I came to Britain at a crucial time in 1958 when the seeds of *Look Back in Anger* were beginning to flower. . . . I am proud that I played some part in the recognition. The working man was a fit subject for drama, and not just a foil in a play on middle-class manners.' Quoted in Edwin

Eigner, 'British Television Drama and Society in the 1970s', in James Redmond, ed., *Themes in Drama* (Cambridge: Cambridge University Press, 1979), p. 212. See also Caughie, op. cit., pp. 18–19.

11 For the most influential exposition of this argument, see Walter Benjamin, 'The Work of Art in the Age of Mechanical Reproduction', in *Illuminations*, trans. Harry Zohn (London: Fontana, 1973).

12 'Dublin Discussion on the Media', *Christus Rex*, vol. xix, no. 1 (1965), pp. 17–18.

13 Ibid., pp. 24–5.

14 Ibid., p. 24.

15 Christopher Murray, 'Irish Drama in Transition 1966–1978', *Études Irlandaises*, no. 4, Nouvelle Serie (December 1979), pp. 289–90. See also Terence Brown, *Ireland: A Social and Cultural History, 1922–79* (London: Fontana, 1981), pp. 319–20.

16 Hilton Edwards, 'The Problems and Possibilities of TV Drama', *RTV Guide*, 26 January 1962, p. 4.

17 Hilton Edwards, 'Drama on Television', *Aquarius* (1973), p. 108.

18 See Annual Reports for 1962 and 1963. In 1965 the shortage of original scriptwriters for television is also cited.

19 'How will Irish drama be affected by the coming of Telefís Éireann?', *RTV Guide*, 26 January 1962, p. 3.

20 See Healy's comment: 'I'm absolutely all for television. Any extra market for dramatists is definitely a good thing. Television is a much more flexible medium than the theatre, and the plays we will see from abroad will help our young writers to get away from the kitchen sink [i.e. kitchen comedies?] to explore new settings. I believe that television will encourage our writers to show us aspects of Irish life that are neglected by the theatre', ibid.

21 Letter from Richard Elvine, *RTV Guide*, 27 November 1964, p. 2.

22 Letter from Chloe Gibson, *RTV Guide*, 4 December 1964, p. 2.

23 'Memorandum on Television to (i) the Minister for Posts and Telegraphs (ii) Radio Éireann, from the Social Study Conference Ninth Annual Summer School, August 1961', reprinted in James J. Campbell, *Television in Ireland* (Dublin: M. H. Gill & Son Ltd., 1961), pp. 27–8.

24 See the detailed report of the Conference in Ita Meehan, 'The Opinions of the Citizen', *Christus Rex*, vol. xvi, no. 2 (1962), p. 103.

25 Ibid.

26 Ibid., p. 105.

27 Campbell, op. cit., p. 8.

28 Ibid., p. 10.

29 Ibid.

30 'Memorandum to the Minister for Posts and Telegraphs', ibid., p. 26. It is interesting to find precisely these aspects of *Tolka Row* singled out for mention, albeit in a more affirmative sense, by the television critic for *The Irish Catholic* some years later: 'I suspect, for example, that the recent editions of *Tolka Row* watched primarily as entertainment, brought to many people who have little time for "serious" programmes, some serious ideas about the general public attitude to psychiatry and mental health; about the plight of some of our people struck by poverty; and about the average citizen's concern or lack of concern with the basic precept of charity' (T. J. M. S., 'Success of the Indirect Approach', op. cit.).

31   'Memorandum to the Pilkington Committee on Broadcasting from the Social Study Conference (Ireland), August 1961', ibid., p. 22.
32   Tom O'Dea, 'A Taste of Summer', *Irish Press*, 20 April 1968, p. 11.
33   'Profile: Christopher FitzSimon', *RTV Guide*, 18 February 1966, p. 7.
34   For comments of the nostalgic milieu of *Coronation Street*, see Raymond Williams, *Television: Technology and Cultural Form* (London: Fontana, 1974), p. 61, and Richard Dyer, 'Introduction' to Dyer et al., *Coronation Street* (London: British Film Institute, 1981), pp. 4–5. For a critique of the 'consumerist' basis of American soap opera, see Peter Conrad, *Television: The Medium and its Manners* (London: Routledge and Kegan Paul, 1982), pp. 66–87, and 'A Screenful of Dollars', *Observer*, 16 May 1982, p. 28.
35   Dennis Porter, 'Soap Time: Thoughts on a Commodity Art Form', in H. Newcombe, ed., op. cit., p. 125.
36   R. Dyer 'Introduction', in Dyer, op. cit., pp. 4–5 and Marion Jordan, 'Realism and Convention', ibid., pp. 31–3.
37   Charlotte Brunsdon, '*Crossroads* – Notes on Soap Opera', *Screen*, vol. 22, no. 4 (1981), p. 34.
38   'Tolka Row', *RTV Guide*, 22 January 1965, p. 12.
39   Christopher FitzSimon, 'Tolka Row', *RTV Guide*, 17 May 1968, pp. 6–7.
40   See Martin McLoone, '*Strumpet City* – The Urban Working Class on Irish Television', in Martin McLoone and John MacMahon, eds., *Television and Irish Society: 21 Years of Irish Television* (Dublin: RTE/IFI, 1984), p. 44.
41   Norman Smythe, 'Tolka Row', *RTV Guide*, 23 September 1966, p. 7.
42   Carolyn Swift, 'Old Friends and New Faces', *RTV Guide*, 6 December 1967, p. 16.
43   'Video News', *Munster Express*, 27 October 1967, p. 11.
44   Christine Geraghty, '*Brookside* – No Common Ground', *Screen*, vol. 24, nos. 4–5, July–October, 1983, p. 137.
45   Brian Devenney, 'Television Commentary', *Irish Independent*, 21 October 1967, p. 11.
46   Carolyn Swift, '150 Episodes of *Tolka Row*', *RTV Guide*, 10 November 1967, p. 11.
47   Peter Cleary, 'Passing of *Tolka Row*', *Sunday Independent*, 3 March 1968, p. 25.
48   This is not to say that *Tolka Row*, or for that matter other representations of urban life which display residual rural structures, necessarily distort the nature of working-class experience in Dublin. It may be, indeed, that *Tolka Row* was attempting to articulate what A. J. Humphreys refers to as the 'radical continuity between the general pattern of the family in Dublin and the rural community' (Alexander J. Humphreys, *New Dubliners: Urbanisation and the Irish Family* [London: Routledge and Kegan Paul, 1966], p. 234. See also pp. 250–1). Humphreys instances religious belief, kinship, solidarity, filial piety and neighbourliness as cases in point, but draws attention nevertheless to the far-reaching effects on family organization, paternal authority, marriage patterns, and welfare dependency brought about by the loss of the family's function as a unit of economic production.
49   'Profile: Maura Laverty', *RTV Guide*, 13 May 1966, p. 15. It is interesting to note that Rita Nolan is represented as having rural origins – in County Kildare – while Gabby Doyle and Maggie Bonar are from Donegal, to which they return at the end.
50   See the interesting letter by Paddy Corrigan to the *RTV Guide*, 31 May 1968, p. 2.

51   Brian Devenney, 'A Critic's Top Ten', *RTV Guide*, 29 April 1966, p. 4.

52   Wesley Burrowes, *The Riordans* (Dublin: Gilbert Dalton, 1977), p. 6. The analysis of *The Riordans* in the following section is greatly indebted to Mr. Burrowes' lively account of his association with the serial.

53   Ibid., pp. 2–3.

54   'The Riordans: Telefís Éireann's new serial begins at 7.15 on Monday', *RTV Guide*, 1 January 1965, pp. 12–13.

55   Burrowes, op. cit., p. 18.

56   It would seem that a large measure of the success of a British serial such as *Angels*, which was set in a hospital, was due to the fact that it was located in the workplace. However, even in this situation there is a clear demarcation between the public occupations and the private lives of the characters – something which does not hold in the family unit farm. *Crossroads*, set in a motel, would perhaps be the nearest to a combination of workplace and personal lives in a British serial.

57   Rev. H. Murphy, D.D., 'The Rural Family: The Principles', *Christus Rex*, vol. vi, no. 1 (1952), p. 7.

58   Ibid., p. 10.

59   Conrad M. Arensberg, *The Irish Countryman* (New York: American Museum Science Books Edition, 1968), pp. 66–7.

60   Burrowes, op. cit., p. 92.

61   Ibid.

62   For an excellent account of the narrative structure of the serial, see Christine Geraghty, 'The Continuous Serial — A Definition', in R. Dyer, op. cit., pp. 9–27.

63   Burrowes, op. cit., p. 86.

64   Ibid., p. 91.

65   Ibid. See also his comment elsewhere: 'I have been criticised for not tying up loose ends in plots or not striving for a satisfactory solution. This is precisely because they are not plots. They are characters in real-life situations and as you well know, life doesn't tie up its loose ends.' ('Riordans characters act real-life situations', *Irish Farmers' Journal*, 25 November 1967, p. 24.)

66   Burrowes, op. cit., pp. 91–2.

67   Ibid., p. 101.

68   See the classic sociological analysis of the central importance of the family in the Irish social structure, Conrad M. Aresberg and S.T. Kimball, *Family and Community in Ireland* (Cambridge: Harvard University Press, 1940).

69   See Jean O'Halloran, 'Theme and Process in Television Drama: The Case of Irish TV', (Unpublished dissertation, Dublin City University, 1983), p. 51.

70   Arensberg and Kimball, op. cit., p. 174.

71   David Fitzpatrick., 'Class, Family and Rural Unrest in Nineteenth-Century Ireland', in P.J. Drudy ed, *Ireland: Land, Politics and People* (Cambridge: Cambridge University Press, 1982), p. 55.

72   O'Halloran, op. cit., p. 32.

73   Frances O'Rourke, 'Facing up to the Half-Way Halt', *Sunday Press*, March 11, 1984, p. 15. Similar sentiments are contained in an article one week earlier, Maryanne Heron, 'Whatever have we done to sex in Ireland', *Irish Independent*, 3 March 1984, p. 7.

74   *Northside Express*, 1 December 1983, p. 4.

5 From Megalith to Megastore: Broadcasting and Irish Culture

1 Cited in Maurice Gorham, *Forty Years of Irish Broadcasting* (Dublin: Talbot Press, 1967), p. 24.
2 Bertolt Brecht, 'Radio as a Means of Communication', *Screen*, vol. 20, nos. 3–4 (1979–80), p. 24.
3 Walter Benjamin, 'The Work of Art in the Age of Mechanical Reproduction', in *Illuminations*, trans. Harry Zohn (London: Fontana, 1970).
4 See Marcus de Burca, *The G.A.A.: A History* (Dublin: Cumann Luthchleas Gael, 1980), p. 217.
5 Gorham, op. cit., p. 90.
6 Rev. R. S. Devane, S. J., *The Imported Press: A National Menace – Some Remedies* (Dublin: James Duffy, 1950), pp. 5–6, 9.
7 Seán Mac Réamoinn, 'Traditional Music', *Radio Éireann Handbook* (Dublin: Radio Éireann, 1955), p. 27.
8 Seamus Ó Braonáin, 'Seven Years of Irish Radio', *The Leader*, 29 January, 1949, pp. 11–12.
9 Garret FitzGerald, 'Radio Listenership and the TV Problem', *University Review*, vol. ii, no. 5, p. 44.
10 Brennan, op. cit., 15 January 1949, p. 20.
11 Herbert I. Schiller, *Communication and Cultural Domination* (New York: M.E. Sharpe, 1976), p. 10 (my italics).
12 Raymond Williams, 'Most Doctors Recommend', *The Listener*, 27 November 1969.
13 See Desmond Fisher, *Broadcasting in Ireland* (London: Routledge, 1978), p. 32.
14 Harri Pritchard Jones, *Wales/Ireland: A TV Contrast* (Dublin: Conradh na Gaeilge 1974), p. 7.
15 D. George Boyce, *Nationalism in Ireland* (London: Croom Helm, 1982), p. 354.

6 Coming Out of Hibernation? The Myth of Modernization in Irish Culture

1 Oliver MacDonagh, *States of Mind* (London: Allen and Unwin 1983), ch. 1.
2 Paul Bew, Peter Gibbon and Henry Patterson, 'Some Aspects of Nationalism and Socialism in Ireland: 1968–1978', in Austen Morgan and Bob Purdie, eds., *Ireland: Divided Nation, Divided Class* (London: Ink Links, 1980), p. 160.
3 John Healy, 'Why Charlie Controls the 25th Dáil', *In Dublin: Election '87* (special issue), 7 February 1987, p. 15.
4 Declan Kiberd, 'The Moral Superiority of Rural Villages', *Irish Times*, 9 December 1986.
5 Fintan O'Toole, 'Going West: The Country versus the City in Irish Writing', *The Crane Bag*, vol. 9, no. 2, 1985, pp. 112–13.
6 See Raymond Williams, *Marxism and Literature* (Oxford: Oxford University Press, 1977), pp. 121–8. It is important to note that Williams' careful elaboration of the concept of residual ideology would challenge the view that it could function as a *dominant* ideology.
7 Kerby Miller, 'Emigration, Ideology and Identity in Post-Famine Ireland', *Studies*, vol. 75, no. 300, Winter 1986, p. 517.

8   Ibid., p. 518.

9   'Getting away from Outworn Shibboleths of Irishness', *Sunday Independent*, 9 November 1980.

10 See T. A. Boylan and M. P. Cuddy, 'Regional Industrial Policy: Performance and Challenge', *Administration*, vol. 32, no. 3, 1984.

11 Umberto Eco, *Travels in Hyperreality* (London: Picador, 1987), ch. 1.

12 See Eoin O'Malley's critical discussion, 'Reflections on Ireland's Economic Identity', *Studies*, vol. 75, no. 300, Winter 1986, p. 485.

13 Johann Arnason, 'The Modern Constellation and the Japanese Enigma: Part 1', *Thesis Eleven*, no. 17, 1987. See also Robert J. Smith's similar observation on the alleged survival of pre-industrial values into the modern era: 'This phenomenon is not a simple transfer into modern corporatism of an established tradition . . . it too is a new device that meets new needs of industrial society as the Japanese perceive it' (*Japanese Society: Tradition, Self and the Social Order* [Cambridge: Cambridge University Press, 1983], p. 66).

14 Edward Said, 'Orientalism Reconsidered', in F. Barker et al., *Literature, Politics and Theory* (London: Methuen, 1986), p. 218.

15 Declan O'Connell, 'Sociological Theory & Irish Political Research', in Kelly, O'Dowd, Wickham, eds., *Power, Conflict & Inequality* (Dublin, 1982), p. 196.

7 Labour and Local History: The Case of Jim Gralton

This essay was inspired by the first Gralton commemoration held in Carrick-on-Shannon and Effernagh, Co. Leitrim, April 1986, and two publications: Pat Feeley's *The Gralton Affair* (Dublin: Coolock Free Press, 1986), and Des Guckian, *Deported: Jimmy Gralton, 1886–1945* (Carrick-on-Shannon: Gralton Committee, 1988). It is dedicated to the memory of Packie Gralton, who died in 1992.

1   Raymond Williams, 'The Practice of Possibility' (Interview with Terry Eagleton), *New Statesman*, 7 August 1987, p. 20.

2   Antonio Gramsci, *Selections From Cultural Writings*, David Forgacs and Geoffrey Nowell Smith, eds., (London: Lawrence Wishart, 1985), pp. 30, 43.

3   See George Ritzer, 'The McDonaldization of Society', *Journal of American Culture*, 6 (1983), pp. 100–7.

4   For an insightful critique of the manner in which new media technologies under capitalism are destroying our experience of space and time, see Joshua Meyrowitz, *No Sense of Place: The Impact of Electronic Media on Social Behaviour* (New York: Oxford University Press, 1985).

5   Quoted in Fergus O'Farrell, 'The Country of the Mind: Irish Local History Reviewed', *The Irish Review*, no. 3 (1988), p. 121.

6   Raymond Williams, *Towards 2000* (Harmondsworth: Penguin, 1985), p. 181.

7   Raymond Gillespie and Gerard Moran, eds., *A Various Country: Essays in Mayo History* (Westport: 1987), ch. 1.

8   Aodh de Blacam, *From a Gaelic Outpost* (Dublin: Catholic Truth Society, 1921), p. xi.

9   D. A. Binchy, 'Two Blasket Autobiographies', *Studies*, vol. 23 (1933).

10 C. Desmond Greaves, *The Irish Transport and General Workers' Union: The Formative Years, 1909–23* (Dublin: Gill and Macmillan, 1982), pp. 216–17.

11   Fr. Michael O'Flanagan, *The Strength of Sinn Féin* (Dublin: Sinn Féin Standing Committee, [1917]), p. 7. See also C. Desmond Greaves, *Liam Mellowes and the Irish Revolution* (London: Lawrence and Wishart, 1971) pp. 113–14.

12   Michael O'Callaghan, *For Ireland and Freedom: Roscommon's Contribution to the Fight for Independence* (Boyle: Roscommon Herald, 1964), p. 28.

13   J. Dunsmore Clarkson, *Labour and Nationalism in Ireland* (New York: Columbia University, 1925), pp. 435–6.

14   Gralton's involvement in land seizures was explicitly compared to Fr. O'Flanagan's activities in an obituary written by his friend, Charlie Beirne. See Feeley, op. cit., p. 68.

15   Ibid., p. 20.

16   Fr. R. S. Devane, 'The Dance-Hall', *The Irish Ecclesiastical Record*, vol. xxxvii, February 1931, p. 179.

17   Ibid., p. 173.

18   One of the few points of factual disagreement in the two biographies of Gralton concerns the attitudes of Gralton's sister, who was a nun in New York, to his activities. Pat Feeley suggests he experienced strong hostility from his own family (p. 35), while Des Guckian paints a far more cordial picture (p. 23).

19   Cited in Jude Flynn, *Life and Times of Father Peter Conefrey* (Cloone, Co. Leitrim, 1983), p. 37.

20   Feeley, pp. 35–6.

21   *The Republican File*, 13 February 1932.

22   *The Republican File*, 20 February 1932.

23   Donal Nevin, 'Labour and the Political Revolution', in Francis MacManus, ed., *The Years of the Great Test, 1926–39* (Cork: Mercier Press, 1967), p. 61.

24   F. S. L. Lyons, *Ireland Since the Famine* (London: Fontana, 1973), p. 501. This threat of de Valera's is ridiculed in *Worker's Voice*, 11 February 1933.

25   *Worker's Voice*, 19 November 1932, p. 2.

26   James Hogan, *Could Ireland Become Communist?* (Dublin: Cahill & Co., 1935), p. 60. In view of the importance it attaches to the Gralton affair, it is surprising that Hogan's book is not mentioned in either Feeley's or Guckian's account of Gralton.

27   Frank Ryan and Michael Price had agreed to speak at the Rotunda meeting, but were withdrawn by the Army Council at short notice.

28   *Workers' Voice*, 4 March 1933, p. 3.

29   Lenin, *Collected Works*, vol. 4, pp. 211–12, (cited in Carmen Claudin-Urondo, *Lenin and the Cultural Revolution* (Sussex: Harvester Press, 1977), p. 57).

30   Cited in Horace B. Davis, *Nationalism and Socialism*, (New York: Monthly Review Press, 1967), pp. 95, 111.

31   See Arthur Griffith, 'Preface to the 1913 Edition' of John Mitchel's *Jail Journal*, (reprinted in John Mitchel, *Jail Journal*, with critical introduction by Thomas Flanagan), (Dublin: University Press of Ireland, 1982), pp. 370, 371.

32   For a view of community as a symbolic construct rather than a form of organic cohesion, see Anthony P. Cohen, *The Symbolic Construction of Community* (London: Routledge, 1985).

33   *Worker's Voice*, 4 March 1933. Margaret Cousins' imprisonment had already featured in the previous week's *Workers' Voice*.

8 The Politics of Silence: *Anne Devlin*, Women and Irish Cinema

1   James Joyce, *Stephen Hero*, ed. Theodore Spencer (London: Ace Books, 1961), p. 54. For a discussion of silence in Joyce's early writings see Jean-Michel Rabate, 'Silence in *Dubliners*', in Colin MacCabe, ed., *James Joyce: New Perspectives* (Brighton: Harvester Press, 1982). For a more general discussion, see Susan Sontag, 'The Aesthetics of Silence' in *A Susan Sontag Reader* (Harmondsworth: Penguin, 1983). Silence as a feminist strategy is explored in E. Ann Kaplan, *Women and Film: Both Sides of the Camera* (New York: Methuen, 1983), ch. 7.

2   Popular accounts of Anne Devlin are legion. For some recent examples, see Eamonn MacThomáis, *The Lady at the Gate* (Dublin: Joseph Clarke, 1971), pp. 120–31, and the re-issued pamphlet by Hester Piatt, *Anne Devlin: An Outline of Her Story*. Revisionist accounts of Robert Emmet are themselves subjected to a debunking exercise in Anthony Cronin's lively article, 'The Bould Robert Emmet' in *An Irish Eye* (Dingle: Brandon, 1985).

3   See Emmet Larkin, 'The Devotional Revolution in Ireland, 1850–75', *American Historical Review*, 77, pp. 625–52.

4   Marina Warner, 'What the Virgin of Knock Means to Women', *Magill*, September 1979, p. 39. See also Marina Warner, *Alone of All Her Sex: The Myth and Cult of the Virgin Mary* (London: Quartet, 1978), pp. 190–1.

5   Patrick Pearse, 'Robert Emmet and the Ireland of To-day' in *Collected Works of Padraic H. Pearse: Political Writings and Speeches* (Dublin: Phoenix Publishing Co., 1924), pp. 83–4.

6   Over forty plays were written about Robert Emmet, and innumerable novels. His story was set to music in two operas and features in many of the earliest Irish films. See Maureen S. G. Hawkins, 'The Dramatic Treatment of Robert Emmet and Sarah Curran', in S. F. Gallagher, ed., *Women in Irish Legend, Life and Literature* (Gerrards Cross, Bucks.: Colin Smythe, 1983).

7   See James Hope's letter to R. R. Madden: 'At the time that politics were first mooted in the North . . . the mass confided in the *writers and speakers*, as men who were necessarily competent to the direction of public affairs, and laid more on them than they were able to perform, had they even been all honest men. . . . The cause of Ireland was the [sic] confined to a few individuals. The masses had no idea of the possibility of managing their own affairs', *The Memoirs of Jemmy Hope* (Belfast: British and Irish Communist Organization, 1972), pp. 7–8.

8   The notion of the female body as 'choric' discourse is central to contemporary French feminism, especially the work of Julia Kristeva. In *About Chinese Women* (London: Marion Boyars, 1977), Kristeva draws a connection between the 'marginal speech' of women who exist outside the symbolic order of time and language, and pregnancy, which is characterized as an 'escape from the bonds of daily social temporality, interruption of the regular monthly cycles: woman deserts the surfaces – skin, eyes – so that she may descend to the depths of the body, to hear, taste, smell the infinitesimal life of the cells' (pp. 35–6).

9   Describing the association between Glenmalure in Co. Wicklow and Michael Dwyer, James Plunkett writes: 'At the farthest end of the glen, just across the river, the ruins of a cottage are another reminder of Dwyer. A woman lived there who had the habit, now and then, of coming out on to the roadway in front to

comb her hair. If she did so, the look-out post high up the mountain knew the military were up to something and took precautions.' (*The Gems She Wore: A Book of Irish Places* [London: Arrow, 1978], p. 78).

10   For a related discussion, see Kevin Barry, 'Cinema and Feminism: The Case of *Anne Devlin*', *The Furrow*, vol. 36, no. 4, April 1985, p. 248.

11   David Will sees in this image an invocation of Delacroix's 'Liberty at the Barricades'. See David Will, 'New Strategies for the Anti-Colonial Cinema', *Cencrastus*, no. 19, Winter 1984, p. 39, and his interview with Pat Murphy, in *Framework*, nos. 26–27, pp. 132–8.

9 'Lies that tell the truth': *Maeve*, History and Irish Cinema

1   For a valuable discussion which seeks to relate *Maeve* to developments in feminist film theory, see the review article by Claire Johnston and the subsequent interview with Pat Murphy in *Screen*, vol. 22, no. 4, 1981.

2   Standish O'Grady, *History of Ireland: The Heroic Period*, vol. 1, (London: Sampson Law, Searle Marston, & Rivington/Dublin: E. Pansonby; 1878), p. x.

3   Cited in Philip L. Marcus, *Yeats and the Beginning of the Irish Renaissance* (Ithaca, New York: Cornell University Press, 1970), p. 235.

4   Philip L. Marcus, *Standish O'Grady* (Lewisburg: Bucknell University Press, 1970), p. 35.

5   For some interesting comments on Queen Maeve's legendary promiscuity, see P. MacCana, 'Women in Irish Mythology', and M. Ní Bhrolcháin, 'Women in Early Irish Myths and Sagas', in *The Crane Bag* issue on 'Images of Irish Women', vol. 4, no. 1, 1980. It is interesting to note in passing that the sexual licence displayed by the other great heroines in early Irish mythology, Deirdre and Grainne, also posed problems for fellow revivalists of O'Grady's such as P. W. Joyce and Katherine Tynan.

6   See Yeats' comment in the early days of the Revival: 'If we can but take that history and those legends and turn them into drama, poems and stories *full of the living soul of the present* . . . we may deliver that new great utterance for which the world is waiting' (My emphasis – cited in Marcus, *Yeats and the Beginning of the Irish Renaissance*, p. 258).

7   Standish O'Grady, *History of Ireland: Critical and Philosophical* (London: Sampson Law, 1881), p. 51. It is clear that in investing ruins and antiquities with organic cohesion, O'Grady is, in effect, attempting to mask over the fragmentation of the Irish past, what James Joyce referred to as the 'broken lights' of popular memory.

8   O'Grady, *History of Ireland: The Heroic Period*, vol. 1, pp. v–vi.

9   O'Grady, *History of Ireland: Critical and Philosophical*, p. 57.

10   Perspective is explicitly compared to viewing reality through a glass window in the pioneering writings of Leonardo and Alberti. For a wide-ranging analysis of the relationship between narrative and visual perspective, see Stephen Heath's influential essay 'Narrative Space', in *Screen*, vol. 17, no. 2, 1976.

11   For some interesting comments on the relationship between narrative and the 'deferment of pleasure', see Bill Nichols, *Ideology and the Image* (Bloomington: Indiana University Press, 1981), pp. 73–80.

10 Narratives of No Return: James Coleman's guaiRE

1   W. B. Yeats, *Autobiographies* (London: Macmillan, 1955), p. 416.

2   See Yeats, *Plays in Prose and Verse* (London: Macmillan, 1931), p. 423.

3   Ibid., p. 72.

4   'At Dunguaire Castle, the past is relived again and again . . . when guests from all over the world assemble at the nightly banquets set out by the Shannon Free Airport Development Company whose property the castle now is', James Patrick Hynes, *White-Shrouded Fort: A History of Guaire, the Hospitable, King of Connaught, and his Descendents* (Mold: Studio 365, 1980), p. 61.

5   See B. A. Stolz and R. S. Shannon, eds., *Oral Literature and the Formula* (Ann Arbor: Center for the Coordination of Ancient and Modern Studies, 1976).

6   See Lady Ferguson, *The Story of the Irish before the Conquest*, second edition (Dublin: Sealy, Bryers and Walker, 1889), p. 15.

7   Marina Warner, *Monuments and Maidens: The Allegory of the Female Form* (London: Picador, 1987), p. 11.

8   Sigmund Freud, *On Sexuality* (Harmondsworth: Pelican Freud Library, 1977), vol. 7: no. 223. Freud is quoting an old legal tag, in Latin: '*Pater semper incertus est*', while the mother is '*certissima*'.

9   James Joyce, *Ulysses* (New York: Modern Library, 1946), p. 205. See also Karen Lawrence, 'Paternity, the Legal Fiction', in Robert D. Newman and Weldon Thornton, eds., *Joyce's Ulysses: The Larger Perspective* (Newark: University of Delaware Press, 1987), pp. 89–97.

10   Elizabeth Butler-Cullingford, '"Thinking of Her . . . as . . . Ireland": Yeats, Pearse and Heaney,' *Textual Practice*, 4, no. 1, 1990, p. 6. Cullingford observes that such personifications may project 'male anxieties . . . of the need to control and subordinate the female sex', anxieties introducing a fault line in the native patriarchal order – the weakness induced by colonization.

11   Sir George Baden-Powell, *The Saving of Ireland: Industrial, Financial, Political* (Edinburgh and London: William Blackwood and Sons, 1898), p. 291. See also David Cairns and Shaun Richards, *Writing Ireland: Colonialism, Nationalism and Culture* (Manchester: Manchester University Press, 1988), ch. 3.

12   Anne Owens Weekes, *Irish Women Writers: An Uncharted Tradition* (Lexington: University Press of Kentucky, 1990), pp. 15–16.

13   See Eileen Hunter, *Christabel: The Russell Case and After* (London: Andre Deutsch, 1973). The controversy was reactivated after Russell's death, in 1976, with litigation between her first son and her husband's next son.

14   Lynne Cooke, 'A Tempered Agnosia', *James Coleman*, exhibition catalogue (Lyons: Musée d'Art Contemporain, 1990).

15   See Michael Newman, 'Allegories of the Subject: The Theme of Identity in the Work of James Coleman', in *James Coleman: Selected Works*, exhibition catalogue (Chicago: The Renaissance Society at the University of Chicago, 1985), p. 44. Foucault's argument recalls F. W. Maitland's famous dictum, 'For the first time, the Absolute State faced the Absolute Individual', quoted in Ian Watt, *The Rise of the Novel* (Harmondsworth: Penguin, 1970), p. 63.

16   Jo Anna Isaak, *The Ruin of Representation in Modernist Art and Texts* (Ann Arbor: U. M. I. Research Press, 1986), p. 23.

17 Paul Muldoon, *Quoof* (London: Faber and Faber, 1983), p. 39. See also Clair Wills, 'The Lie of the Land: Language, Imperialism and Trade in Paul Muldoon's *Meeting the British*', in Neil Corcoran, ed., *The Chosen Ground: Essays on Contemporary Poetry of Northern Ireland* (Chester Springs, Pa.: Dufour Editions, 1992), pp. 136–49.

18 See Christine Buci-Glucksmann, 'Catastrophic Utopia: The Feminine as Allegory in the Modern', in Catherine Gallagher and Thomas Laquer, eds., *The Making of the Modern Body: Sexuality and Society in the Nineteenth Century* (Berkeley: University of California Press, 1987), pp. 220–9.

19 See Nell McCafferty, *A Woman to Blame: The Kerry Babies Case* (Dublin: Attic Press, 1985). Joanne Hayes' own book, *My Story* (Dingle: Brandon Books, 1985), was withdrawn from circulation due to a legal action following the state tribunal into her case.

20 Erich Auerbach, 'Figura', *Scenes From the Drama of European Literature* (Manchester: Manchester University Press, 1984), p. 30.

11 Identity Without a Centre: Allegory, History and Irish Nationalism

1 James Joyce, 'The Dead', *Dubliners* (Harmondsworth: Penguin, 1992), p. 225.

2 Benedict Anderson, *Imagined Communities: Reflections on the Origin and Spread of Nationalism* (London: Verso, 1983), p. 30.

3 E. J. Hobsbawm, 'Some Reflections on *The Break-Up of Britain*', *New Left Review*, 105, September–October (1977), pp. 4–7.

4 The Dublin *Daily Express* had an explicit editorial commitment to 'reconcile the rights and impulses of Irish nationality with the demands and obligations of imperial dominion' (Stephen J. Brown, *The Press in Ireland: A Survey and Guide* [Dublin: Brown and Nolan, 1937], p. 35).

5 E. J. Hobsbawm, *Nations and Nationalism since 1870* (Cambridge: Cambridge University Press, 1991), pp. 164, 169, 181.

6 Terry Eagleton, 'Ecriture and Eighteenth-Century Fiction', in Francis Barker, et al., eds., *Literature, Society and the Sociology of Literature* (Colchester: University of Essex, 1977), p. 55.

7 Susan Sontag, *Against Interpretation* (New York: Delta, 1966), p. 13. For a related example in art criticism, see Michael Fried's exhortation that modernist works should 'seek an ideal of self-sufficiency and what I call "presentness" . . . Effects of presentness can still amount to grace.' ('How Modernism Works: A Reply to T. J. Clark', in W. J. T. Mitchell, ed., *The Politics of Interpretation* [Chicago: University of Chicago Press, 1983], pp. 232–4.)

8 Rosemary Radford Reuther, 'A World on Fire with Faith', *New York Times Book Review*, 26 January 1992. According to Malise Ruthven, it is no coincidence that many fundamentalists have a scientific training: 'For all the jeremiads that fundamentalism, Islamic and Christian, lances at Western "materialism", it is fundamentalism that is hard, factual and philistine . . . Fundamentalism is the most materialistic of contemporary ideologies, a throwback to the mechanistic values of the Victorians.' (*A Satanic Affair: Salman Rushdie and the Wrath of Islam* [London: The Hogarth Press, 1991], p. 142.) It is striking that Ruthven discerns in fundamentalism the 'presence' and self-validating meaning that Sontag and Fried associate with high modernism.

9 Archbishop MacHale's questioning of papal infallibility was partly motivated by his nationalism, in that it was bound up with the dissident 'Gallican' movement which sought a degree of national autonomy within the church, as opposed to the 'Ultramontanist' tendency to centralize power in Rome.

10 Wakes, keening (a form of ritual lamenting performed by females at wakes) and patterns (popular, and frequently ribald religious festivals which commemorated local patron [hence 'pattern'] saints at holy wells) were subject to systematic interdiction by the post-Famine church. See S. J. Connolly, *Priests and People in Pre-Famine Ireland* (Dublin: Gill & Macmillan, 1982), and the excellent overview in his pamphlet *Religion and Society in Nineteenth-Century Ireland* (Dundalk: Dundalgen Press, 1985).

11 Seán O'Faoláin, *King of the Beggars: A Life of Daniel O'Connell* (Dublin: Poolbeg Press, 1980), p. 29. For the accommodation between Catholicism and the colonial administration, see Tom Inglis, *The Moral Monopoly: The Catholic Church in Modern Irish Society* (Dublin: Gill and Macmillan, 1987), ch. 5, and David Lloyd, *Nationalism and Minor Literature: James Clarence Mangan and the Emergence of Irish Cultural Nationalism* (Berkeley: University of California Press, 1987), Introduction and ch. 2.

12 'Dialogue with Jacques Derrida', in Richard Kearney, *Dialogues with Contemporary Continental Thinkers* (Manchester: Manchester University Press, 1984), p. 116.

13 'The Intent of British Imperialism', *The Times* (London), 1 January 1877, reprinted in Hans Kohn, ed., *Nationalism and Realism: 1852–1879* (Princeton: Van Nostrand Company, 1968), pp. 135–6.

14 Sir George Baden-Powell, *The Saving of Ireland: Industrial, Financial, Political* (Edinburgh: William Blackwood and Sons, 1898), p. 221.

15 The romantic attempt to impose Burkean ideas of continuity on Irish history is critically analysed in Tom Dunne, 'Haunted by History: Irish Romantic Writing 1800–50', in Roy Porter and Mikulas Teich, eds., *Romanticism in National Context* (Cambridge: Cambridge University Press, 1988). See also my discussion in ch. 12, pp. 157ff.

16 Derrida, op. cit., p. 117.

17 See, for example, the sustained critique of Daniel Corkery's classic *The Hidden Ireland* (1924) in Louis Cullen's *The Hidden Ireland: Reassessment of a Concept* (Gigginstown: The Lilliput Press, 1988).

18 Tom Dunne, 'The Gaelic Response to Conquest and Colonization: The Evidence of the Poetry', *Studia Hibernica*, 20 (1980), p. 11.

19 Richard Peet, *Global Capitalism: Theories of Societal Development* (London: Routledge, 1991), p. 112.

20 Aodh de Blacam, *Towards the Republic: A Study of New Ireland's Social and Political Aims* (Dublin: Thomas Kiersey, 1919), pp. 22, 23. I trace the development of this critical, 'decentred' version of Irish nationalism in two sections of Seamus Deane, ed., *The Field Day Anthology of Irish Writing* (Derry/London: Field Day/Faber and Faber, 1991), vols. ii and iii.

21 Dunne, op. cit., pp. 11–12.

22 Karl Marx, *Capital: A Critique of Political Economy*, trans. Ben Fowkes (Harmondsworth: Penguin, 1976), vol. 1, p. 91.

23 Colin Leys, 'Conflict and Convergence in Development Theory', in Wolfgang J. Mommsen and Jurgen Osterhammel, eds., *Imperialism and After: Continuities and Discontinuities* (London: Allen and Unwin, 1986), p. 321.

24 See Vincent P. Pecora, 'The Limits of local Knowledge', in H. Aram Veeser, ed., *The New Historicism* (New York: Routledge, 1989).

25 William Roseberry, 'Balinese Cockfights and the Seduction of Anthropology', *Social Research*, 49 (1982), p. 1021, cited by Aletta Biersack, 'Local Knowledge, Local History: Geertz and Beyond', in Lynn Hunt, ed., *The New Cultural History* (Berkeley: University of California Press, 1989), p. 82.

26 Patrick O'Farrell, 'Millenialism, Messianism, and Utopianism in Irish History', in P. J. Drudy, ed., *Anglo-Irish Studies*, ii., 1976, p. 53; Tom Garvin, 'Defenders, Ribbonmen and Others: Underground Political Networks in Pre-Famine Ireland', *Past and Present*, 96 (1982), pp. 134, 140.

27 Michael Beames, *Peasants and Power: The Whiteboy Movements and their Control in Pre-Famine Ireland* (Brighton, Sussex: The Harvester Press, 1983), pp. 73, 97. See also Maureen Wall, 'The Whiteboys', in T. Desmond Williams, ed., *Secret Societies in Ireland* (Dublin: Gill & Macmillan, 1973), p. 16.

28 Natalie Zemon Davis, *Society and Culture in Early Modern France* (Stanford: Stanford University Press, 1991), p. 149. See also Beames, op. cit., pp. 98–101.

29 The combination of patriarchy and paternalism in the political theory which informed Jacobitism is discussed from a feminist perspective in Carole Pateman, *The Sexual Contract* (London: Polity Press, 1988).

30 James S. Donnelly, jun., 'The Whiteboy Movement, 1761–65', *Irish Historical Studies*, xxi, no. 81 (1978–9), pp. 27–8.

31 Zemon Davis, op. cit., p. 219. For a discussion of the difficulties in separating literal and allegorical levels in ethnography, see James Clifford, 'On Ethnographic Allegory', in James Clifford and George E. Marcus, eds., *Writing Culture: The Poetics and Politics of Ethnography* (Berkeley: University of California Press, 1986), p. 119. See also my discussion above, pp. 18–22.

32 Wall, op. cit., p. 16. As Louis Cullen remarks, for all the nebulousness of the visionary poetry of the period, some of the poems are so homely and topical that 'we are almost listening to the conversations in some circles in Munster, in effect to the loose talk which alarmed Protestants in Cork or Clare, the two great counties of literary composition in Irish' (Cullen, op. cit., p. 48).

33 See, for example, John Hand's account: 'Since the days when it became treason to love their country, the Irish poets usually adopted allegory, such as we find in "Dark Rosaleen". They sang of Ireland as the "Dark Little Rose", the "Shan Van Vocht" [i.e., the poor old woman] . . . and under a hundred other names.' ('Street Songs and Ballads and Anonymous Verse', in *Irish Literature*, vol. 8, [New York: Collier & Sons, 1904], p. 3266.)

34 Cited in Edward Hayes, *The Ballads of Ireland*, vol. 1 (London: Fullerton & Co., 1855), p. xxvii.

35 Hayes, ibid., p. xxi.

36 Rev. Samuel O'Sullivan, 'Thugee in India and Ribbonism in Ireland', in *Remains of Rev. Samuel O'Sullivan, D. D.*, vol. 3 (Dublin: McGlashen, 1853), pp. 197–8.

37 Hayes, op. cit., p. xxxiv.

38 James Joyce, *Portrait of the Artist as a Young Man* (Harmondsworth: Penguin, 1992), pp. 205, 67.

39 Richard Ellmann, *James Joyce* (New York: Oxford University Press, 1965), p. 10.

40 Joyce, op. cit., p. 101.

41   James Joyce, *Ulysses* (New York: Modern Library, 1946), p. 192.

42   Seamus Deane, 'Silence and Eloquence', *The Guardian*, 12 December 1991.

43   James Joyce, 'The Dead', p. 213. (All subsequent page references in parentheses in text.)

44   Ellmann, op. cit., p. 257.

45   Daniel O'Connell may be seen as the first political leader to systematically align the dominant strands in Irish nationalism with the *state* rather than the *nation*, although, as we have noted above (n. 11), the state in question was that of a colonial administration. The O'Connell monument is thus placed on a continuum with the other icons of colonial rule that tend to attract Gabriel's eye on the Dublin skyline: the Wellington monument, the Fifteen Acres, and the gloomy facade of the Four Courts which 'stood out menacingly against the heavy sky'.

46   Pierre Nora, 'Between Memory and History: *Les Lieux de Memoire*', *Representations*, 26, Spring (1989), p. 13.

47   Donal O'Sullivan, *Songs of the Irish* (Dublin: Mercier Press, 1981), p. 130.

48   James Joyce, *Stephen Hero*, ed. Theodore Spencer (London: Ace Books, 1961), p. 68.

49   Joyce wrote that 'This party under different names: "Whiteboys", "Men of 98", "United Irishmen", "Invincibles", "Fenians", has always refused to be connected with either the English political parties or the Nationalist parliamentarians. They maintain (and in this assertion history fully supports them) that any concessions that have been granted to Ireland, England has granted unwillingly, and, as it is usually put, at the point of a bayonet.' (James Joyce, 'Fenianism: The Last Fenian', in Ellsworth Mason and Richard Ellmann, eds., *The Critical Writings of James Joyce* [London: Faber and Faber, 1959], p. 188.)

50   See David Lloyd, 'Adulteration and the Nation', in *Anomalous States: Irish Writing and the Post-Colonial Moment* (Dublin: Lilliput Press, 1993).

51   William Thackeray, *The Irish Sketch Book and Critical Reviews* (London: Smith, Elder & Co., 1880), p. 221.

52   Clifford, op. cit., pp. 110, 120.

53   Mikhail Bakhtin, *Problems of Dostoevsky's Poetics*, ed. and trans. Cary Emerson (Manchester: Manchester University Press, 1984), p. 81.

12 Race Against Time: Racial Discourse and Irish History

1   This educational aid, along with other amusing board games such as 'Trading with the Colonies', can be inspected at Strokestown Park House, Co. Roscommon. I am grateful to the curator of the house, Luke Dodd, for drawing my attention to these relics of 'old decency'.

2   Homi K. Bhabha, 'Difference, Discrimination and the Discourse of Colonialism', *The Politics of Theory* (Colchester: University of Essex, 1983), pp. 199, 203–4. Revised versions of the essay appear in *Screen*, vol. 24: no. 6 (1983), and in Frances Barker et al., eds, *Literature, Politics and Theory, Papers from the Essex Conference, 1976–84* (London: Methuen, 1986).

3   Frances E. Kingsley, ed., *Charles Kingsley, His Letters and Memories of His Life*, vol. iii (London: Macmillan & Co. Ltd., 1901), p. 111 (cited in G. J. Watson, *Irish Identity and the Literary Revival* [London: Croom Helm, 1989] p. 17).

4   Cited in Francis Hackett, *Ireland: A Study in Nationalism* (New York: B. W. Huebsch, 1919), p. 227.

5   Sheridan Gilley, 'English Attitudes to the Irish in England, 1780–1900', in C. Holmes, ed., *Immigrants and Minorities in British Society* (London: Croom Helm, 1978), p. 91. Gilley's work has been conscripted into the front ranks of contemporary polemical exchanges over anti-Irish racism. As the historian Roy Foster expresses it: 'Innocent and sometimes naively hilarious works of piety about the Fenians or Young Irelanders, written by amateur historians on the British left, fall into a much cruder category [of propaganda]. They are joined by the half-baked "sociologists" employed on profitably never-ending research into "anti-Irish racism", determined to prove what they have already decided to be the case. Historians like Sheridan Gilley may have scrupulously and sympathetically explored the definitions of historical "racism" and rejected them for the Irish but this matters [little] to such zealots.' (Roy Foster, '"We are all Revisionists now"', in *The Irish Review*, 1 (1986), p. 3.)

6   *The Times*, 17 December 1867 (cited in Gilley, op. cit. p. 96). These sentiments are endorsed by Gilley: 'When the Irish conformed to English values they were quietly accepted in England. But that is surely the point: it was the Irish rejection of English values, which – rather than race – aroused English dislike of them' (p. 93). What this argument overlooks is the extent to which those who failed to conform to English values were not only deemed to be outside English civilization, but to be beyond 'the pale of humanity', in Goldwyn Smith's felicitous phrase. For some of the less welcome implications of this acceptance of dominant English values, see the discussion below of how the Irish embraced racist ideologies, pp. 175–7.

7   Gilley's criticism is directed mainly at works such as L. P. Curtis's influential study *Apes and Angels: The Irishman in Victorian Caricature* (Newton Abbot: David & Charles, 1971).

8   See Nicholas Canny, *The Elizabethan Conquest of Ireland: A Pattern Established* (Hassocks, Sussex: Harvester Press, 1976): 'Events in Ireland, 1565–76, have a significance in the general history of colonization that transcends English and Irish history. The involvement of men in Irish colonization who afterwards ventured to the New World suggests that their years in Ireland was a period of apprenticeship' (p. 15). See also D. B. Quinn's pioneering work, *The Elizabethans and the Irish* (Ithaca: Cornell University Press, 1966), and K. R. Andrews, N. Canny and P. E. H. Hair, eds., *The Westward Enterprise: English Activities in Ireland, the Atlantic and America, 1480–1650* (Detroit: Wayne State University Press, 1979).

9   Cited in Quinn op. cit., p. 119. Mountjoy's statement was a response to a modest proposal that the entire native population of Ireland be transported to the Plantations of America.

10   Quinn, ibid., pp. 25, 153, 24.

11   Cited in Nicholas Mansergh, *The Irish Question, 1840–1921* (London: Unwin University Books, 1965), p. 23.

12   Anthony Buckley, '"We're Trying to Find our Identity": Uses of History among Ulster Protestants', in Elizabeth Tonkin, Marion McDonald and Malcolm Chapman, eds., *History and Ethnicity*, ASA Monograph 27 (London: Routledge, 1989), p. 187.

13   According to Canny: 'We find the colonists in Virginia using the same pretexts for the extermination of the Amerindians as their counterparts used in the 1560s and 1570s for the slaughter of segments of the native Irish population . . . no determined effort was ever made to reform the Irish, but rather, at the least pretext – generally resistance to the English – they were dismissed as a "wicked and faythles

peopoll" and put to the sword. This formula was repeated in the treatment of Indians in the New World' op. cit., (p. 160).

14   Michael Rogin, 'Liberal Society and the Indian Question', in *Ronald Reagan the Movie and other Episodes in Political Demonology* (Berkeley: University of California Press, 1987), p. 153.

15   Ibid., p. 142.

16   Jacques Derrida, *Of Grammatology*, trans. Gayatri Chakravorty Spivak (Baltimore: The Johns Hopkins Press, 1977), p. 136.

17   Derrida, ibid., p. 198.

18   John Locke, *An Essay Concerning Human Understanding*, vol. 2 (London: Dent, 1974) p. 258. For a useful exposition of Locke's theory of history, see Ian Haywood, *The Making of History* (Rutherford: Fairleigh Dickinson University Press, 1986).

19   David Hume, 'The Natural History of Religion', in Richard Wollheim, ed., *Hume on Religion* (London: Fontana, 1968), pp. 79–80.

20   David Hume, *A History of England*, new edition, vol. 5 (London, 1796), pp. 397–8.

21   Jeoffry [sic] Keating, *The General History of Ireland*, trans. Dermod O'Connor (Dublin, 1841), p. 53. Keating's history was composed in Irish and was first translated by O'Connor in 1723.

22   Charles O'Conor, *Dissertations on the History of Ireland* (1753), third edition (Dublin, 1812), pp. 78, ix, 77.

23   Thomas Campbell, *Strictures on the Ecclesiastical and Literary History of Ireland* (Dublin, 1789), p. 9.

24   Charles Gavan Duffy, *Young Ireland: A Fragment of Irish History, 1840–1850* (London, 1880), p. 44 (cited in David Lloyd, *Nationalism and Minor Literature: James Clarence Mangan and the Emergence of Irish Cultural Nationalism* [Berkeley: University of California Press, 1987], p. 68). It is worth pointing out that the title of Duffy's book – 'Fragment' – belies the seamless unity he sought to impose on Irish history.

25   Douglas Hyde, 'The Necessity for De-Anglicizing Ireland', in *The Revival of Irish Literature* (London, 1894), p. 121.

26   Rev. C. J. Herlihy, *The Celt Above the Saxon* (Boston: Angel Guardian Press, 1904), p. 171.

27   Gilley, op. cit., p. 81.

28   Conor Cruise O'Brien, *States of Ireland* (London: Hutchinson, 1972); F. S. L. Lyons, *Culture and Anarchy in Ireland, 1890–1939* (Oxford: Oxford University Press, 1979).

29   See Griffith's virulent defence of slavery in 'Preface to the 1913 Edition' of John Mitchel's *Jail Journal*, reprinted, with critical introduction by Thomas Flanagan, (Dublin: University Press of Ireland, 1982), pp. 370–1.

30   Thomas MacDonagh, *Literature in Ireland* (Dublin: The Talbot Press, 1919), p. 57.

31   George Sigerson, *Modern Ireland* (London, 1868); *Barla of the Gael and Gall* (London: Unwin, 1925), first published in 1897. I have dealt with MacDonagh and Sigerson at greater length in the sections which I have edited in vols. 2 and 3 of Seamus Deane, ed., *The Field Day Anthology of Irish Writing* (London: Faber and Faber, 1991).

32   Hume, 'The Natural History of Religion', p. 80.

33   'The Individuality of a Native Literature,' *The Nation*, 21 August 1847, p. 731 (cited in Lloyd, op. cit., p. 72).

34   Joseph Cooper Walker, *Historical Memoirs of the Irish Bards* (1786), 2nd edition, vol. 1 (Dublin, 1818), p. 55.

35   For the Jacobite background of Ossian, see Albert Boime, *Art in an Age of Revolution, 1750–1800* (Chicago: University of Chicago Press, 1987), pp. 214–27.

36   Donal McCartney, 'The Writing of History in Ireland, 1800–30', in *Irish Historical Studies*, 10 (1957), p. 359. For an extended discussion of the differences between Irish and English conceptions of history, see Oliver MacDonagh, *States of Mind: A Study of Anglo-Irish Conflict, 1780–1980* (London: Allen and Unwin, 1983), ch. 1.

37   Fredric Jameson, '*Ulysses* in History', in W. J. McCormack and Alistair Stead, eds., *James Joyce and Modern Literature* (London: Routledge & Kegan Paul, 1982), p. 129.

38   David Frisby, *Fragments of Modernity* (London: Polity Press, 1985), p. 45.

39   For Nietzsche's aversion to historicism, see Frisby, op. cit., p. 32ff.

40   *The Voice of the Nation: A Manual of Nationality*, by the writers of *The Nation* newspaper (Dublin: James Duffy, 1844), p. 156.

41   George Simmel, 'Die Ruine', in *Zur Philosophie der Kunst* (Potsdam, 1922) pp. 127–88 (cited in Louis Hawes, *Presences of Nature: British Landscape, 1780–1830* [New Haven: Yale Center for British Art, 1982]).

42   William Drennan, *Glendalloch and other Poems* (Dublin: William Robertson, 1859), p. 279.

43   'Lament over the Ruins of the Abbey of Teach Molaga', in D. J. O'Donoghue, ed., *Poems of James Clarence Mangan* (Dublin: O'Donoghue, 1903), pp. 26–7. For a detailed and perceptive reading of this poem, see Lloyd, op. cit., 90ff.

44   Wyndham Lewis, *Time and Western Man* (London: Chatto and Windus, 1927), pp. 99–100, 106–7.

45   Lewis, ibid., pp. 109, 175, 181.

46   This is not to contradict Derrida's insistence that all speech carries with it the disruptive effects of writing: the point is, rather, that models of speech in societies which dominated Western thought operated, as Spivak puts it, 'on an implicit phonocentrism, the presupposition that speech is the immediate expression of the self'. The argument here is that the same powerful cultures were not so willing to grant this self-validating phonocentrism to the speech of subaltern cultures. It is precisely, therefore, the phonocentric presuppositions of dominant cultures, particularly in their imperial or colonial manifestations, which are thrown into disarray by subaltern modes of communication such as rumour. See the section on 'Rumour' in Gayatri Chakravorty Spivak, 'Subaltern Studies: Deconstructing Historiography', in *In Other Worlds: Essays in Cultural Politics* (New York: Methuen, 1987) pp. 211–15, as well as Jameson's remarks on gossip as a means of 'dereification', op. cit., p. 135.

47   Spivak, ibid., p. 213. Spivak remarks in the course of her discussion that in certain cases, e.g. the codes of law, written texts operate on an implicit phonocentrism, a description that would seem to apply to the valorization of scripture and *written texts* in Locke's and Hume's approaches to religion and history.

48   Lewis, op. cit., pp. 7–8.

49   Lewis, ibid., p. 122 (quoting from his own book, *The Art of Being Ruled*, ch. vi, part xii).

50   Ibid., p. 118.

51   Jameson, op. cit., pp. 135–6.
52   Franco Moretti, 'The Long Goodbye: *Ulysses* and the end of Liberal Capitalism',
      in *Signs Taken for Wonders* (London: Verso, 1983), pp. 189–90.
53   Wyndham Lewis, *The Lion and the Fox* (London: Grant Richards, 1927), p. 322.
54   See Guy Debord, *Society of the Spectacle* (Rebel Press, AIM Publications, 1987),
      paragraphs 158, 162: 'The spectacle, as the present social organization of the
      paralysis of history and memory, of the abandonment of history built on the
      foundation of historical time, is the *false consciousness of time* . . . *thus spatial
      alienation*, the society that radically separates the subject from the activity it
      takes from him, separates him first of all from his own time'.
55   *The Ethics of Hunger Striking*, by a Catholic priest (London: Sands, 1920), pp.
      14–15.
56   G. J. Watson, op. cit., p. 28.

13 Montage, Modernism and the City

1   John Eglinton, 'Mr. Yeats and Popular Poetry', in John Eglinton, W. B. Yeats, A.
     E., W. Larminie, *Literary Ideals in Ireland* (London: Fisher Unwin, 1899), p. 43.
2   Franco Moretti, *Signs Taken for Wonders*, trans. Susan Fischer, David Forgacs,
     David Miller (London: Verso, 1983), p. 190. Moretti does at least proceed from
     'effect to cause', acknowledging that the paralysis of Irish culture was due in no
     small measure to its dependency on a stagnant British empire.
3   James Wills and Freeman Wills, *The Irish Nation: Its History and its Biography*
     (Edinburgh: A. Fullerton & Co., 1876), vol. 1, p. 3.
4   Sergei Eisenstein, *The Film Sense*, trans. Jay Leyda (London: Faber and Faber,
     1968), p. 181.
5   For a recent discussion of the sense of catastrophe in Irish history, see Brendan
     Bradshaw, 'Nationalism and Historical Scholarship in Modern Ireland', *Irish
     Historical Studies*, vol. xxvi, no. 104, November 1989.
6   L. P. Curtis, jun., *Anglo-Saxons and Celts: A Study of Anti-Irish Prejudice in
     Victorian England* (Bridgeport, Connecticut: Conference on British Studies,
     1968), p. 51.
7   A. Nicholas Vardac, *From Stage to Screen: Theatrical Origins of Early Film: David
     Garrick to D. W. Griffith* (Cambridge, Mass: Harvard University Press, 1949);
     John L. Fell, *Film and the Narrative Tradition* (Berkeley: Unversity of California
     Press, 1986).
8   See Sergei Eisenstein, *Film Form*, trans. Jay Leyda (London: Faber and Faber,
     1963), p. 223.
9   James Joyce, 'Ireland, Island of Saints and Sages' in Ellsworth Mason and
     Richard Ellmann, eds., *The Critical Writings of James Joyce* (London: Faber and
     Faber, 1959), p. 165.
10   James Joyce, *Ulysses*, (New York: Modern Library, 1946), p. 209.

14 Unapproved Roads: Ireland and Post-Colonial Identity

1   See one correspondent's view in a letter to the *Irish Times*: 'As the college must share
     its special year with events commemorating the Famine, the highlighting of Queen

Victoria – who stood almost aloof from the Great Hunger of the people at that time – is an unfortunate choice. Her association with the university could have been adequately recognized in a less dramatic way.' (T. J. Maher, 'Queen Victoria's Statue', 30 January 1995). It is important to point out, however, that the statue was not restored to its former site but was rather 'reframed' by the curators of the exhibition behind a glass case in the corner of a display room, as part of a more general exhibition. As I argue below, this changes significantly the 'meaning' of the statue, and certainly calls into question its previous imperious position.

2   The factors which influenced the Irish government's failure to commemorate the centenary of the Famine are discussed in Mary E. Daly, 'Why the Great Famine got Forgotten in the Dark 1940s', *Sunday Tribune*, 22 January 1995. For the neglect of the Famine by academic historians, see Cormac O'Grada's valuable introduction to the re-issue of R. Dudley Edwards and T. Desmond Williams, eds., *The Great Famine* (Dublin: The Lilliput Press, 1995), first published in 1956.

3   Thomas McEvilley, 'Here Comes Everybody', *Beyond the Pale: Art and Artists on the Edge of Consensus* (Dublin: Irish Museum of Modern Art, 1994), p. 13.

4   At the Irish Museum of Modern Art, 1994–5.

5   The *banshee* (literally, 'female fairy') was a harbinger of death for certain families, and her wail struck terror into all those who heard it.

6   Cecile Bourne, 'Interview [with Alice Maher]', *Familiar: Alice Maher* (Dublin: The Douglas Hyde Gallery, 1995), p. 23.

7   Bill Ashcroft, Gareth Griffiths and Helen Tiffin, *The Empire Writes Back: Theory and Practice in Post-Colonial Literatures* (London: Methuen, 1989), p. 33.

8   In one of the few discussions of the Irish contribution to colonialism, Hiram Morgan points out that in relation to India 'those Irish who received commissions and commands were from the Protestant elite' and argues that the same holds in relation to Australia: 'In Australia the Catholic Irish were numerous but it was the Anglo-Irish "imperial class" who exercised most influence. . . . The Catholic Charles Gavan Duffy did become Prime Minister of Victoria in 1871–2 but he was a rare bird in his day.' (Hiram Morgan, 'Empire-Building; An Uncomfortable Irish Heritage', *The Linen Hall Review*, vol. 10, no. 3, Autumn 1993, pp. 8, 9.)

9   As Vijay Mishra and Bob Hodge point out in their trenchant review of *The Empire Writes Back*, 'What an undifferentiated concept of post-colonialism overlooks are the very radical differences in response and the unbridgeable chasms that existed between white and non-white colonies . . . there is, we feel, a need to make a stronger distinction between the post-colonialism of settler and non-settler countries.' (Vijay Mishra and Bob Hodge, 'What is Post-Colonialism?', in Patrick Williams and Laura Chrisman, eds., *Colonial Discourse and Post-Colonial Theory* [New York: Columbia University Press, 1994], pp. 285, 288.) As I argue below (note 18), there is also a need in an Irish context to show the radical differences *within* white societies, and particularly to question the assumption which equates whiteness with the settler community, or the culture of the colonizer.

10   Morgan, op. cit., p. 9. As Mishra and Hodge point out, 'complicit post-colonialism' is that which does not challenge the standards of the imperial centre but rather seeks to emulate them, gaining admittance to the canon (p. 289). That the most considerable achievements in Irish literature derived their impetus from *resisting* the

canon is the argument of David Lloyd's *Nationalism and Minor Literature: James Clarence Mangan and the Emergence of Irish Cultural Nationalism* (Berkeley: University of California Press, 1987) – a book, significantly, not included in the extensive reader's guide and bibliography to *The Empire Writes Back*.

11 Considered in this light, there may well be some truth in the observation that the only reason the Irish are not racist at home is that there are not enough racial minorities or non-Europeans in the country to make immigration a social problem. The key question here, however, is why Ireland is in this situation? The answer is clear: because it itself is in the anomalous position of being the only ex-colony in the European Union, and hence is not advanced enough industrially to act as an economic magnet for immigrants from developing countries. This is a radically different proposition from the naïve assumption that certain peoples or cultures are inherently bigoted, and only lack the opportunity for their racism to assert itself.

12 Edmund Spenser, 'A Briefe Note on Ireland' (1598), cited in Theodore W. Allen, *The Invention of the White Race*, vol. 1 (London: Verso, 1994), pp. 63, 210. Spenser's advice to the Queen was a follow-up to the Lord President's suggestion that 'the Irish should be constrained first to taste some great calamity, so as to render them more assured and dutiful thereafter'. See Pauline Henley, *Spenser in Ireland* (Cork: Cork University Press, 1928), p. 164. It is this historical backdrop which gave such force to accusations of genocidal intent with regard to the nineteenth-century Great Famine.

13 David R. Roediger, *The Wages of Whiteness: Race and the Making of the American Working Class* (London: Verso, 1991), p. 134.

14 Cited in McEvilley, 'Here comes Everybody', p. 21.

15 Roediger, op. cit., p. 144. See also Reginald Horsman, *Race and Manifest Destiny: The Origins of American Racial Anglo-Saxonism* (Cambridge, Mass.: Harvard University Press, 1981).

16 Ella Shohat and Robert Stam, *Unthinking Eurocentrism: Multiculturalism and the Media* (New York: Routledge, 1994), p. 42.

17 In this connection, the amnesia shown by the Irish state towards the Famine in 1945 was matched by the embarrassing fifteen-minute ceremony which passed for a commemoration of the 75th anniversary of the Rising, in 1991.

18 As Theodore Allen argues in the related context of slavery, such judgements betray an assumption that, somehow, colonization is more suitable for 'Third-World' countries: 'It is only a "white" habit of mind that reserves "slave" for the African-American and boggles at the term "Irish slave trade"' (Allen, p. 258).

19 Anne McClintock, 'The Angel of Progress: Pitfalls of the Term "Post-colonialism"', in Williams and Chrisman, eds., *Colonial Discourse and Post-Colonial Theory*, p. 294.

20 Donald Horne, *The Public Culture* (London: Pluto Press, 1986), p. 154.

21 Cited in James M. Blaut, *The National Question: Decolonising the Theory of Nationalism* (London: Zed Books, 1987), p. 144.

22 For some pertinent comments on this, see Shohat and Stam, op. cit., p. 43.

INDEX

Abbey Theatre 58
Achebe, Chinua 174
agrarian insurgency 140–44
allegories of identity *see also guaiRE* 7, 18–22
Allen, Theodore 211 n18
American culture *see also* Anglo-American
    culture 13, 23–9
Anderson, Benedict 134, 135, 137
Andrews, Eamonn 44
Anglo-American culture *see also* American
    culture 75, 77–8, 96
Anglo-Saxonism 176
Anne Devlin (Murphy, P.) 4, 107–16
Aran Islands, Synge and 23, 24, 29, 30–31, 32
Arden, John 46
Arigna 99, 100, 102–3
Arnason, Johann 91
Arnold, Matthew 9, 150, 156, 162, 167
art 23, 172–4
Atwood, Margaret 174
Auden, W. H. 8
Auerbach, Erich 133
Aughrim 144

Baden-Powell, Sir George 131, 137
Bakhtin, Mikhail 10, 147
Ballagh, Robert 23, 86
Ballroom of Romance, The 83
banshee 173
Barthes, Roland 158, 161
Battle of Little Big Horn 14
BBC 45, 46–7, 70
Beames, Michael 140
Beaumont, Gustave de 151–2
Beckett, Samuel 6
Behan, Brendan 47
Belfast Frescoes 178, 179
Benjamin, Walter 72, 131, 132, 162, 167
Bernstein, Edward 105
Bew, Paul 83
Bhabha, Homi 149
Binchy, D. A. 97
Blacam, Aodh de 97, 138

Blaney, Neil 84
Bord Fáilte 86
Boucicault, Dion 6, 167
Boyce, George 81
Bracken 67–9, 77
Bradshaw, Brendan 6, 17
Brecht, Bertolt 72
Brennan, Seamus 72, 75–6, 78
British drama and television 46–47
broadcasting *see also* media; radio; television
    British *see* BBC
    Broadcasting Act 1960, Section 31 79–80
    and state control 71, 73–7
    Irish language 75–7
    and national identity 70–73
Buckley, Anthony 152
Burke, Edmund 137, 176
Burke, Kenneth 9
Burrowes, Wesley 57, 58, 61, 64
Butler-Cullingford, Elizabeth 131
Byrne, Gabriel 64, 78–9
Byrne, Seamus 47

Camden 151
Campbell, James J. 50
Campbell, Thomas 154
Canny, Nicholas 150
Capra, Dominic La 189 n45
Carleton, William 6, 15
Carlyle, Thomas 150
Caughie, John 45
Celticism 9, 81, 156
censorship 79
Charon 132
cinema *see also Anne Devlin; Maeve* 80,
    117–18, 123–4, 165–9
Clandillon, Seamus 71, 72, 73
Clark, Samuel 11
Cleary, Peter 56
Clifford, James 21, 147
Coleman, James 129–33
colonial discourse 149
colonialism 131, 149–51

Conefrey, Fr Peter 101–2
Connolly, James 103, 138
Cooke, Alistair 70
Cooke, Lynn 132
Cooper Walker, Joseph 157
Corkery, Daniel 34
Cornewall Lewis, George 34
Coronation Street 52–3
Cousins, Margaret 106
cowboys as heroes 24, 25–9, 32
Coxhead, Elizabeth 191 n24
Cullen, Cardinal 86
Cullen, Louis 204 n32
cultural nationalism 96–7
Curran, Sarah 108, 110
Curtis, L. P. 167

D'Alton, Cardinal 44
Dada 166
Daily Express 165
Dallas 52, 53, 69
dance-halls 100–1
Darnton, Robert 17
Davis, Natalie Zemon 141, 142
de la Tour 115
Dead, The 134–5, 143–6
Deane, Seamus 203 n20
Debord, Guy 209 n54
Defenderism 140
Denning, Michael 19
Derrida, Jacques 137, 153, 161
Devane, Fr R. S. 75
Devenney, Brian 55
Devlin, Anne *see also* Anne Devlin 107–8
devotional revolution 86, 136
diaspora 175–6
Dickens, Charles 167–8
Doherty, Willie 177–8
Donaghy, Lyle 104
Donnelly, James 141
Douglas, James 49
Drennan, William 159
Dublin Opinion 171
Duffy, Charles Gavan 155, 175
Dun Guaire Castle 129–30, 131
Dunne, Tom 137–8, 139
Dynasty 52

E.T. 39, 41
Eagleton, Terry 135
Easter Rising 3, 8, 99, 108, 140
Eastwood, Clint 26

Edwards, Hilton 47–8
Eglinton, John 165, 168, 169
Eisenstein, Sergei 166
Eliot, T. S. 82
Ellmann, Richard 144
Emerson, Ralph Waldo 176
emigration to United States 98
Emmet, Robert 107–8, 109–10, 111
Engels, Friedrich 179–80
Enlightenment 89–90, 135–6
Evergreen Memories 177, 178

Fading Dreams 177–8
Falkiner, C. Litton 5
Fanon, Franz 162
Faupel, Rev Luke 46–7
Feeley, Pat 99, 102
Fell, John L. 167
female allegory 130–1, 132
feminist politics 20–21, 108–10, 116, 124–5
Fenians (Irish Republican Brotherhood) 140, 146
Fianna Fáil 1932–3 73, 74, 103–4
film *see* cinema
Finberg, H. P. R. 96
First Programme for Economic Expansion 82
FitzGerald, Garret 76
Fitzpatrick, David 66
FitzSimon, Christopher 52
folk rituals 18–19
Foran, Thomas 99
Ford, John 24, 39
Foster, Roy 14–15
Foucault, Michel 132
Freud, Sigmund 40, 131
Fried, Michael 202 n7
Frisby, David 158
frontier myth *see also* myth of the west 8, 14, 187 n29
fundamentalism 136

Gaelic Athletic Association 73, 96
Gaelic culture 138
Gaelic games 72–3
Gaelic League 81
Gaelic Revival 81
Gageby, Douglas 77
Garvin, Tom 140
Gate Theatre 58
Gavan Duffy, Charles 155, 175
Geertz, Clifford 140
Gellner, Ernest 137
Gentle Gunman, The 117

Gibbon, Peter 83
Gibson, Chloe 48, 49
Gilbert, Humphrey 151
Gillespie, Raymond 96
Gilley, Sheridan 150, 152, 155–6
Gilroy, Paul 6
Glenroe 77
Glorious Revolution 166
Gonne, Maud MacBride 102
Gorham, Maurice 74
Graham, Dan 132
Gralton Defence Committee 104, 106
Gralton, James 5, 97–106
Gralton, Packie 102
Gramsci, A. 95
Gray, Ken 64
Great Famine 1845–8 171–2
Green, Alice Stopford 5 6
Griffith, Arthur 30, 32, 99, 105–6, 156
guaiRE 129–33

Hand, John 204 n33
Haughey, Charles 81
Hayes, Edward 20, 143
Hayes, Joanna 133
Healy, Gerald 47, 48
Healy, John 84
Henry, Paul 23
Herlihy, Fr C. J. 155
Higgins, F. R. 104
Hinde, John 11, 38, 39, 40–43
historical experience 12–18, 21–2
historical tradition 153–63
Hobsbaum, E. J. 7, 135, 137, 138, 147
Hoch, Paul 29
Hodge, Bob 210 n9&10
Hogan, James 104
Hoggart, Richard 46
Homans, Peter 26
Hope, James 199 n7
Horne, Donald 179
Hroch, Miroslav 19–20, 21
Hume, David 153–4, 155, 157
Humphreys, A. J. 194 n48
hybridity 172, 174, 176, 180
Hyde, Sir Douglas 71, 72, 155, 156

IDA 86, 88–9, 91, 93
individualism 24–6
Industrial Revolution 89
industrialization *see also* IDA 88–93
   Japan 90–91

internationalism 82–5, 95, 180
Investment in Education 1965 83
IRA 104, 140
Ireland, myth of the west and 29–35
Irish Independent 84, 104
Irish Museum of Modern Art 172, 180
Irish Press 51, 73, 77
Irish Republican Brotherhood (Fenians) 140
Irish Times 64, 77
Irish Transport and General Workers' Union
   (ITGWU) 98, 99
Irish World 14
Irish/Native American analogies 150–53, 176
Isaak, Jo Anna 132
ITGWU 98, 99

Jackson, Andrew 152
Jameson, Fredric 158, 161
Japan and modernization 94–5
jazz 101–2
Johnson, Barbara 7
Johnson, Thomas 99
Johnston, Denis 104
Jones, Harri Pritchard 80
Joyce, James 6, 82, 107, 131, 134, 136,
   143–4, 146, 160–61, 162, 163, 165
Judge, Michael 49

Keating, Geoffrey 8, 154
Keating, Sean 23
Kennedy, President J. F. 13
Kerry babies controversy 133
Kiberd, Declan 84–7
Kiernan, Dr T. J. 75
Kindness, John 178
King's Threshold, The 129
Kingsley, Charles 149–50
Kingston, Lord 99, 100, 102
Kitse, Jim 27
Knights of Columbanus, seminar June 1964
   46, 48
Knock 108
Kohn, Hans 7
Kristeva, Julia 199 n8

La Capra, Dominic 189 n45
Land War 1881 11
Larkin, Emmet 28, 86
Late Late Show, The 4, 11, 12, 44, 57, 77, 78–9
Laverty, Maura 47, 54, 56
Lawlor, Iris 55
Leicester School 96

Lemass, Sean 77, 79, 82, 83
Lenin 105
Lévi-Strauss, Claude 153
Lewis, George Cornewall 34
Lewis, Wyndham 160, 161, 162–3
Leys, Colin 139
Literary Revival, The 8, 9, 24, 25–6, 28, 47,
        118, 168
Lloyd, David 146, 159
Locke, John 7–8, 153
Lynch, John 99
Lyons, F. S. L. 16, 17, 156

Mac Conghail, Muiris 37
Mac Hale, Archbishop 202 n9
Mac Réamoinn, Seán 75
Macardle, Dorothy 102
MacBride, Maud Gonne 102
MacDonagh, Oliver 82
MacDonagh, Thomas 156
MacEntee, Sean 74
MacNeill, Eoin 29
Macpherson, James 157
MacSwiney, M ire 104
Madden, R. R. 110
Maeve (Murphy, P.) 4, 108, 117–27
Mahaffy, J. P. 163
Maher, Alice 173
Man of Aran 117
Mangan, James Clarence 159–60
Marcus, Philip 118
Marx, Karl 4
Marxism 95, 105, 138, 139
materialism 9, 10
Maturin, Charles 6, 15
McCabe, Eugene 49
McCartney, Donal 158
McClintock, Anne 179
McEvilley, Thomas 172
McGeehan, Patrick 102
McLoone, Martin 54
McLuhan, Marshall 184 n2
McMahon, Sean 32
McSwiney, T. 162
McSwiney, Terence 129
Meagher, John 84
media *see also* broadcasting; radio; television
    Anglo-American culture 75, 78
    censorship 79
    and national identity 10–11, 70
    and tradition 72–3
Méliès, Georges 37

memory 119–20, 172–4
Miller, Kerby 85, 86
Minister for Posts and Telegraphs 75, 79
Mishra, Vijay 210 n9&10
modernism *see also* protomodernism 6, 165–9
modernization 82–96
Mohill demonstration 102
Molloy, M. J. 47
Molly Maguires, the 18, 19, 141
Molyneaux, James 8
montage
    and Eisenstein 166–7
    and Joyce 165, 168–9
Moody, T. W. 16
Moore, Tom 167
Moran, Gerard 96
Moretti, Franco 161, 162, 165–6, 168
Morgan, Hiram 210 n8
Morgan, Lady 15
Morison, Fynes 151
Morrison, Toni 172, 185 n9
Morrisroe, Bishop 100
Morton, Thomas 151
Mountjoy, Lord 151
Muldoon, Paul 132
Murphy, Pat 4, 107–16, 117–127
Murphy, Rev H. 59, 60
music, traditional 73, 75, 172
myth of the west 13–14, 18–35, 85
myths
    frontier 8, 14, 187 n29
    popular history 16–18
    of the west *see* myth of the west

Napier, Philip 172
narrative
    forms 118–22
    and television 50
Nation, The 157
national identity *see* nationalism national
        narratives 12–18
nationalism *see also* national identity,
    anti-colonial 6–8
    contemporary 105
    cultural 96–7
    and identity 134–47
    and Marxism 95
    and media 10–11
    and post-colonialism 105–6
Nationality 99
Native American/Irish analogies 150–53, 176
native historians 154–5

neo-traditionalism 89
Newman, Sydney 192 n10
Nietzsche 158, 159
Nora, Pierre 145
North Down by-election, June 1995 8
Northside Express 69
nostalgia 82–5

O'Brien, Conor Cruise 79, 156
O'Brien, William 15–16, 19
Ó Caoimh, Padraig 73
Ó Caollaí, Maolsheachlainn 80
O'Connell, Daniel 136, 140
O'Connell, Declan 93
O'Connor, Frank 82, 104
O'Conor, Charles 154
O'Dea, Tom 51
O'Donnell, Peader 104
O'Donovan, John 48
O'Faoláin, Seán 3, 82, 136
O'Flanagan, Fr Michael 99
O'Grady, Standish 15, 118, 120, 121, 133
O'Halloran, Jean 67
Ó Hehir, Michael 72
O'Kelly, Seán T. 103
O'Neill, Shane 151
O'Neill, Terence 83
Ó Riada, Seán 78
O'Rourke, Francis 69
O'Sullivan, Donal 145
O'Sullivan, Rev Samuel 143
O'Toole, Finta 85
Olcott, Sidney 117
oral culture 153
oral tradition 161
Osborne, John 46
Ossian 157–8, 159
Outside Broadcast Unit 58
Owens Weekes, Anne 131

Panofsky, Erwin 29
Parkman, Francis 152–3
Patterson, Henry 83
PAYE protest 1979 92
Pearse, Patrick 29, 32, 108
Peet, Richard 138
Philadelphia coalfields 19
photography 37, 39, 119, 177–8
Pike Theatre 47
Pinter, Harold 46
Playboy of the Western World, The 31–5
Plunkett, James 199 n9

political unity 139
Politicians, The 45
politics of representation 8–12
popular history, myths of 16–18
post-colonialism 171–80
post-industrial revolution 91
post-nationalism 105
postcards 38–43
Price, Alan 31
print culture 134–6, 138, 146
Promise of Barty O'Brien, The 3
protomodernism 6

Queen Victoria 171
Quinn, D.B. 150

race 155–6
racism 149–51, 175–6
Radford Reuther, Rosemary 136
radio 72, 73, 74, 76
Radio Éireann *see* radio
Raleigh, Walter 151
Reagan, Ronald 13, 92, 96
reductionism 9
Reith, Lord 70
Republican Congress 5
republicanism 102
Reuther, Rosemary Radford 136
Reynolds, Patrick 102
Ribbonism 140, 143
Riordans, The 4, 11, 12, 51, 57–67, 68, 77, 78
Rising of the Moon, The 117
Rituals of the Memory 119
Rodgers, W.R. 35
Roediger, David 176
Rogin, Michael 152
romanticism 14, 96, 158–60
Rory O'More 117
Roseberry, William 140
Rousseau 153
RTE *see* television 47, 48, 52
RTE Annual Reports 48, 52
RTV Guide 48, 53
Ruggheimer, Gunnar 57
rural/urban divide 84–6
Russell, Lady Christabel 131, 132
Ruthven, Malise 184 n2, 202 n8
Ryan's Daughter 117

Said, Edward 92
Sands, Bobby 172
Schiller, Herbert 77

Scots Irish see Ulster Scots
Scott, Walter 159
Second Vatican Council 83
Seven Days 57
Shakespeare 162, 168
Sheehan, Canon 29, 30
Shohat, Ella 176
Sigeson, Dr George 156
silence 107–8, 112–14, 116
Simmel, George 159
Sinn Féin 99
Sitting Bull 14
Slotkin, Richard 12, 13
Smith, Anthony D. 10
Smith, Robert J. 196 n13
soap operas see television serials
Social Study Conference, Ninth Annual 49
socialism 95, 106
Sontag, Susan 135
Spenser, Edmund 154–5, 176
Spivak, Gayatir Chakrovorty 161
Stack, Austin 102
Stam, Robert 176
Stoker, Bram 6
Strachey, William 151
Strumpet City 77
Stuart, Francis 104
Sullivan, A.M. 15, 155
Sweeney, Maeve see Maeve
Swidler, Ann 187 n30
Swift, Carolyn 54, 56
Synge, J.M. 11, 23–35

T.J.M.S. 192 n5, 193 n30
Táin Bó Cuailgne 118
TAM see Television Audience Measurement
Telefís Éireann see television 44
Telefís Feirme 58
television
    and cultural identity 77–82
    current affairs on 44–5
    drama 44, 45–69
    drama, British 45, 46–7
    and family 49–50, 53–7, 59–67, 68–9
    influence of 4
    and narrative 50
    serials 51–7
    single plays 45–51
    and social life 49–50
Television Audience Measures (TAM) 80
Thackeray, William 146–7
Thatcher, Margaret 166
Thierry, Augustin 142

Thompson, E.P. 186 n20
Thornley, David 192 n3
Thurot 141
Titanic, The 178–9
Tolka Row 4, 51–7, 68, 77
traditional music 73, 75, 172
2RN see Radio Éireann 70

Ulster Protestants 152
Ulster Scots 14
Urban/rural divide 84–9

de Valera, Eamon 44, 82, 103
Vardac, A. Nicholas 167
Vatican Council
    1870 136
    Second 83
Vaugh, James 102
Victoria, Queen 137
Victorian era 171–2
violence 33–4, 123

Walcott, Derek 174
Walker, Joseph Cooper 157
War of Independence 129
Warner, Marina 108, 130
Watson, G.J. 30
Webb, Sidney 105
Weber, Max 34
Weekes, Anne Owens 131
Weinshemer, Joel C. 17
Wesker, Arnold 46
west, myth of the see myth of the west
Western genre 13
Western imperialism 137
White, Patrick 174
Whiteboys, the 18, 20, 140–42, 146
Whittaker, T.K. 77, 82
Wilde, Oscar 11
Wilde, Sir William 18
Williams, Raymond 9, 46, 79, 85, 95, 96
Wizard of Oz, The 38
Woolacott, Martin 4
Worker's Voice 102, 104

Yadov, Alok 185 n13
Yajnik, I.K. 106
Yeats, Jack 23
Yeats, W.B. 8, 24, 25, 129, 165, 200 n6
Young Ireland movement 140
Young, Derek 62

Zemon Davis, Natalie 141, 142